THE
RACE
QUESTION
IN
CANADA

THE CARLETON LIBRARY

A series of Canadian reprints and new collections of source material relating to Canada, issued under the editorial supervision of the Institute of Canadian Studies of Carleton University, Ottawa.

ANDRÉ SIEGFRIED

THE
RACE
QUESTION
IN
CANADA

EDITED AND WITH AN INTRODUCTION BY

FRANK H. UNDERHILL

The Carleton Library No. 29 / McClelland and Stewart Limited

The Canadian Publishers

McClelland and Stewart Limited

25 Hollinger Road, Toronto 16

PRINTED AND BOUND IN CANADA
BY
T. H. BEST PRINTING COMPANY LIMITED

Contents

PART TWO

THE POLITICAL LIFE OF CANADA

I – The Constitution and Its Operation

II – The Parties, Their Psychology and Programmes

PART THREE

THE BALANCE OF RACES AND CIVILIZATIONS IN CANADA

PART FOUR

CANADA'S EXTERNAL RELATIONS

Introduction to the
Carleton Library Edition

André Siegfried is the Tocqueville of Canada. If we Canadians had shown the intense interest in ourselves which our American neighbours have shown in themselves ever since the Pilgrim Fathers landed, and if, being interesting to ourselves, we had continuously attracted the interest of inquiring students from other countries, Siegfried's volumes on Canada would have become classics, as Tocqueville's two volumes on democracy in America have become. The penetrating light which Siegfried's analysis throws upon the permanent elements in the relations of English and French within Canada, and upon the delicate and shifting balance between British and American influences on our Canadian way of life, would be widely appreciated. His remarkable combination of the qualities of historian, political economist, social psychologist, geographer and philosopher, would be admired.[1] His passion for studying the interactions of religion and politics, and his conception of America as a new civilization, would recall the example of Tocqueville, and he would be hailed as second only to his earlier countryman among those Europeans who have studied this continent.

But most Canadians are still ignorant of Siegfried's name; whereas Americans have been discussing Tocqueville vigorously ever since his first volume appeared in 1835. In fact, each successive generation of Americans, as it becomes aware of the new problems of its own age, discovers fresh insights in Tocqueville. Thus the phenomenon of our Canadian neglect of Siegfried throws some light on one important difference between us and the Americans. We are less mature than they are. English Canadians and French Canadians alike, we have shown little taste for that realistic and critical self-knowledge which is the mark of maturity.

Siegfried was the author of two main works on Canada. The first was published in 1906 in Paris as *Le Canada, les deux races:*

[1] In the June, 1959, number of the *Revue française de science politique* François Goguel wrote a tribute to André Siegfried, who had presided over the editorial board of that review since its foundation. Remarking that Siegfried was a stranger to the traditional divisions between academic disciplines, he said that the great lesson of his work is to put scholars on guard against the danger of excessive specialization and against the seduction of too elaborate techniques of research.

problèmes politiques contemporains, and in 1907 in an English translation in London as *The Race Question in Canada.* The second came out in 1937 just before World War II, entitled simply *Canada.* It was brought up to date and republished in a second edition in 1947 under the title of *Canada: An International Power.* While the 1937 and 1947 volumes are to be found fairly easily by anyone in Canada who wants to consult them, the first book – which is more distinctive and illuminating – has long been out of print. It is this first work which is here republished.

Almost every paragraph in it is exciting today because the book deals with the question over which we are brooding so uncomfortably just now: the problem of the terms on which English Canadians and French Canadians are to live side by side for the next hundred years. Page after page is likely to provoke exclamations by the contemporary reader on how contemporary the book is, even when the changes of sixty years have made some of the passages completely out of date.

It is a sad reflection on the slowness with which Canadians have evolved toward maturity that this book, which has so much to say to us today, was published in 1907 not in Canada for Canadian readers but in Britain for British readers. At least we can take comfort from the fact that Siegfried's first work, on democracy in New Zealand, which was published in Paris in 1904, apparently stimulated no demand for an English translation till 1914, and the translation was then also published in Britain for British readers.

Canadians, of course, have always been interested in what outsiders have had to say about them – as one can see at any time in the nineteenth century by the eagerness with which Canadian newspapers reprinted English and American comment on Canadian affairs. But the interest, so far as political comment went, was likely to be that of political partisans seeking confirmation of their own views, especially of their own low opinion of their political opponents, rather than the interest of genuine students of politics looking for new insights into their own problems. And the Siegfried type of analysis was too impartially unflattering to all parties to be of much use for local party purposes.

The book did, however, attract favourable and serious notice among Canadian intellectuals. *Queen's Quarterly* seems to have missed it. But *The University Magazine* (published by a committee of McGill, Toronto, and Dalhousie professors) had a review in April 1907, by F. P. Walton, Dean of Law at McGill, which welcomed *The Race Question in Canada* as "a fine example of the admirable lucidity of the French mind" and found that it was "singularly accurate in its statement of facts and general view of tendencies." Later, in 1908, *The University Magazine* printed an article by Siegfried himself, in French, on the political parties of France.

The Review of Historical Publications relating to Canada, forerunner of the present *Canadian Historical Review*, contained in 1906 a long and striking appraisal of the original French edition of the work, written by W. L. Grant, at that time Beit Lecturer in Colonial History at Oxford. "Perhaps for the first time Canada has been treated scientifically. There is something almost inhuman in M. Siegfried's detachment; his analysis approaches the calm and the neutrality of a vivisectionist. Himself a Frenchman, a Protestant and an anti-clerical, little in the book identifies him with any race, religion or political creed. Yet, while dispassionate, he is not colourless; he is merciless but not unsympathetic; he has abstained from excessive simplification and not endeavoured to confine Canadian national life within a limited number of pigeonholes. . . . Almost every aspect of Canada's national life is treated with sympathy." Grant's one serious criticism was that Siegfried, in concluding that the future relations of Canada with Britain would be an indefinite continuance of the present relations, "perhaps hardly does justice to the ideal of a full national life within the British Empire."

When in 1907 the English translation of *Les deux races* appeared, the *Review of Historical Publications* included a short note on it, calling the book "a frank and passionless analysis of Canadian thought today" and "the most scientific treatise on the subject that has yet appeared." Notice, please, this reference to "Canadian thought," which correctly describes the nature of the Siegfried work. Perhaps the long neglect of Siegfried in Canada has been due to the fact that there were not enough Canadians in 1907 and later who considered that Canadian politics involved thought.

Whatever the reasons may have been, after this first welcome Canadian scholars seemed to drop Siegfried; and Canadian politicians and journalists seldom paid any attention to him. *The Race Question in Canada* has long needed reprinting; and a new edition of it could not come at a more fitting time than in the midst of our current anxieties about bilingualism and biculturalism.

André Siegfried was born in 1875 in Le Havre, and died in 1959 within about a month of reaching his eighty-fourth birthday. The Siegfried family came from Mulhouse in Alsace where they were engaged in the cotton trade. André's father, Jules Siegfried, made his fortune when, on the outbreak of the American Civil War, he quickly realized that a fresh source of supply of raw cotton must be found, and extended his firm's activity to India. In 1870, when the Germans annexed Alsace, the Siegfried firm moved to Le Havre. Jules Siegfried was a vigorous entrepreneur with broad interests, somewhat resembling the great cotton magnates of Manchester in the mid-nineteenth century. He was an admirer of Cobden, and his son André, explaining his father's political beliefs, put him down as a liberal in the English sense.[2] He visited America during the Civil War and was the guest of President Lincoln, who took him along on an official tour of the Northern military lines. In his adopted city of Le Havre he moved from business into politics and served as mayor of the city. The Siegfrieds were Protestants, strong republicans after 1870, and supporters of lay control over education. Jules Siegfried built up a successful system of state schools in Le Havre. Then he moved on to Paris where almost continuously from 1885 to his death in 1922 he served as a deputy or senator.

Jules Siegfried was accustomed to entertain on a big scale in his Le Havre and Paris homes; and there André met many of the leading political figures of France and foreign countries. His father, though he served on many committees and commissions, only won ministerial office once. For a few months he was a member of the Ribot government in 1892-93, where, fittingly, he held the portfolio of Minister of Commerce. It was precisely at this time that Sir Charles Tupper from Canada negotiated a trade treaty with France, a treaty famous in our history because it was the first to be negotiated by a Canadian plenipotentiary in practical independence of imperial control. Jules Siegfried was in charge of the French side of the negotiations, and at home young André heard a good deal of talk about Canadian affairs. This incident gave him his first interest in Canada.

When he had completed his university studies André was encouraged by his father to enter public life. The father was a man of action, and educated the son as an English upper middle-class boy would be trained for public affairs. Four times André stood for election to the Chamber of Deputies – in 1902, 1903,

[2] See his book, *Mon père et son temps: Jules Siegfried, 1836-1922* (Paris, 1946).

1906 and 1910 – and four times he was defeated. Evidently his tastes were not quite those of his father, though he was wont later to pride himself on the fact that he got his understanding of politics from studying men as well as books. At any rate he became a student rather than an active politician. As he put it, "la volupté de comprendre me paraît aussi belle que l'ivresse de l'action."

On a trip around the world in 1898 he first visited Canada, and he was here twice again before publishing his book in 1906. In 1904, as the section on political parties shows, he spent a long time in the country during the general election of that year. He won his doctorate by two studies, one on democracy in New Zealand and the other on Gibbon Wakefield. Then, after these works on two of the British dominions, he started a detailed examination in several volumes of the politics of the various geographical regions of France, "a psychological and political geography of France" as he described it. But World War I broke out after he had completed only one volume, that on the West of France. During the war he served for several years with the British forces as an interpreter. Then in the early twenties he was a member of the League of Nations secretariat for a time, and served in various missions for the French government. Some of this work took him once more to the English-speaking countries. In 1924 appeared the first of his two books on Britain,[3] and in 1927 the first of his two books on the United States.[4]

In 1929 he lectured at the summer Institute of Politics in Williams College, Williamstown, Massachusetts. On this occasion I heard him deliver some delightful lectures on French party politics, which in 1930 formed the basis of another book: *France, A Study in Nationality*. He sat during the month of the Institute's sessions in a round-table at which Canadians (English Canadians) and Americans discussed the relations of their two countries. At the conclusion of our discussions he told us that he had sat silent during these Anglo-Saxon arguments because he realized that he was a stranger in our midst, that we shared certain interests in which he could not participate, and that our controversies were merely family quarrels that did not go very deep.

This theme, the development of the Anglo-Saxon world, led by the United States, toward a civilization different from that of

---

[3] *L'Angleterre d'aujourd'hui* (*Post-War Britain*) (London, 1924).
[4] *Les Etats Unis d'aujourd'hui* (Paris, 1927). This work appeared in the United States under the title *America Comes of Age* (New York, 1927).

France and Western Europe, became more and more prominent in his later thinking. Aspects of it can be found in his second book on Britain in 1931[5] and his second book on Canada in 1937. By the end of World War II the new North American civilization dominated all his reflections. It was, he admitted, Western, but it was not European; it was collectivistic rather than individualistic, the results of the overwhelmingly continental environment of the Americas as contrasted with the smaller-scale environment of the Mediterranean in which humanity was not dwarfed by its surroundings. The development of this theme is to be found in his Romanes lecture at Oxford in 1945 (*La Civilisation occidentale*; the lecture was delivered in French), in his 1947 volume on Canada, and above all in his 1955 volume on *America at Mid-Century*.

In the preface to his Williamstown book Siegfried explained to his American audience that his visits to the principal Anglo-Saxon countries had given him "an opportunity to observe democracy as practised with the Anglo-Saxon spirit and methods." "Instead of the aggressive and somewhat negative individualism of the Latin civilization, I saw political societies based on social co-operation. At bottom it seemed to be a contrast between the Catholic and Protestant state of mind, religion leading to extraordinarily different consequences."[6] This shows a rather more sympathetic attitude to the Anglo-Saxon type of politics than he had shown sóme twenty years earlier in his first book on Canada.

But he was also becoming more and more of a Frenchman. "Our democracy," he concluded his Williamstown lectures, "is Latin in origin, and therefore unlike the Anglo-Saxon democracies where practical social accomplishments are the first consideration. Their program is to increase the comfort and welfare of mankind, but they do not worry very much about its intellectual freedom. They have a practical aim, which they expect to achieve through moral co-operation. . . . This democratic formula which arose from Puritanism is an Anglo-Saxon invention and has no connection with our rational conception. Politically the Anglo-Saxon state is moral rather than intellectual; and although it fully recognizes the rights of man, it drags in social duties which from our point of view seriously hamper his liberty. . . . It is a different conception of society, customs, life, and of the individual himself. . . . The emphasis in the one case is laid on the individual who thinks, and in the other on the individual

[5] *England's Crisis* (London, 1931).
[6] *France, a Study in Nationality* (New Haven, 1930), p. vi.

who lives. . . . Yet, if mankind is ever again preoccupied with the question of the individual, his thoughts, and his right to think for himself, it is not talk about vacuum cleaners, refrigerators and adding machines, that will move the world. French idealism, with its motive power still intact, will regain its old interest."[7]

One Anglo-Saxon reader, at least, tends to react to Siegfried's reiterated emphasis on the individualism which is fostered by the French type of civilization by reflecting that nearly every society in western history since the Greeks has insisted that in its membership alone is to be found a genuine belief in true individualism. Siegfried became more and more a pessimistic French conservative in his old age. He looked back nostalgically to the old French conceptions of civilization as he understood them, though he was aware that the future lay with the new American civilization. "Are we wrong," he asked in his book on the United States in 1955, "to look backwards, like Lot's wife?" At least he knew the penalty which Lot's wife suffered, which is more than can be said for most elderly political philosophers.

Long before his old age Siegfried had received many honours. In 1944 he was elected to the Académie Française. He spent years as a popular lecturer, first in the École Libre des Sciences Politiques and then in the Collège de France. He wrote for *Le Figaro* and contributed to many journals in France and abroad. He was the author of many books on a wide variety of topics – Switzerland (a very enlightening study), the Mediterranean, South Africa, Latin America, Protestantism,[8] the character of peoples,[9] and various aspects of geography.

[7] *Ibid.*, p. 112.
[8] His sketch of the history of Protestantism was part of a book on *Les forces religieuses et la vie politique* (Paris, 1951) in which he collaborated with André Latreille, who wrote on Catholicism while Siegfried wrote on Protestantism.
[9] Siegfried was no doubt somewhat too fond of wide generalizations about the characters of different societies. Boyd Shafer in his book, *Nationalism: Myth and Reality* (New York, 1955) has some very effective criticism of this kind of writing: "Attempts to describe the national characters of the various peoples . . . seldom go far beyond the random guesses of such intelligent men as the eighteenth century's David Hume. For the most part they are the prejudices of racialists like Gobineau and Houston Stewart Chamberlain, the superficialities of psychologists like Le Bon, and the entertaining guesses of shallow popularizers like Madariaga and Siegfried" (p. 228, paperback edition). Shafer mentions the Siegfried books on the United States, France, England, New Zealand and Latin America; but, being an American he is, presumably, unaware of the books on Canada.

After this brief sketch of the main course of Siegfried's thinking, it is now possible to consider the implications of the young André Siegfried's views on Canada in 1906.

Siegfried's study of Canada as he saw it in 1904 and earlier, and as he read its history, contains many statements which historical critics today might question. He uses the word "race" freely in a way that modern anthropologists would deplore. He lumps together all English-speaking citizens as "Anglo-Saxons." But his general accuracy is well established, and it is not necessary to correct the minor mistakes of the book.

What makes his writing so interesting is clear enough. He is, on the one hand, a Frenchman with a sentimental attachment to the French society in North America, eager to observe the French characteristics that have survived several centuries of life across the Atlantic. But he is also a Protestant who has been living, at home in old France, through the great political-religious struggle of the Third Republic that ended in the separation of church and state. In this struggle all his sympathies were on the secularist, anti-clerical side, so that he is specially sensitive to and critical of the aspects of Quebec society which suggest clerical control or interference. He assumes that modernity necessitates the independence of politics and its separation from religion; and today that assumption seems to be accepted by those elements in Quebec society who are carrying through its quiet revolution.

Like most Frenchmen, he also assumes that French civilization is the model that other countries should copy, as it has been ever since the seventeenth century. Thus he shows impatience with the muddled compromises of Anglo-Saxon Canada regarding the relationship between politics and religion. One of the things that makes his writings fascinating to read in chronological succession is his gradual discovery that the rest of the world is no longer going to follow France as a political, intellectual and spiritual leader. He becomes steadily sadder as he grows older, but he recognizes the inevitability of what is happening. Reading him helps one to understand that President de Gaulle's resentment at the French loss of leadership is no mere personal outburst of a grandiose romanticism.

In 1906 this assumption of France's natural intellectual leadership imparted another bias to Siegfried's analysis of Canadian politics. He assumes that political parties, if they are to be healthy and creative, should be divided, as they are in France, on ideological lines. Both his earlier book on New Zealand and his book on Canada are slightly patronizing about parties in Anglo-Saxon communities. His unsparing and devastating analysis of the Canadian party system is, along with his description of the Quebec Catholic theocracy, the most striking part of his book. I gather that it offended most of the non-academic Canadians who read it in 1907. But it is unanswerable. One can only suggest that the differences between an ideological and a non-ideological party system are not completely clear-cut. Government in a political democracy requires the building up of a majority in a representative legislature. This majority may be constructed in the form of one of our Canadian heterogeneous parties or in the form of a French coalition of parties. A Canadian critic of the French system might uncover numerous coalitions of the Third Republic in which the absence of principle was not less conspicuous than in one of the heterogeneous, non-ideological, majority parties of Canada. The appetite for power is likely to dissolve principle in Latin as well as in Anglo-Saxon minds. The Canadian governmental majority party, like the French governmental majority coalition, is a gathering together of diverse elements. In Canada this gathering together or coalition is formed before the general election; in France the coalescing occurs after the election.

Siegfried found that Canadian parties, lacking principles or ideology, won office by the lowest kind of appeal to material interests. He returns again and again to this theme of the materialism of Canadian politics. It was only gradually as he grew older that he came to see that the practice in Anglo-Saxon communities of seeking material prosperity for everyone may have some moral idealism in it. By 1955 he was declaring that the great economic development of America, brought about by the dynamic American spirit and the supreme American capacity for organization, was one of the creative achievements of the modern world. It is this understanding of the American spirit, so difficult for the European to comprehend, that makes *America at Mid-Century* one of his finest works.

This second book of his on the United States should be read by Canadians in conjunction with his first book on Canada, the other example of his writing at its best. For by the fifties he had concluded that American civilization, rather than British or French, is the leader which the rest of the world is going to follow. His two books on England are very critical of Britain's difficulty in modernizing herself, in adjusting to the new conditions of the post-1914 world. And these conclusions influence the trend of his thinking about the future of Canada, a nation on the American continent. In 1906 he thought that Canada could continue to balance successfully between British influences, with some assistance from France, and the influence of the United States. By the forties he was worrying about the fact that Canadian nationality is a political nationality only, that it possesses no distinctive individual culture, and that English Canadians and French Canadians are not sure that they want a distinctive common culture.

Siegfried's first book on the United States – *America Comes of Age* – has a long section on American Puritanism which is not particularly sympathetic but which, in its grasp of the fact that Puritanism is the essential basis of modern America, goes much deeper than does his slightly ironical sketch of early twentieth-century Ontario Protestant Puritanism. But how could any observer from outside be other than ironical about the smug, materialist, fundamentalist, unintellectual worship of God and Mammon which marked our Ontario Protestant churches at the turn of the century – unless he were to become vehement and indignant? The underlying basic weakness of the civilization of English-speaking Canada is that the Puritanism which reached Canada at the beginning of the nineteenth century from the United States and Britain arrived without any intellectual baggage, and so has never been able to do for us what seventeenth-century Puritanism did for American civilization.

Siegfried's studies of Canada miss several points to which one wishes he could have devoted longer study. One may, of course, ignore the fact that he has practically nothing to say about the Maritime Provinces. But his prolonged examination of French Canada, even though it brings out so starkly the deep and wide gulf between French and English in this country, does not quite prepare the reader for the intensity of the present strain between the two peoples.

Siegfried largely neglected the influence of the Riel affair. He first studied Canada in the midst of the Wheat Boom when the country was recovering from the bitter earlier divisions over Riel, over schools, over French Catholic ultramontanism, over the Boer War, and before it had plunged into the still more bitter divisions caused by World War I. So he assumed a degree of success in English-French relations which succeeding events have not confirmed. He missed in his later books, because they were directed mainly to Canada's new international position, the accentuation of the tribal, isolationist, nationalism of Quebec as the French province passed from the age of Laurier and Bourassa, who are obviously the heroes of *The Race Question in Canada*, to the age of Groulx. He did remark shrewdly in 1937 on the disquieting fact that one tended to discuss English-French relations in Canada as if they were foreign relations, and that the best that had been achieved was "a modus vivendi without cordiality." In 1947 he remarked that the citizen of Quebec finds Toronto to be as foreign as New York. He failed to note the perhaps more important fact that the citizen of Toronto finds Quebec more foreign than New York.

In addition, after his promising start in *The Race Question* in which he inquires into the absence of an effective labour movement in Canadian politics, Siegfried fails in his later books to show much interest in the third parties which sprang up after World War I and which undermined the solidity of the classical two-party system that he had described in 1906. After predicting in 1906 that the new West would refuse to follow the lead of Ontario and Quebec, he shows little interest or insight into later Western political movements. The prairie wheat farmer fails to move him to enthusiasm. He has only dire predictions about a form of agriculture that lacks, he thinks, the close communion of the European peasant with his land.

Several times he failed to sense movements in Canadian opinion that were just about to emerge when he happened to be in Canada. The 1906 book fails to foresee the anti-American outburst of the Reciprocity election in 1911. He was in America in the early months of 1914 and wrote letters back to a French paper about his trip across the continent. As late as June 12, from Montreal, he was writing that the British imperialists were mistaken if they expected to drag their colony into the terrible vortex of European militarism.[10] In the 1947 book, emphasizing the new dependence of Canada on the United States for her security, he remarked that Canadians saw their position as that of an ally rather than of a protectorate. This seemed sensible enough at the end of the forties, but hardly prepares one for

---

[10] See *Deux mois en Amérique du Nord à la veille de la guerre* (Paris, 1916), p. 27.

what Canadians are reading in their papers in the 1960's. But the contemporary historian, with his advantages of hindsight, should beware of too many criticisms of predecessors who displayed an imperfect foresight.

There is one other bit of writing by Siegfried which would surely be very entertaining and enlightening if we could see it. Did he keep a journal or diary with notes of his interviews and observations during those many tours in which he studied the Anglo-Saxons? What did he note down at the moment about the characters of leading Canadians, and of ordinary Canadians, as he saw them and listened to them talking? What did they say to him in private? If records of this kind survive, one wonders whether a collection of them in print might not make almost as fascinating a volume as the Pierson volume on Tocqueville and Beaumont in America.

I have made several changes in the text of the 1907 English translation of *Les deux races*. The English translator at that time produced a volume for English rather than for Canadian readers; and he knew much less about Canada than Siegfried knew. He changed Siegfried's francs into pounds rather than into dollars; he spoke of corn rather than of wheat; he misspelled many names of men and places which are more familiar to us in Canada than they were to him in England; he spoke regularly of the Confederacy when we speak of Confederation; he referred to provincial parliaments rather than to provincial legislatures; and he talked about the Reds and Blues of Quebec, not knowing, apparently, that we English Canadians, in our easy familiarity with the French language, were already referring to them as Rouges and Bleus. I have made the necessary changes where these references occur.

Siegfried quotes frequently from the text of speeches or documents in the English language; and, of course, he translates them into French. In 1907 his English translator, instead of consulting the official English text, usually translated Siegfried's French back into his own English. This did not necessarily change the meaning of what was said; but some of the speeches and extracts from documents that have been much quoted in our history look rather strange in this garb. I have made appropriate corrections here as well.

The English translator took many opportunities to squeeze two or three Siegfried sentences into one of his own. And he was apt to condense Siegfried's paragraphs on incidents in Canadian history that he presumably thought too local to be worth all the space that Siegfried gave them. He lacked Siegfried's untiring interest in religion and in the varieties of religious experience, Catholic and Protestant. I have substituted a fuller and more literal translation of Siegfried's writing at a good many of these places, because the original English translation was apt to spoil the precision and subtlety of his analysis, and sometimes muted the sardonic overtones of some of his sentences.

FRANK H. UNDERHILL
Carleton University,
November 1965.

INTRODUCTION

1: Canada's Problem: Its Chief Factors

Canadian politics is a tilting-ground for impassioned rivalries. An immemorial struggle persists between French and English, Catholics and Protestants, while an influence is gathering strength close by them which some day may become predominant – that of the United States. In this complex contest, the subject of my book, the whole future of Canada is at stake.

There is no need to begin by evoking memories of history which will be present to all minds. By way of preface it will suffice to set out as clearly as possible the chief factors of what may be called the Canadian problem. It is, as I have implied, a very complex one. Hence its difficulty. Hence its profound interest.

I

In the first place, and above all, it is a racial problem. Great Britain conquered our French possession in the New World, but she failed either to annihilate or to assimilate the colonists whom we left behind. From the 60,000 they numbered in 1763, when the Treaty of Paris put our defeat on record, their numbers have swollen until they constitute to-day a people of 1,650,000 souls, upholding proudly, under the alien rule they have loyally accepted, their creed, their language, and their traditions. Their special domain, their impregnable stronghold, is the province of Quebec, in which they muster 1,322,000 out of 1,648,000 inhabitants.[1] To these we have to add the descendants of our Nova Scotians – our Acadians – some 140,000, to be found in the Atlantic provinces, and the members of the many important communities founded by our race in different corners of the boundless prairie. Here, however, our compatriots must always be in a minority, it would seem: it is the basin of the St. Lawrence that must remain the theatre for the working out of French destinies in the New World.

The British element in Canada, less prolific than ours, has grown unceasingly through immigration, until it has come to be in a majority. Out of the total of 5,371,000 inhabitants for the

[1] All these figures are taken from the Canadian census of 1901.

whole colony, 3,061,000 were, in 1901, of British origin. In Quebec, as we have seen, an insignificant minority, they number in Ontario 1,732,000 out of 2,182,000. There is a pronounced feeling of jealousy between these two provinces, which together form the heart of the Dominion. The dominant race suffers the presence of the French because it cannot do otherwise, but it sets up its own tongue and religion and form of civilization against theirs. An open warfare is in progress, the bitterness of which it were useless to seek to disguise.

The first part of this book will be devoted to an account of this rivalry in all its causes and manifestations.

The Church of Rome is assuredly the most powerful factor in the formation of the French-Canadian people. We shall see how they have been upheld by it, how it has developed them and disciplined them in their struggle, leaving its mark on them for ever. The English in Canada have been affected in the same way by the influence of the various Protestant Churches, or, more exactly, by the influence of the spirit of Protestantism. This also will come under our consideration, serving to show us how religious questions are at the root of all Canadian differences and divisions.

From the Church we shall go to the school, wherein the battle will be found raging no less fiercely. Here we shall see the same adversaries engaged in the same strenuous struggle: first of all, the Roman clergy refusing to cede to the state – the English state – the education of the Catholic children; then the French people as a whole resolute in their defence of their separate schools and colleges, held by them essential to their integrity as a separate people; while on the other side we shall see the Canadians of British parentage extolling the public schools of English type, of which they would fain make a crucible for the creation of a new race, united in language, customs, and thought.

We shall then proceed to examine the national sentiments of these two races, formed separately by their priests, pastors, and teachers, discovering for ourselves something of all the endless complications and contradictions and refinements of which the Canadian mind is constituted.

What are the feelings of these Frenchmen, conquered by force of arms, but conceded their full rights as citizens, towards the land beneath whose flag they pass their lives? And what place does the land of their fathers still hold in their hearts? What is their attitude towards their British fellow-sub-

jects, side by side with whom they live but with whom they are
engaged so unceasingly in such fierce conflict? What is their
outlook – adherents as they are to the old faith – upon English
Protestantism and the progress of free thought? We shall not
find it easy to make our way through the maze.

The English in Canada, though not so difficult to analyse,
are yet far from easy to understand. Their antipathy to their
French neighbours does not involve either hostility against
France or an unalterable fidelity to England. Many of them,
fascinated by the prestige of their mighty neighbour, are in
danger of forgetting the links that bind them to Great Britain;
and indeed it looks as though Canada might – almost imperceptibly – pass over to the United States. The Canadians themselves do not look forward to this eventuality with ease of mind,
but it would seem as though they were making ready for it.

These are the delicate and intricate matters into which we
must inquire before we venture to discuss that somewhat artificial entity designated officially by the Confederation of 1867
as the Canadian People.

II

This brings us to the second part of the book. After we
have studied the two races apart, we shall study them together
in their common political life, ruled over by the same government and subject to the same laws: no longer French and
English, but just Canadian citizens.

We shall see how the Constitution of 1867, the basis of
Confederation, endeavoured to combine national unity with the
profound diversity of the provinces, separated as they are by
distance, race, language and religion; and how rival peoples,
forced by destiny to work in double harness, gradually arrived
at an understanding in the fields of parliamentary business and
general administration. The organization of parties upon the
basis of compromise and not of racial strife will show us the
wisdom of the leaders and the discipline of their followers.
Nowhere else is the influence of British traditions to be found
exerting itself more effectively or with better results.

On the other hand we shall note how the neighbourhood of
the United States makes itself felt whenever there are great
popular consultations of the voters and wide movements of
opinion. In order to realize to what extent the habits of thought
and action of the New World have transformed Canada, we

must penetrate into the everyday details of its electoral processes and watch the political machine at work, eliciting the
considerations which really weigh with the voters. We must
follow the representatives of the public into parliament and
inquire into the motives by which they are actuated. Only thus
shall we succeed in discerning the difference between colonial
civilization and English civilization.

The individuality of Canada will emerge before our eyes
from this picture of the life of its political capital; and as we
proceed to study the characteristics of the different parties it will
stand out more clearly still.

III

But the artificial unity which is the work of the Confederation has not solved the problem of the races. Under its cover
they have continued to live and to struggle. To whom is the
country ultimately to belong? To the French, ever growing in
multitude by virtue of their philoprogenitiveness? To the English, unceasingly reinforced by armies of immigrants? Rivals in
numbers, but rivals also in their customs and ideas. Is the
French-Canadian form of civilization sufficiently in keeping
with the times to achieve the victory, or must we reconcile
ourselves to the idea that Canada has passed for ever into
Anglo-Saxon hands? In truth this question has been answered
already, and is out of date. But the future has to reply to another
almost as grave.

The *tête-à-tête* of Quebec and Ontario cannot continue
for ever. Whilst this Anglo-French antagonism persists in the
East, scarcely modified by the years, a new Canada is being
developed in the West. Out there it is not the French with whom
their ancient opponents are confronted. It is the civilization of
America whose exuberance, force and vitality threaten to sub-
merge everything.

IV

It will remain for us, in conclusion, to inquire into the
foreign affairs of Canada considered as an individual nation.
Here again there are many problems for the future to solve.

The nature of the colonial bonds that tie the Dominion to
Great Britain is not eternal. If they are drawn closer, that will
mean the triumph of imperialism; which we shall study in all

its diverse phases and all its aspects, political, economic, and military. If they are broken, that will involve independence, with its attendant insecurity and danger — always latent — of absorption by the States. If they relax merely, insensibly, we shall have an indefinite prolongation of the actual state of things, with the door, however, wide open to American customs and ideas.

These are the alternative contingencies that depend upon the working out of the manifold and complex factors which we shall be studying in the first three sections of this book.

PART ONE

THE PSYCHOLOGICAL FORMATION OF THE TWO RACES

I–THE CHURCH

2: The Catholic Church – Its Administrative Methods

Of the 5,371,000 inhabitants of Canada, 2,229,000 are Catholics, and of these 1,429,000 belong to the single province of Quebec. The Church of Rome has its stronghold, therefore, upon French soil, and if we except the Irish element, which is somewhat numerous, it may be said that, speaking generally, the French of Canada are Catholic and the British Protestant. This fact contains the key to the entire political situation of the Dominion. There need be little fear of our exaggerating the part played by religion; both with Protestants and Catholics it is immense. In the case of the French Canadians the ascendancy of the Church is so great that it may be regarded as the principal factor in their evolution.

It has been too much insisted upon that separation between church and state has become the rule in the New World. That is true as regards the Protestants, but it is not quite accurate as regards the Church of Rome, at least in Quebec, where it is in enjoyment of a privileged system of government.

Let us make haste to acknowledge that upon the banks of the St. Lawrence the Catholic Church has achieved a place apart, that it has always proved a loyal and powerful protection to its disciples, and that our race and tongue owe to it perhaps their survival in America. This unique position has enabled it, ever since the British conquest of Canada, to wrest special privileges from the victors. In many respects the Old World rights which it still maintains are a recognition of services rendered to our nationality. Little wonder, then, if the Church is doubly dear to the French of Canada, who see in it not merely the exponent of their faith but also the accredited defender of their race.

Guarantees in regard to religious points figured largely in

the treaties which handed over our old colony to England. The capitulations of Quebec in 1759 and of Montreal in 1760 began by protecting the vanquished from all danger of that religious persecution of which they stood most in dread. The Treaty of Paris in 1763 confirmed these preliminary stipulations, and formally recognized the right of the French Catholics to keep up the practices of the Church of Rome within the limits of English law. Finally the Quebec Act, passed in 1774 by the imperial parliament, established definitively the civil, political, and religious rights of the French in Canada.

The status of the Catholic Church in Canada may be regarded, therefore, as due to a species of Concordat. The Quebec Act is really a treaty almost as much as a law. This was almost inevitable in a bilingual country in which two races live side by side without mingling.

The privileges of the Catholic Church in Canada are as follows: To begin with, it is accorded a kind of official recognition. The Quebec Act, regardful of the old French traditions, and confirmed in this by the *Code Civile* of 1877, cedes to the Catholic clergy the right to gather in and retain and disburse the time-honoured revenues due to them, provided that these revenues are to be exacted only from those who profess the religion of the Church of Rome.

The Protestants are entirely immune, therefore, from such rates. But it is otherwise with those who do not make an explicit declaration either that they have been converted to Protestantism or that they have ceased to belong to any faith. Catholics, liberal or liberated, religious free thinkers, if there be any such, are subjected to a certain mild form of intimidation, inasmuch as the law forces them either to obey the behests of the clergy or else nerve themselves to a kind of small apostasy, severely regarded by the public opinion, and in any case an ungrateful proceeding.

Unless they make this public profession, the Catholics are subjected to the payment of a tithe, or rather of a twenty-sixth bushel of wheat from their crop, for these dues are only acknowledged officially in the country districts. Here they have all the appearance of a regular tax, the clergy being empowered to enforce their payment by legal processes. In the towns their place is taken by a poll-tax not usually recognized by the law; from time to time, however, the courts have admitted its obligatory character, and as its levy is seldom or never challenged, it may be bracketed with the tithe. It will be seen, therefore, that in regard to this matter the separation between church and state does not exist.

There are other cases also in which the clergy are able to have recourse to the arm of the law for the recovery of their dues. When, for instance, there is question of erecting a new church, the bishop, assisted by a building committee, levies a special tax upon the members of the parish concerned, and he can secure a bill from the legislature for its enforcement.

No Protestant, I repeat, is liable to be thus taxed, but it is difficult for a Catholic, however unorthodox, to escape. Willy nilly, all must pay, and prosecutions, though rare, are by no means unheard of. No one protests. The French Canadians are devoted to their Church, free-thinkers are few, priest-baiters almost unknown. Therefore there is no talk of suppressing this ancient practice surviving from the France of yore.

It might be supposed that these important privileges would be balanced by a certain restriction of the liberties of the Church. That is not so. Its hierarchy and entire organization are absolutely free from control, or even supervision, at the hands of the state. We shall be able to take stock of all its essential features without so much as mentioning the name of the civil power.

The Canadian parish, the unit of the ecclesiastical state, is formed more or less upon the basis of the French parish. It is administered by a *curé* and a vestry board, composed of acting and honorary church-wardens; these boards are renewed by process of co-option, but it is the bishop through the *curé* who has the chief say as to their constitution. And though they are autonomous bodies to a certain extent, it must not be ignored that they are largely controlled – and to an ever increasing extent – by the bishop.

The allotting of ecclesiastical appointments also is carried out in complete freedom. The appointing of the *curés* lies with the bishops; that of new bishops with the Pope, who makes his selection from a list of three names (*dignus, dignior, dignissimus*) which is presented by the bishops already on the bench. No intervention from outside takes place, though the presence of an Apostolic Delegate involves the possibility of semi-official negotiations. But the Church is sufficiently strong in Canada to discountenance interference, and its pride would be hurt by certain kinds of suggestions. One does not easily forget the tone of ironical contempt with which Canadian ecclesiastics are wont to speak of the "Concordat," under which a M. Dumay, a freemason, had the appointing of the bishops in France!

The creation and delimitation of new dioceses is equally free from interference by the state. These are matters for Rome. Ottawa has nothing to say about them. It is not even necessary to notify them to the Canadian government. Thus the Church really achieves that perfect condition of complete independence of which its high functionaries love to talk. It lives outside the jurisdiction of the civil power; *above* it, the ecclesiastics sometimes maintain and always feel. No one ventures to assert in Canada, as in France, the supremacy of the state.

The very conception of a civil state does not seem indeed to have ever taken root in French Canada. One has no difficulty in seeing that it never went through its 1789. The reins of government are still in the hands of the clergy, and this seems to the public quite natural. It is the same with education: there are Catholic schools and Protestant schools, but there are no secular schools in our sense of the word. The dead are buried in denominational cemeteries: a Catholic who has died without receiving the last sacraments is not allowed to be buried in a Catholic cemetery; his family have to solicit a grave for him in a Protestant or Jewish cemetery. Such cases have occurred more than once. But in this respect also, though there have been protests enough, there has been no genuine effort at reform. This gives some idea of the mutual sentiment of toleration existing between the Churches. The condition of having no religion is simply not taken into account.

Most of the understandings come to in other countries with the Holy See have tended to check the intervention of the clergy in politics. In Canada the freedom of the priest in this respect is absolute. There is no law to prevent him from holding forth from the pulpit on the most burning questions of the day. As to the bishops, they are free to throw all the weight of their authority into the balance either by means of pastoral letters or of collective mandements. They have intervened in this way from time to time, and the government has had no power to cope with them effectively. The utmost that could be done has been to annul certain elections in which clerical interference has gone beyond all reasonable limits and has taken the form of refusing the sacraments to influence votes. But these cases have been very rare, and even the leaders of the Liberal party, though opposed by the Church, recognized the priest's right to take part in the electoral contests.

The clergy may congratulate themselves, therefore, on their position in face of the law. The law not merely places no obstacles in their way, but on the contrary it supports them. Only in their household, so to speak, have they rivals to contend with – namely, the members of the religious orders.

At the time of the cession of Canada it was stipulated that the sisterhoods should not be disturbed. There was no such provision as regards the Jesuits, Recollets, and Sulpicians, but the new rulers treated them in the most tolerant fashion. The Jesuit community, however, ceased to exist towards the end of the eighteenth century, and by an existing law their property passed into the hands of the state. The other orders developed, unfettered in any way, and the Sulpicians, in particular, throve remarkably.

In the course of the last twenty years the multiplication of religious confraternities in Canada has taken on considerable proportions; the Jesuits have returned, and have even been endowed to the extent of $680,000 by the Quebec legislature as indemnity for the former confiscation of their goods. In addition, the fame of Canada as a Catholic country, the liberal tendency of its ecclesiastical rule – to say nothing of the anti-clerical laws promulgated in France–have had the effect of attracting thousands of monks and nuns to the Dominion. They have to go through some formalities, it is true, before becoming established, but these are formalities and nothing more; they must obtain a bill from the provincial legislature, but this is rarely refused them; and they must submit to the jurisdiction of the bishopric. This done, they are free to receive offerings and legacies, without trammels of any kind upon their activities.

Their activities are very diverse in form. For the most part they win the goodwill and approval of the public. Some orders give up their lives to prayer and meditation, amply supported by alms. Others devote themselves to education: the Sulpicians, for instance, have most of the seminaries under their sway; the Jesuits play an important role in secondary education; the Christian Brothers find their occupation in the management of primary schools; while there are many who, availing themselves of the exemption from taxation which they enjoy, earn their livelihood just like laymen by setting up printing works or kitchen gardens, taking in washing, etc. They find a large field for their energies also in hospital work and charitable duties of all kinds in a country in which the province of the secular administration is not yet very clearly marked out. Finally, these orders sometimes are moved to build chapels, and it is in this connection that they come into direct conflict with the secular clergy.

Chapels are apt to be formidable rivals to parish churches. This has been discovered in Canada as elsewhere. The monks are well equipped for making way. They have all their time at their disposal, and are able to win adherents among rich and poor alike by their visits and good offices. The poor have recourse to them as their special protectors, as regards both body and soul. The rich are attracted by a stamp of elegance which distinguishes certain confraternities.

These are not the remarks merely of a foreign visitor. They come from the bishops and *curés* themselves. The bishops, especially, look with alarm at a competition which in some cases seems fraught with danger to them. They have even gone so far as to appropriate for their congregations certain chapels which seemed in too great demand; and, in order to avert the evil, they have sought to discourage the immigration of the members of religious orders in too great numbers. Not openly, but by means of hints, they convey a friendly warning to new arrivals and to intending comers that Canada, though a big place, has but a small population, and that for its still somewhat restricted flocks there is not scope for an unlimited supply of shepherds. If you *must* come, they say, at least go farther west and open out the prairie!

You may even hear people in close touch with the Church, but enjoying a greater freedom of speech than its dignitaries, complain openly of this troublesome invasion, and talk of the possibility of introducing a law dealing with the whole question of religious confraternities – a law which would meet with no very determined opposition from the bishops and *curés*. But these are wild words, the outcome of jealousy and ill-humour. Against the common enemies, Protestantism and Free Thought, all the forces of Catholicism are united and as one man. There may be diverse currents, but they are turned by the Vatican in the one direction.

The Catholic Church in Canada is in truth in a condition of deep submission to the Holy See. It bent the knee, not perhaps without reluctance but to the full, to that new order of things by which, thirty or forty years ago, the Church became an absolute centralized monarchy. We shall note many evidences of this in the course of the chapters that follow.

3 : The Catholic Church – Its Fear of the English Protestant Influence

All the old beliefs have been preserved as it were in ice among the French of Canada, and it would seem that the great stream of modern thought has as yet failed, with them, to shake the rock of Catholic belief. It is rare to find a body of the faithful so submissive in their attitude; and it is not merely the country folk who are to be found rallying round their priests, but also the townsfolk and the industrial population generally. Indifference is to be met with, of course, here as everywhere, but it hardly ever takes on the form of disrespect. We are far indeed from modern France.

In a bilingual country peopled by two races it is natural that the limits of religious jurisdiction should be very clearly drawn; this is the normal result of historical conditions, no less than of a very consistent and resolute line of policy followed by the Roman clergy since the first days of the conquest – the policy of isolation.

Dispersion and absorption are the two dangers which menace unceasingly the unity of our race in Canada. Therefore it was that the Church, profoundly convinced that to keep the race French was to keep it Catholic, came to look upon isolation as the chief safeguard for a racial individuality threatened on all sides by the advances of the New World. Therefore it is that it has put out all its efforts to segregate its flock from the rest of America. Instead of attempting the difficult and ungrateful task of making converts in the enemy's camp, it has devoted all its energies to retaining its hold over the souls belonging to it from the far past. In this work the two influences it has most to fear are those of French Protestantism and Anglo-Saxon free thought. To keep its members out of the reach of these two powerful tendencies is the programme which it continues to have constantly before it.

The first of these two dangers is the more threatening, for the solid body of French Catholics is beaten upon at all points by the on-coming waves of the Anglo-American ocean. English and Protestant have become almost synonymous terms in a country in which there are doubtless many English Catholics but in which French Protestants are practically non-existent. And it were vain to ignore the fact that conversion to Protestantism involves generally the passing of the convert into the ranks of the English body: the two things go together. In order to prevent these defections, the Catholic Church has done everything in its power to lessen the contact of the two races. The development of the French Canadians may have suffered from this division, but to it is due in great degree the astonishing persistence of their distinctive individuality.

Natural circumstances facilitate the accomplishment of this programme. Victors and vanquished, English and French, might well be expected to avoid rather than seek out occasions of intercourse: everything, or almost everything, tends to keep them apart.

The fact of their speaking different languages in particular constitutes a real barrier between them, which the clergy naturally do nothing to break down: the state of things produced by it is all in their favour.

This, however, does not apply to the bourgeoisie; for business, like the learned professions, demands a thorough knowledge of English. The colleges for secondary education managed by the Church have had to recognize this necessity, with the result that almost all Canadians of the upper or even the middle classes are now able to speak both languages quite well; they are in consequence more exposed to the influences of the neighbouring form of civilization.

But the great mass of French Canadians are unacquainted with any foreign tongue. They will probably remain so, and the Church can be at rest in regard to them as long as they do, for they are proof against the influence of the English-speaking races. Monseigneur Laflèche, Bishop of Trois-Rivières, has expressed his view upon the whole subject in a phrase that has become famous: "My children, be well up in French, but not *too* well up in English!"

Language constitutes the outworks protecting Catholicism in Canada. When these have been overcome, the stronghold of the Church is open to new attacks in the shape of the social intercourse that ensues between the two races, and above all in mixed marriages.

It is impossible to prevent all intercourse between two races living together in the same cities. The Church has realized this, and has reserved all her strength for the prevention as far as practicable of marriages between Catholics and Protestants. To this end she imposes severe conditions: the ceremony must take place only in the Catholic Church, and an undertaking must be given that the children shall be brought up in the Catholic faith.

This attitude is easy to understand, and its effects are clear. The Church wishes to keep its boundaries intact and well defined. She would prefer to lose a single individual member altogether rather than sanction the admission of a Protestant upon any other terms into a Catholic family. Otherwise the result might be the formation of dubious groups, half Catholic, half Protestant, likely to tend later towards free thought and to be lost entirely to Rome.

The success of this policy has been well-nigh complete. Mixed marriages are few, and in all cases the question of religion is settled one way or the other. It is not the clergy alone who are responsible for this solution. The whole Canadian community, Protestant as well as Catholic, supports them in the matter. Both races seem to feel that it is necessary to be either French or English, Protestant or Catholic – that it is not possible to be both at once, or to maintain a state of equilibrium between the two. Both armies have made prisoners in the strife, but each has in the long run held good its position.

The situation of the French Protestants between these opposing forces is a very difficult one. The French Protestant is something of a paradox in Canada. There is no place for him. The moment comes for him sooner or later when he must choose between his race and his religion. It is not easy for him to keep to his religion: no French-Canadian girl will be allowed to marry him unless he be prepared to hand over his children to the Church of Rome. If he wishes to remain a Protestant he is almost bound to marry an Englishwoman, and the result is that even if he himself resists British influences and remains French, his children will be barely able to speak his language, and will develop almost certainly into Anglo-Saxons.

It is in the second generation that these changes show themselves most notably. The examples are so convincing that one does not need to study French-Canadian society very long in order to come across them. Here is a Frenchman, very Protestant but at the same time very French, who settles in Canada. He has been successful, his sons are brought up there and share his ardent patriotic sentiments. When the time comes for them to marry, they naturally consider that an English-Canadian wife would be a stranger; and in order not to betray a whole body of traditions, they marry French-Canadian girls, yielding to the conditions laid down by the clergy. Their children will be Catholics; eventually they will hardly know that their father has been a Protestant.

Now, consider the case of a French Protestant who is Protestant above all. Not wishing at any price to become a Catholic, he is logically led to marry an English-Canadian girl of his own faith. What happens in his household? Something that he should have foreseen. Only English is spoken there; and if, on his express wish, his children learn French, they know it only as a foreign language. Very soon in that family our civilization will be only a memory.

It is true that there are some small French communities in Canada belonging to the Reformed Church – small colonies perhaps it would be more correct to designate them, for they have nothing Canadian about them. Their moral elevation of character and their cohesion are worthy of all praise, but their position is a precarious one owing to the state of things I have described.

It would be quite a mistake to suppose that the Canadian Catholic clergy are animated by any anti-English feeling in their policy of isolation. What they are guarding against is Protestantism and liberalism. That is why they look askance at the Americans also, even the American Catholics who are suspected of too great independence in their attitude towards the Holy See. Therefore it is that the neighbouring peoples are kept apart almost as by water-tight partitions. The Canadian Catholic spirit follows its own course, and knows no other guidance than that of Rome. In these circumstances it is not surprising that Protestant, Jewish and deist America should be an object of even greater alarm than England, as being more alive and less conservative. The policy of annexation has no more resolute opponents than the clergy of Quebec, for they realize that on the day the province should be swept into the American vortex there would be an end to its old isolation, and it would be overwhelmed by the torrent of new ideas. It would mean the end of Catholic supremacy in this corner of the world, perhaps the deathblow to the French race in Canada.

Such, then, in its main outlines, is the policy of isolation so effectively pursued by the Canadian Catholic Church. It is becoming a more and more difficult one in the face of the unceasing advance of methods of communication and the progress of education and the growth of the power of the press. However, the clergy are not relaxing their efforts, and they maintain their desperate struggle for the upper hand in the matter of the schools. And if they do not win over many Protestants they still retain their authority over their own flocks.

Up to the present their defences have not suffered much at the hands of their English opponents. Let us see now how they have fared face to face with the revolutionary France of 1789. Their resistance in this direction we shall find is not less persistent or less energetic.

4: The Catholic Church –
Its Fear of Modern France

In the eyes of the Catholic clergy of Canada modern France, viewed either from the standpoint of its administrative methods or of its free-thinking tendencies, is a source of danger not less great than Protestant England. It symbolizes to them the secular theory of government, the triumph of modern ideas, the hated principles of the Revolution. France to them is an object lesson, a nation adrift to which a wide berth must be given. We may evoke the deep and sincere sympathy of the Canadian priests personally and individually, but the Catholic Church of Canada in the very name of its principles can regard the France of 1789 with no other feeling than alarm.

Despite their rapid and complete submission to English rule, the French priesthood cherished none the less for some time after the conquest of Canada a certain feeling for our *ancien régime*. But with the Revolution the divorce became complete. While the Church in France lost all its privileges the Church in Canada retained them, precisely because it had ceased to be French. From its distant stronghold upon the St. Lawrence it looked on in safety at the crisis of 1793. It was inevitable that it should congratulate itself on having ceased to belong to a country whose impiety and lawlessness it condemned.

The development of our democracy in the course of the nineteenth century has resulted but in the strengthening of this disapprobation. To 1789 and 1793 succeeded 1848 and 1871. The Third Republic, after some hesitations, decided to act in independence of, and, when necessary, in opposition to Rome. The secular school, the law against religious societies, the rupture with the Pope, the separation of church and state, have marked the principal stages of this movement.

That the example of France is one to be avoided rather than imitated is the view not merely of the Catholic clergy but of all Catholic French Canadians. Even the liberals among them do not feel drawn towards our present social condition. They come to France and enjoy themselves among us and see things to admire, but they refuse to take us for a model.

The Catholic newspapers of the colony – none of which could live without the approval of the priests – never cease to proclaim our decadence and ruin under the régime of the free-masons. Whether it be the *Semaines Réligieuses*, the organs of the bishops, or the independent journals like *La Vérité* of Quebec, or the great dailies like *La Patrie*, *La Presse*, or *Le Journal*, it is always the same refrain: Unfortunate France!

Not everyone in Catholic Canada sympathizes with the following passage from *Le Journal* (November 22, 1904), but there is no mistaking the accents of the Church: "We spoke yesterday of the unhappy condition of France. We give her our pity, because the evil from which she is suffering is a terrible one. We dread it for ourselves, for it is contagious: it is the evil of free-masonry."

La Vérité congratulates Canada on being no longer a colony of France. It goes on: "We have thus escaped, thanks be to God, the horrors of the French Revolution and the still worse horrors, though different in kind, of modern France with its impiety. . . . Let us beware of official France! She is our greatest danger at the present moment. Too many people fail to realize this." And the conclusion follows naturally: "We frankly confess that we do not see the necessity of developing relations between France and Canada."

This conclusion is that of the clergy. It is part of the general policy of isolation which we have described above: since France has become the most intense centre of the revolutionary spirit, the classical land of new ideas, Canadians will do well to hold themselves aloof from a nation so disquieting. Let them confine themselves strictly to French Catholic circles, even though there are many liberals among them; but, to repeat the slogan we have just quoted, beware of official France. The ecclesiastical authorities do not like to say such things aloud, but they leave no one ignorant that this is what they think. And, above all, their actions in all circumstances are in accord with these thoughts.

The Church may keep its faithful members separated from the Anglo-Saxon world by leaving them ignorant of the English language. Against French influence it cannot use the same means, for the community of language is exactly what brings Canada closest to France. On the other hand the danger of geographical neighbourhood does not exist. The distance between the two countries is very great, and few people from the two sides meet.

Nevertheless, these meetings, however little they may multiply, incur the risk of being fruitful in consequences, just as our writings may provoke new orientations and develop ferments of independence. The defence tactics of the clergy in this case are different from those which we explained in the previous chapter. They take care first to supervise and control the reading of books from France; then they choose very carefully those of our citizens whom they invite to Canada; and finally, as far as possible, they discourage the youth of Canada from coming to Paris in search of ideas and slogans. Sometimes they go so far as to suspect even our ecclesiastics of liberalism.

The controlling of the reading of an entire people is a big enterprise, but one before which the Canadian clergy has never recoiled. To this end it possesses an "Index" – an effective weapon of which it avails itself daily. Our principal authors have come under its ban – Musset, Renan, and above all, Zola, "whose name should not be so much as mentioned even from the pulpit, and whose books should not be admitted, not merely into any Catholic, but into any decent, respectable household."[1] Of course, the Index is not all-powerful: the interdicted books find their way into the colony in spite of it. They are not exposed for sale, however, in any of the respectable bookshops, and in the small towns no bookshop that is not respectable has a chance. The condemned authors are ruled out also from those libraries which are under the control of the clergy, and we shall see presently how little disposed the clergy are to allow any library to thrive in independence of them. There are reading-rooms managed by intelligent, broad-minded people, who welcome presents of books from their friends in France, but they are not free to put in circulation whatever works they may think fit. If they were to try, they would very soon be crushed. All such gifts have to be approved by the bishop. Even so, there are extremists who are disturbed at the sight of official France taking note of the social condition of Canada. *La Vérité* goes so far as to condemn the reading of the *Revue des deux Mondes*. A propos of the presentation of thirty-three yearly volumes of the *Revue* to one of these reading-rooms by a generous Rouen lady, the Quebec journal remarks: "Is it to be supposed that there is nothing reprehensible in these thirty-three annual vol-

[1] Letter from Mgr. Bruchesi, Archbishop of Montreal, 1903, cited by M. G. Giluncy, *L'Européen*, October 31, 1903.

umes? To imagine so is to know very little of the history and character of the *Revue*." (May 15, 1904.)

The clergy are not less cautious when there is question of nominating a Frenchman from France for any post in the Dominion. They require elaborate guarantees as to his soundness of views. Laval University, for instance, has for some years past had French professors of literature. Candidates for these posts are examined very rigorously not only in regard to their special qualifications but also in regard to their tendencies of mind. Nevertheless, the original French temperament asserting itself in them, some of them are held to be too liberal, too bold – in a word, too French. Sometimes they are not allowed a complete liberty of speech. One of them who had begun to treat of the nineteenth century in the first year of his professorship was shunted to the seventeenth century in his next. And he was really a sober-minded, moderate man. Every professor of advanced ideas must consider himself sacrificed in advance if by chance he has succeeded in being chosen.

The same may be said of any publicist anxious to spread radical doctrines in Canada. His propaganda will meet with effective opposition from the clergy, and if he accepts the support offered him by the English he will do for himself altogether. With the French he could only make way either with the support or at least the toleration of the Church. M. Brunetière's talents alone would not have sufficed to win him the triumphs that fell to his lot at Montreal and Quebec; he needed also his reputation for Catholic sympathies, and even so there were some sections in Quebec who thought him somewhat too advanced.

It should be borne in mind that this opposition to the France of to-day, and all that she stands for, originates with the Church. Left to themselves, the majority of Canadians, especially in the towns, would be very glad to see and listen to even the boldest of our public men.

Even our French priests are not always welcome in Canada, as I have said already. In a curious article in *La Revue du Clergé Français* a French priest, Père Giquello, formerly editor of the *Semaine Réligieuse* of Tours, tells us of the great disillusionment he experienced in regard to this colony. "In the Canadian dioceses," he writes, "there is no room for priests from France. . . . The Canadian clergy have adopted the Monroe Doctrine, and their motto is 'Canada for the Canadians.' Even when there is not a full complement of seminarists for a diocese, French priests will find themselves ruled out on principle. Try for yourself. Present yourself to one of these Canadian bishops to whom we give so cordial a welcome here in France. You will be very well received, he will say all kinds of nice things to you. Encouraged by his sympathetic and benevolent demeanour, you will offer him your zealous services; you will tell him of your ardent wish to undertake the duties of a priest; you will even put before him your qualifications and any talents you may possess. Now will come the change! The episcopal countenance, a moment ago so radiant, is clouded over. The eyebrows are drawn together, a hard line is visible at the corners of the lips, you receive a downright refusal, and are discourteously bidden good-day. I guarantee that eight times out of ten the interview will take this course."[2]

The clergy, as I have said, are equally against the sending of Canadian youths to France for the completion of their studies. They look with disfavour, for instance, upon endowments in connection with the University of Paris. They prefer the universities of Lille, Fribourg, or Louvain as being more Catholic and not in France.

The question was raised very distinctly à propos of medical students. Our countrymen in Canada have always displayed brilliant aptitudes for the career of medicine. It is only natural, therefore, that the most distinguished among them should wish to complete their studies in Paris, where they have the double advantage of speaking their native tongue and finding a Faculty of the highest class. Many are the young Canadians who have come freely for this purpose. The Church could do nothing to prevent them.

But one fine day it was suggested that it would be a desirable thing to institute scholarships for the medical students at Laval University which should cover the expenses of their voyage to France. The idea was an excellent one and quite practicable, and the French government welcomed it with the greatest favour. But nothing was done. Why? The Archbishop of Montreal did not conceal the reason from the people of his entourage: he was afraid of the evil influences that Paris life might have upon the winners of the scholarships. *La Vérité*, that *enfant terrible* of the ultramontane party, did not hesitate to blurt out what certain anxious Catholics were thinking to themselves. "The idea has been put forward of establishing a college in Paris for French-Canadian medical students. This idea has

[2] P. Giquello, "Choses Canadiennes," *Revue du Clergé Français*, December 15, 1904.

given rise to serious disquiet. For if the capital of France is a centre of science, it is also, alas! a centre of corruption and impiety. If the project can be carried out without peril to the faith of our future physicians, well and good. If not, let it be put aside, for it is of infinitely greater moment that we should have physicians a little less learned but sound in matters of religion, than a little more learned and without faith." (July 15, 1904.)

The Church is quite logical in taking up this attitude, and it is to be feared that any other such proposal would meet in the same way with determined if not open opposition. Should it be found necessary to supplement the higher education of Canada in any particular branch, it is to be feared that other centres of French culture, such as Switzerland or Belgium, where the progress of the secular modern spirit is less marked, will be chosen in preference to Paris. Is it not a matter for regret that in regard to this question of university education we should not be able to count the Church among the chief champions of a Franco-Canadian rapprochement?

It is not only the lay students, however, who yearn to put the finishing touch to their studies in Europe. The clerical students experience the same desire, and it would seem to be essential in their case. Rome is naturally their ultimate destination; but France is on the way, and they love to stay with us en route.

Close relations used to result from this state of things. Charming and faithful friendships were formed between distinguished representatives of both branches of the Church, and many young Canadian priests learned to love France more than their Superiors would have wished. Their contact with the French clergy taught them that even in ecclesiastic society there is room for a kind of liberalism unknown in Canada.

Perhaps for this reason the Canadian Church has seemed of late to discountenance such intercourse a little. Sojourns at St. Sulpice are no longer recommended. There existed until recently in Rome a Sulpician seminary resorted to by French and Canadians in common. Therein, under one roof, during many months of close companionship, they formed intimacies which were to brighten their whole lives. This mixed institution has recently disappeared, and from a French standpoint the fact is to be deplored. To-day there is a seminary apart for the Canadian students in the Eternal City. Many of the younger members of the Canadian clergy have openly expressed to me their regret at the change. One day perhaps these broad-minded young clericals will be bishops. Then perhaps they will think differently!

Thus it is that in its own defence the Canadian Church is endeavouring to relax rather than to draw closer the bonds uniting it to republican, or even ecclesiastical France. Down to the present it has been more or less successful in its efforts. But it seems scarcely probable that it can persist in these tactics for ever. Intercourse between the two countries increases inevitably every year, and the isolation in which the Church would keep Canada is contrary to the whole logic of the times. It cannot endure.

5: The Catholic Church –
Its Influence in Social Life

Having done all in her power to keep her flock out of the range of pernicious influences, the Catholic Church in Canada proceeds to watch over it and guide it in small matters as well as great. Refusing absolutely to be bound down by the state to a line of non-interference with the liberty of the citizen, she maintains stoutly her right to act as a natural leader. "Not only is the Church independent of civil society – she is superior to it by reason of her extent and of her goal. . . . It is not the Church that is comprised in the State; it is the State that is comprised in the Church."[1]

In every aspect of life, social or political, public or private, the clergy expects to have its say and to give its orders. Its aim is that no position on any question of importance be set forth unless inspired or at least authorized by itself. It condemns the theory of the separation of the two realms, lay and religious; and, since the obstacles in its way are feeble or non-existent, it tends in the province of Quebec to constitute a veritable little theocracy.

So, in French-Canadian society, the individual, the family, worldly relations, are surrounded by a close network of ecclesiastical influences which it is almost impossible to escape. Note that Protestants remain perfectly free. Free thinkers would enjoy the same independence, which is moreover guaranteed by the law, if they were numerous enough for mutual support. But Catholics, whether free thinkers, indifferent or emancipated, can escape only with the greatest difficulty from the fundamental

[1] Collective pastoral letter of the Quebec Episcopate, Sept. 22, 1875.

rules of a society fashioned by Rome. If they do not consent to submit, at least in form, social life becomes impractical for them, or nearly so.

We all know the case, classical amongst us, of the radical or socialist whose wife is a clerical. Every French Canadian who is somewhat emancipated in his religious views will feel the same difficulty as our Frenchman. In his innermost mind he will certainly be able to preserve the ideas that please him; he will even be able in large measure to express them orally or in writing. But he would hardly be able to put them into practice in his family life. Will he succeed in having a civil marriage, supposing that his conscience forbids a marriage in the church? It is not likely. On this point he will have to yield to his fiancée, that is to the clergy, who will thereby already become influential in his new life. Then, if he refuses at first to follow the religious ceremonies, the natural insistence of a pious wife, the tacit disapproval of his conduct by public opinion, will usually end by overcoming his resistance. It is thus that in Montreal certain free thinkers, free-masons perhaps, are regularly dragged to mass. They do not listen, they do not respect the service, they may even bring books and read them ostentatiously. What does it matter? They are there and their presence is in itself an act of submission. One can divine from this example what courage and obstinacy a French Canadian must possess in order to evade even these external forms.

But it is in the teaching of the children that the power of the clergy shows itself irresistibly. There are no lay schools, as we have said already. So it is necessary to choose between the English school of Protestant tendency and the French school of a tendency and character distinctly Catholic. We have explained the cruel problem of conscience which this situation imposes on the Protestant. The free thinker is not less embarrassed, for neither of the two alternatives can satisfy him. Finally, the Catholic – or simply the indifferent husband of a practising wife – has no freedom to hesitate; he cannot act independently without exposing himself to the formidable hostility of the ecclesiastical power; it is difficult, dangerous, impossible. In these conditions it is almost inevitable that every French-speaking child ends by falling under Roman influence.

For the Church this kind of domination is a question of life or death. On this its future depends. So this is the last point on which it is disposed to make the slightest concession. Let the English Protestants for their part do as they please. Let them organize godless schools, the Church will not protest. This does not come within the domain reserved to it. But let there be a threat to lay hands on the French confessional schools, in order to put them under the direction or even the supervision of the state, and then the clergy as one man will charge with all its force.

The submission of the faithful in the school question is strictly part of Catholic obedience. The Church admits no exception, and on this subject it makes no compromise. "Those who do not obey the hierarchy," declared Monseigneur Langevin, "are no longer Catholics. When the hierarchy has spoken it is useless for the Catholic to say the contrary, for if he acts that way he ceases to be a Catholic. Such a person may still claim the title, but I tell you clearly in my capacity as bishop, and with all the authority attaching to the position, that the Catholic who does not obey the hierarchy on the school question ceases to be a Catholic."[2] These words express clearly the rule which has always directed the clergy in the matter of education.

The control of education is not sufficient for the Church. The child, grown into a young man, is exposed on all sides, even in Canada, to the contagion of modern ideas. Through books and newspapers he may come into almost direct contact with the most advanced and revolutionary representatives of the actual world. A redoubling of vigilance is necessary, therefore, to ensure that the man does not deny everything which the schoolboy has learned.

Placing a book on the Index is a first obstacle imposed by ecclesiastical authority in the way of the freedom of reading which is judged dangerous. By this means the purchase of many works which are suspect or declared to be so is rendered difficult. Visiting a library in a small Quebec city, I searched in vain for several masters of the contemporary French novel. They had been placed under interdict and were not there, either in the open or in concealment. I discovered a sufficiently complete collection in the room of the son of the house, hidden behind a curtain. I understood then how the Index functions. The Church had not been able to prevent our literature from penetrating – that would have been impossible. But it had made this literature generally inaccessible, and so at least it saved appearances. One must recognize that this amounts to a good deal.

It is not, however, by means of purchased volumes that new

[2] At Montreal, in 1876. Cited by J. S. Willison in his book, *Sir Wilfrid Laurier and the Liberal Party*, II, 239.

or subversive doctrines are in danger of spreading. It is really through public libraries. So the Church has declared a war without mercy on them. Not that it opposes the creation or existence of every library. But it is insistent on control over all those that are founded, and on supreme control – failing which, it prevents them from being born or destroys them. The history of Canada for the past half-century has furnished several striking examples of this deliberate opposition of the clergy to the free, easy and independent reading of modern books.

The most celebrated case is that of the *Institut Canadien*. This was a scientific and literary society founded in 1849 in Montreal by a group of young men who were mostly of the liberal persuasion. They were all Catholics, but in a spirit of broad tolerance they admitted English Protestants to membership. The movement having made rapid progress, other *Instituts Canadiens*, similar to the first, were established in most cities. By 1854 the province of Quebec had one hundred of them.

The Church became alarmed, and founded rival societies, known as *Instituts Nationaux*, which it kept under strict supervision. By 1858 this tactic had brought about the disappearance of all the *Instituts Canadiens* with the one exception of that of Montreal which still held firm and, while professing its respect for religion, refused to pass under the Caudine Forks. It soon became a veritable *bête noire* to the ecclesiastical authorities.

The first complaint against it was that it had an independent library, with a reading-room in which were two Protestant journals, the Montreal *Witness* and *Le Semeur Canadien*. Then Monseigneur Bourget, Bishop of Montreal, accused them of having in their possession immoral books. The committee replied that in their opinion this charge was without foundation, and that the matter was one for their own judgment entirely.

This meant war. In a pastoral letter, the bishop, having set forth the case clearly, declared openly that the committee had been guilty of two grave offences: first, in claiming to be the sole competent judges of the morality of certain works; secondly, in having declared that they were not in possession of immoral writings when books were to be found in their library which had been placed on the Index. He called upon the committee to withdraw these statements. Unless they did so, Catholics would be forbidden to belong to the *Institut Canadien*.

The situation became inextricable for the members of the society. Catholics for the most part, they would incur very serious consequences by opposing the bishop. In 1863 they suggested a compromise. Let the bishop indicate all the books which he considered immoral and they should be kept under lock and key! To this proposal the bishop made no definite reply. What he really desired was the disappearance of the society, not merely its reform. The committee soon realized this, and in despair appealed to Rome. After a delay of four years, this brought them a fresh condemnation from the Pope: all those who continued to be members of the society or to read its Annual would be deprived of the sacraments. Resistance became impossible. In 1869 the *Institut Canadien* closed its doors. The Church had prevailed over the cause of liberty.

The pretensions of the clergy have not been lessened since then, though they are formulated, perhaps, less aggressively than in this pronouncement by Monseigneur Bourget. They continue to set their face against the starting of public libraries of all kinds without their approval. In 1903 Mr. Carnegie offered a great library to Montreal on the lines of those which he had presented to a number of American cities. Such a boon would have been the more welcome in that Montreal possesses only two mediocre collections of French books. However, the municipal council refused the gift, and their action in the matter is attributed almost universally to clerical influence.

To-day as yesterday, therefore, it remains very difficult to create in Quebec an enterprise of French social education – I will not say against the Church, but beyond its reach. Applying the words of the gospel, "he who is not for me is against me," it exacts complete submission or drives you into open hostility. Controlling the disciplined army of its faithful, it is easy for it to boycott an institution that displeases it. And so, in spite of legislation which, as far as words go, presents all the guarantees of liberalism, the liberty of reading books leaves much to be desired in French Canada.

The liberty of the press is likewise far from being complete. To be sure, no law restricts it. The English newspapers are printed and published in entire freedom from outside interference. To all appearances, that is also the case with the French newspapers, but this is not so in reality. The bishops, with their power of condemnation, are able to exercise almost complete control. Condemnation from the pulpit results in a decrease of sales at once. Should this not suffice, the confessional does the rest. Editors know they can resist for two or three months, but not more. The Church always wins in the end.

There are many liberals or even anti-clericals among the

Canadian publicists who deplore this condition of affairs, but who must trim their sails like all the others so as not to run their journals upon the rocks. All, or almost all, come to an understanding with the clergy. At Montreal, the archbishop calls any editor severely to account who prints anything calculated to hurt the susceptibilities of the Church; a second offence of the same kind would entail very serious consequences. The newspaper directors, mindful of the interests of shareholders, are careful to avoid such conflicts. Sometimes a canon of the cathedral, specially selected for this work, is enabled to read the proofs of articles and to delete whatever may seem to him harmful. In such conditions it will be easily understood that anything in the shape of an anti-clerical campaign is out of the question for the great French-Canadian dailies. It would merely be jeopardizing their existence.

What is not possible for a mass-circulation journal, would this be possible for a journal of combat, which has a narrower circulation and which desires to discuss and propagate ideas? In a word, under existing conditions, could an anti-clerical journal exist in French Canada? Experience has always proved that this is impossible. We may instance the case – now no longer recent – of *Le Pays*, twice condemned and at last crushed by Monseigneur Bourget. More interesting, however, are the experiences of *Les Débats* and *Le Combat*, quite lately condemned and destroyed without any kind of trouble by the Archbishop of Montreal.

Les Débats, now defunct, was run in opposition to the Church, and attacked it in very downright fashion. Many warnings were conveyed to it, but without result. Instead of falling into line with its prudent contemporaries, it persisted in its policy. At last Monseigneur Bruchesi condemned it in a letter read in all the churches in his diocese.

We may claim, [he said], *to have shown all possible forbearance and consideration in our attitude towards* Les Débats. *We regret that our efforts have had no result. Its harmful work has been persisted in, perhaps more audaciously than ever. The journal has been setting forth doctrines in regard to evolution which are bordering on heresy, if not actually heretical. It has insulted disgracefully the venerated name of Monseigneur Ignace Bourget. It has spoken insultingly of Pius IX., and has held the Syllabus up to ridicule. We cannot refer here to all the other offences of which it has been guilty. Lately, when we had occasion to remind Catholics in one of our parishes of the necessity of keeping holy the Lord's Day, Les Débats could find nothing better to do than to endeavour to make fun of our letter. . . . Fathers and mothers, are you going to leave in the hands of your children a poison that is calculated to cause their spiritual death? Bad books and bad newspapers are, as you know well, deadly poisons for the soul. It is our aim to preserve, especially among the youth of our community, – so dear to us and so exposed to peril, – the purity of our faith, the strength of our morals, the practice of our religious duties, as well as a love for the Church and respect for its authority. . . . These are our reasons for wishing to arrest the diffusion of these dangerous publications, capable of causing irreparable evil. By virtue of our episcopal powers and in accordance with the rules of the Index, we therefore forbid the faithful of our diocese to sell, buy, read, or keep this newspaper, Les Débats. . . . This charge shall be read from the pulpit of all churches in which Mass is publicly celebrated, and in the chapter-house of all religious communities, on the first Sunday after its receipt. Given at Montreal, under our hand and seal and the counter-signature of our Chancellor, this twenty-ninth day of September nineteen hundred and three.*

(Signed)   PAUL ARCHBISHOP OF MONTREAL.[3]

Clearly *Les Débats* could not withstand so definite an interdict. It disappeared – but to reappear under a new name, *Le Combat!* *Le Combat* took up the same line as its predecessor, only to experience just the same fate; it could scarcely flatter itself that it could hope for anything else. On the 20th of January 1904, the archbishop launched a second interdict, worded as follows:

On September 29, 1903, I was obliged to forbid the reading of Les Débats. *This newspaper has since then continued to appear under a new title though in the same tone. It claims to be in its fifth year of publication, and the numbering of its new issues corresponds with that of the old. Now you all must understand that it was a dangerous newspaper that I condemned, not merely a name. In consequence, the journal condemned on September 29 remains condemned throughout the diocese whatever title may be given to it, unless and until its directors make submission and promise of amendment. Until the interdict has*

[3] Letter of Mgr. Bruchesi, Archbishop of Montreal, Sept. 29, 1903.

been removed, it is forbidden to buy, sell, read, or keep this newspaper.[4]

Thus Monseigneur Bruchesi officially condemned not merely *Les Débats* and *Le Combat* but any future successor of the same character, whatever its name: it amounted to a general interdict, placed upon an entire order of ideas. As a matter of fact no successor appeared. There was no law to prevent the paper from being continued, but from the moment the archbishop launched his mandate it ceased to have readers.

The interesting point about this episode is that it shows the immense authority wielded by the Church, when there is nothing to resist its will. The doctrines of Monseigneur Bourget and Monseigneur Bruchesi are not personal to them – they are the doctrines of Rome, under Leo XIII and Pius X as under Pius IX. In the *Libertas* Encyclical of Leo XIII they may be found clearly set forth.[5] The Church claims to have the right of restricting freedom of every kind – of worship, of speech, of the press, of education, and even of the conscience. The Catholic clergy succeed better in Canada than elsewhere in carrying this programme into effect, yet freedom in all these things is provided for in the Canadian constitution. Liberty appears in the laws, but does not yet exist in the customs of the people.

6: The Catholic Church – Its Intervention in Politics

The claims of the Church in Canada to authority over the family, education, and printing, make it easy to understand that it is not disposed to remain neutral in the political struggle. Its conception of its own supremacy involves its participation in politics as an absolute duty.

Its spokesmen have expressed their views on this point on many occasions. "It is impossible to deny that politics and religion are closely allied and that the separation of church and state is an absurd and impious doctrine. This is especially true under a constitutional government which, by entrusting full legislative powers to a Parliament, places a very dangerous

---

[4] Letter of Mgr. Bruchesi, Jan. 24, 1904.
[5] Encyclical letter of His Holiness Leo XIII to the patriarchs, primates, archbishops, and bishops of the Catholic world on the subject of human liberty, June 20, 1888 (generally known as the *Libertas* Encyclical).

weapon – a double-edged sword – in the hands of its members."[1] Therefore, to cope with this danger, shall the Church take on itself the guidance of the state? That is the conclusion that follows inevitably from the following phrase, taken from a collective pastoral letter issued by the Episcopate of the province of Quebec: "The priest and the bishop have the right and the duty to speak not only to the electors and to the candidates, but also to the constituted authorities" (September 22, 1875).

By their famous collective pastoral of 1896 on the subject of the schools of Manitoba, the Bishops of the ecclesiastical provinces of Quebec, Montreal, and Ottawa confirm this utterance, and assert with no uncertain voice their right to take part in electoral campaigns: "If the bishops, whose authority issues from God Himself, are the natural judges of all questions which touch upon the Christian faith and morals, if they are the acknowledged heads of a perfect society, sovereign, superior by its nature and its ends to civil society, it follows that it is in their province, when circumstances so demand, not merely to express generally their views and wishes in regard to religious matters, but also to indicate to the faithful or to approve the best means of attaining the spiritual ends in view" (May 6, 1896).

Innumerable members of the clergy have intimated individually to their flocks that it is their duty to follow strictly the instructions of the Church in politics. Thus the Bishop of Rimouski, again on the Manitoba school question, writes to a correspondent: "An elector who is at heart a Catholic and who is anxious to obey his bishop cannot say, 'This is my own opinion and I must vote according to my conscience,' and go against the order of his bishop, without sinning grievously and rendering himself unworthy of the sacraments. That opinion of his is a culpable opinion, and his conscience in this matter is a false conscience. The personal opinion of a voter is not his good conscience if not in conformity with the wishes and instructions set forth by the bishops in their pastoral" (June 12, 1896).

Certain prelates have gone even farther than this. In 1876, Judge Casault having cancelled two elections on the ground of clerical interference, the Bishop of Rimouski (a predecessor of the bishop cited above) did not hesitate to denounce as false and contrary to the teachings of the Church the following propositions involved in the judgment:
1. That Parliament is all-powerful and entitled to make what

---

[1] Pastoral letter of the Bishop of Trois-Rivières, published in the *Journal de Trois-Rivières*, April 20, 1870.

laws it likes, even if they be contrary to the practice of religion.

2. That the freedom of the elector ought to be absolute.

3. That it is within the province of the courts of law to repress what they may consider the abuses of the pulpit or the exercise of the priest's right to refuse the sacraments.

4. That the refusal of the sacraments in connection with voting is an illegal proceeding.[2]

Certainly some of these episcopal declarations, made in the heat of battle, do not exactly represent the policy of the Vatican. Several times, on the complaint of statesmen too violently opposed, the Papacy has intervened with the Canadian hierarchy to moderate the harshness of its attacks. At the close of the great battle of Manitoba, on the official instance of Sir Wilfrid Laurier, now prime minister after his victory, the Holy See sent to Ottawa an apostolic delegate whose instructions would seem to have been to preach calm rather than combativeness. Was it the influence of this ambassador, or was it rather the absence of any burning religious question in the elections of 1900 and 1904? At any rate a certain appeasement has taken place in the last ten years. However there has not been, and doubtless will not be, any disavowal by Rome of doctrines as applied to Canada which in themselves it has never denied. Canadian priests accordingly maintain their political pretensions with energy.

What especially characterizes clerical action in Canadian elections is the total absence of precautions with which it is carried on. The bishops and *curés*, not being bound by any legal text, and persuaded that they are exercising a strict right in mingling in public affairs, do not even take the trouble to hide their intervention. In open pulpit or in letters voluntarily communicated to the press, they take sides frankly, patronize one candidate, condemn another, give orders, issue prohibitions, and even go so far as to have recourse to the weapon of refusal of sacraments, which is very efficacious in a society so observant of religious duties. From Confederation in 1867 down to 1896 one might say that there was not an election in which this intervention in politics did not show itself with the most audacious simplicity. Without recalling at length the character of these contests, let us take certain examples of clerical tactics. These

2 Cited by J. S. Willison, *Sir Wilfrid Laurier and the Liberal Party*, I, 292-98.

will give an understanding of the tone and of the methods habitually employed.

The Charlevoix by-election of 1876 is often recalled to mind. It took place following some passionate polemics between Protestants and Catholics, and was the occasion of a general mobilization of the ecclesiastical forces in favour of the Conservative candidate, Hector Langevin. The Liberal candidate, Pierre Tremblay, was also a Catholic. Nonetheless, the clergy let themselves go against him with unusual violence. In all the pulpits, in all the confessionals, the *curés* devoted themselves to passionate propaganda. "Vote according to your conscience," said one of them, "I approve of that, but according to your conscience as enlightened by your superiors. Do not forget that the bishops of this province assure you that liberalism resembles a serpent in the earthly paradise which creeps close to men in order to bring about the fall of the human race." Such speeches were repeated hundreds of times. The judicial inquiry that took place after the election revealed circumstances still more grave. One witness declared: "I was afraid of damnation if I voted for Tremblay." Another said he had understood that whoever voted for the Liberal candidate was guilty of mortal sin, and in case of death could expect to see himself deprived of the services of a priest. A third explained that he was old, that he would doubtless soon die, and that in these circumstances he would not have wished to vote against the opinion of his *curé*. Finally another declared, under oath, that the *curé* of Saint Hilarion had said aloud in the pulpit that to vote for the Liberal party was to vote against the *curé*, against the bishop, against the Pope himself.[3]

In his book *l'Irlande, le Canada, Jersey*, (p. 218), M. de Molinari cites a still more curious example of pressure. It occurred in a contested election of the same period. In the course of the inquiry a Liberal *habitant* whom the *curé* had threatened with the fires of hell was being questioned. Question: "When did the *curé* tell you that Lucifer had come from hell to enrol your votes?" Answer: "In the preceding election." Q: "Were you afraid of seeing Lucifer?" A: "No. A Catholic ought not to fear Lucifer. He runs away from the holy water, does Lucifer." Q: "What frightened you then?" A: "It was the words from the *curé* which had given me a terrible terror, his accents and his eloquence. I was afraid for the moment, I was seized with fear,

[3] Examples quoted by J. S. Willison, *op. cit.*, I, 289-90.

but I reassured myself." Q: "You said that after all you didn't think that Lucifer would come after you." A: "No, because I was a Catholic, apostolic and Roman; and a Catholic ought not to be afraid of the devil. I have never been afraid of the devil, not me." Q: "You swear that the devil has never prevented you from voting?" A: "No, he has never prevented me from voting. Perhaps if he had appeared to me, he would have prevented me from voting, but he never appeared to me."

This kind of propaganda took place thirty years ago in a remote district. One is permitted to believe that it would not be possible to-day. In 1896, indeed, when the school question was publicly discussed, the action of the clergy had not this rude character. One must state, however, that it was as passionate and energetic.

A collective charge of the episcopate (the same as that to which we have alluded above) began by declaring, in terms undoubtedly veiled but nonetheless perfectly clear, that the Church identified itself with the Conservative cause. The consequence was deduced in all the parishes: Catholics were forbidden to vote Liberal. In the ardour of the struggle, which kept on increasing, the clergy were not long in revealing themselves completely. Obedience to the charge, that is to vote Conservative, became their great, their unique slogan. Many documents establish this fact.

In a letter dated June 12, 1896, the Bishop of Rimouski wrote to a voter: "Sir, you ask me if it is a grievous error to vote against the charge of the bishops on the Manitoba schools. I reply: Yes, it is a grievous error to vote for a supporter of M. Laurier who has not yet declared that he obeys the charge."

Toward the same date the vicar-general of the Archbishop of Quebec wrote to the *curé* of Sainte Ubalde: "In reply to your letter asking if it is a mortal sin not to follow the direction given by the bishops in their collective charge, I am directed by Monseigneur to say to you that it is a grievous error . . . a mortal sin. If anyone says to you: 'In spite of your reasoning I have more confidence in M. Laurier and I shall vote for his candidate,' that voter, unless he has lost his senses, is guilty of a grievous and mortal error" (June 4, 1896).

The Bishop of Trois-Rivières did not hesitate to reveal himself more fully. In the cathedral, in the open pulpit, he violently attacked M. Laurier in person, accusing him of being a rationalist liberal, of adhering to doctrines condemned by the Church (May 17, 1896). The war became more general. It was carried on in all the parishes against all the candidates who did not declare clearly that they submitted to the charge of the bishops.

We shall study later the scholastic and political consequence of the election of 1896, which has remained famous in Canada because of the astonishing clerical pressure of which it was the occasion. Let it suffice to state now that the priests were not the victors in the struggle. With the practical common sense of the Norman peasant now awakened, the French Canadians understood, as they had perhaps not understood twenty years earlier, that the anathemas of the clergy were really too violent to be justified. They reminded themselves that M. Laurier was himself a respectful Catholic and they judged it exaggerated to count the act of voting for him a mortal sin. The Liberal party won a resounding victory in the province of Quebec and in the Dominion as a whole. The clergy, being beaten, immediately prepared for a reconciliation with the victor, and resigned themselves for some years to a semi-abstention from politics.

Since 1896, in truth, clerical interference has been much more reserved. For the moment it is necessary to dismiss to the past most of the incidents which we have just been quoting. Does this mean that they are relinquishing their ideal of political predominance? The Liberals hope so, say so, and believe so, but perhaps they are unduly optimistic. The more guarded attitude of the clergy in electoral affairs may be explained more plausibly by the absence of questions of special importance to the Church. Their position is not less uncompromising than it was. Let some new controversy come along that shall touch them closely and the priests will invade the platforms once again. They will bear themselves more discreetly than in the past, of course, for their unpleasant experience in 1896 has given them food for thought. But they will be found to be animated by the same conviction, energy, and determination as of yore.

There is a passage in the *Immortale Dei* Encyclical of Leo XIII which the Canadian bishops are glad to invoke: "Everything that has in it a sacred element, everything that bears upon the safety of the soul and upon the worship of God – whether by its nature or by reason of its end – comes within the authority of the Church."[4] These lines justify, nay they ordain, the intervention of the clergy in political affairs. It would be vain to imagine that they have any idea of renouncing their right to intervene.

[4] Cited in the collective charge of the bishops, May 6, 1896.

7: The Catholic Church – Its Role in the Political Evolution of Canada

After what we have seen of the formidable organization of the power of the Catholic Church in Canada, one can easily understand that it must be a great factor in the evolution of the entire colony. It would be impossible to secure anything like a state of equilibrium without the co-operation of the Catholic clergy. England knows this well. From the very morrow of the conquest of Canada, the Church had decided on the policy it would take up, and has kept to it ever since. This policy, it will be remembered, consists of the following three articles:

1. Complete and final acceptance of British rule.
2. Complete and final severance from France.
3. The passionate defence of the integrity of the French-Canadian race.

The Church of Rome has never cherished any exclusive attachment to any one nation. When our defeat in Canada was seen to be irrevocable she thought only of providing for her own future, and securing from the victors the maintenance of her ancient privileges. This done, she ranged herself deliberately on the British side.

Guided by her, the French Canadians became loyal subjects to the new rulers, and were soon ready to take part in the defence of their new country. During the American War of Independence they fought for England, and all attempts to win them over to the opposite camp failed completely. The Church set them an example of loyalty, and the priests encouraged them from the pulpits. In the war of 1812 the Bishop of Quebec ordered the offering up of public prayer for the success of the English cause, and the seminarists, taking up arms, mounted guard on the walls of the capital. Should such an eventuality come about again to-day, the attitude of the clergy would be in no way different: even against France they would devote themselves, body and soul, to the defence of British rule.

British rule, in truth, has proved entirely to their taste, and a tacit understanding seems to have been arrived at by the two powers, civil and ecclesiastic. On the one hand, the Church keeps the French Canadians submissive, loyal, and calm. In return, the English government has left it almost free to exercise its authority just as it may please in the Catholic part of the colony, which thus remains for it a sort of preserve rarely trespassed on by the foreigner.

This *entente* may be said to constitute one of the most solid elements in the foundation of the structure of British rule in Canada. It is true that whenever its own interests have been at stake the Church has defended them fiercely, at the risk of destroying Canadian unity. But it has generally abstained from associating itself with insurrectionary movements in which religion had no stake. Thus in 1837, when Papineau raised his great revolt on behalf of French liberties, the Church would have nothing to say to him, and took its stand uncompromisingly on the side of British rule.

Its regard and respect for British sovereignty are complete and manifest. In its religious services it calls down the blessing of God upon its English rulers. Never a word escapes it against the King of England. Rarely indeed has foreign rule been accepted more absolutely.

The clergy act in the matter with their own eyes open. True, the country parishes produce many priests who in their ignorance, their almost complete isolation, are unable to appreciate the real condition of things. To them there is not much difference between the two Frances, that of Europe and that of America. Frenchmen unalloyed, they continue in their simple honest fashion to detest *les Anglas*, as they call them in their picturesque Norman tongue.

The chiefs of the clergy take a higher and a wider view, looking at the matter not through sympathetic or hostile eyes, but having regard only to interest, to the great political interest of the Church. These leaders do not hesitate to congratulate themselves openly, even in the presence of visitors from France, on no longer belonging to France. Such is their language on being questioned, and often they volunteer the opinion without being questioned. Here are words which I have heard more than once from important Canadian ecclesiastics: "This country, sirs, is for us the country of Cockaigne. The sovereignty of Britain suits us perfectly. Thanks to it the position of our Church is excellent, secure, and, I believe, definitively established. We enjoy complete liberty. . . . I do not wish to hurt your feelings, for I love France; but permit me to say to you that for no consideration on earth would we wish to fall under her domination again."

This decisive language can be heard daily in Canada, and

it denotes exactly the attitude of the clerical authorities. They have no particular affection for the English, who are Protestants and foreigners, and they dread the effects of English influence upon their flocks; but they have a feeling of real gratitude towards the British government, and they display it by their enduring fidelity.

In these conditions, the Catholic Church would derive no benefit from a revival of French rule; on the contrary it would have much to lose. Children of 1789, we could scarcely leave them the privilege of its tithes or its exemption from taxation; our democratic tendencies would inevitably assert themselves on the banks of the St. Lawrence. The result would be a sort of bankruptcy for the Church. No wonder the Canadian priests hold us in dread and avoid us.

Let us repeat that, taken individually and left in some degree to their own innermost preferences, the French-Canadian ecclesiastics love France. They come here with joy, they feel themselves at home, they consider our country in spite of everything as a mother country. When it is crushed by defeat or adversity, they do not withhold their most intense sympathy, whilst saying aloud that its misfortunes are the punishment for its sins. At bottom, in the depths of their hearts they nurse an irresistible inclination for the prodigal son who was once the eldest son of the Church. But these sentiments stop at the threshold of the political domain, and there they count for nothing.

Still, it will be objected, has not the Catholic Church made itself the champion of the French race in Canada? Is it not she who has maintained there our language and our nationality? Assuredly; and no one would dream of saying the contrary. But care must be taken to distinguish once more between France and French Canada, between the French cause and the French-Canadian cause. To the first the Church is indifferent, perhaps hostile. To the second, since 1763, it has given its most complete devotion.

Without the support of the priests, our compatriots in Canada would undoubtedly ere now have been dispersed or absorbed. The village church formed a centre for them when their own country abandoned them and withdrew from them even the social authorities round which they might have organized their resistance. It is the country *curé* who by dint of daily instruction has kept alive in them those modes of thought and manners of living that form the individuality of the French-

Canadian civilization. It is the Church that by taking under her care the collective interests of the people has enabled them to withstand successfully all attempts of the English at persecution or seduction. The bonds between the clergy and the laity in French Canada are as strong to-day as they were a hundred years ago. Now as then the maintenance of Catholicism would seem to be the most essential condition of the continuance of our race and tongue in the Dominion.

This fact raises grave problems for the future. The protection of the Church is precious, but the price paid for it is exorbitant. Its influence has made the French Canadians serious, virtuous and industrious, as well as prolific. Their domestic qualities are the admiration of all; their health and strength show no signs of diminution. But, on the other hand, are not the intellectual bondage in which the Church would keep them, the narrow authority she exercises, the antiquated doctrines she persists in inculcating, all calculated to slow the advance of the race and to handicap it in its rivalry with the Anglo-Saxons long since freed from the past and its outworn forms?

That is the question asked anxiously by all who visit the banks of the St. Lawrence. But what can be done? For either the French Canadians will remain strict Catholics, and thus find it difficult to keep pace with the rapid progress of their British fellow-subjects, or else they will break loose from the bonds of the Church and, thus losing the marvellous force of cohesion they derive from her and becoming more accessible to outside influences, they will suffer grave fissures in the venerable structure of their unity. That is the disquieting dilemma in which we are left by our study of Canadian Catholicism.

8: Protestantism

If Catholicism is one of the essential factors in the development of the French Canadians, Protestantism does not count for less in that of the English race in the Dominion. In the preceding pages we have taken note of the domain of the Church of Rome, and in doing so have surveyed the frontiers of the rival religion. We have seen how clearly the lines of demarcation are drawn, dividing the colony into two distinct regions separated from each other by origin, language, and creed.

As in England and Australia and the United States, it is

undoubtedly the Protestant religion that has had the chief influence upon the formation of the character of the English, also in Canada it has stamped itself so strongly alike upon the individual, upon the family, and upon public life, that the laws and politics of the country bear marks of its effect. However, as we are dealing now with a Church and clergy very different from the Catholic, the whole condition of things differs from that which we have just been studying. And this fact accentuates the contrast, already so striking, between the two Canadas.

British Canada taken as a whole may be called a Protestant country. The Catholics, French or Irish, as we have seen, are in a minority, numbering only 2,229,000 out of 5,371,000. Subtracting some 50,000 non-Christians – agnostics, Jews, Japanese, and Chinese – we have a total of 3,092,000 Protestants, nearly three-fifths of the whole.

Quebec is the only province with a Catholic majority. Everywhere else the Protestant majorities are enormous.

	Inhabitants	Protestants
Quebec	1,649,000	21,000
Ontario	2,182,000	1,800,000
Maritime Provinces	893,000	594,000
Manitoba	255,000	219,000
N.W. Territory	160,000	120,000
British Columbia	178,000	136,000

Thirty years ago the future of Protestantism in the West might have been in doubt; at that time the Church of Rome hoped to annex Western Canada by furthering emigration from Quebec. But the attractions of the industrial states of New England were stronger, and to-day the hope of thus conquering Western Canada has been abandoned by the clergy themselves; they stand up firmly for the rights of the faithful in those parts, but they have reconciled themselves to the idea that the region has passed beyond their grasp. The French Catholic population constitutes one great island as it were in the lower valley of the St. Lawrence and an archipelago in the Atlantic provinces, Ontario and the West. Much the greater part of the colony is distinctively English.

As in all the Anglo-Saxon countries, Protestantism in Canada is divided into a very small number of large sects and an infinite variety of small ones. The Methodists, Presbyterians, Anglicans, and Baptists constitute nearly nine-tenths of the whole.

Methodists	917,000
Presbyterians	842,000
Anglicans	681,000
Baptists	292,000
Other sects	360,000

Of these smaller sects the official census enumerates thirty-seven, of which the most important are the following:

Lutherans	93,000
Congregationalists	28,000
"Disciples of Christ"	15,000
Salvation Army	10,000
Adventists	8,000

The smaller sects are ordinarily full of zeal and activity, but with a few exceptions they are lacking in funds and have not sufficient weight to exercise much influence. It is only the four larger sects that can be said really to count.

The Methodists, with their 917,000 members, constitute nearly a third of the entire Protestant population of the Dominion. The province of Ontario, in which their numbers amount to 666,000, is their stronghold. Their strong organization, the cohesion of all their branches, and their great financial resources give them a power and importance unsurpassed by any other of the non-Catholic religious bodies.

The Methodists – it is said of them alike by way of praise and of blame – represent the respectable bourgeoisie, the class of people who having made the most of their opportunities in this world are conscious that they have also made satisfactory provision for their welfare in the next. Throughout Ontario, and especially in Toronto, they occupy a position of importance; they are not the most fashionable people of the town – for there is an Anglican "smart set" which regards itself as very superior in the mundane hierarchy – but they are more solid, more wealthy, they have more prosperous commercial establishments and finer churches. At the same time, they have a very keen sense of their role as Englishmen and Protestants, having carried with them from England the conviction of the inevitable supremacy of their race and the indisputable superiority of their religion.

Such is the twofold patrimony which they guard stoutly in the face of the French Canadians whom Providence has given them for neighbours. Canadian Methodism may be said to form the centre of anti-French, aggressive Protestantism. It is the

Methodists who keep up the cry, "No French domination! No Popery!" We shall see presently what effect this state of mind has upon the elections.

The Presbyterian Church, with its 842,000 members, comes next. As everywhere else, it is the Church of the Scots, that prosperous, industrious, and sympathetic race. In Nova Scotia and Manitoba it takes the lead among the Protestant sects, in Ontario it comes after Methodism. Wherever it is to be found predominant it stamps the life and habits of the public with its imprint of somewhat gloomy sternness. Winnipeg, which comes especially under its influence, is one of the most puritanical cities in the Dominion. It is a Western city, overflowing with energy and cosmopolitan to the last degree, yet there is nothing about it of the free, light-hearted tone that characterizes most of the other American cities of mushroom growth. This is particularly noticeable on Sundays.

Apart from their uncompromising morality, the Presbyterians are the most agreeable of companions. Their cordial bearing and their hospitality are proverbial; moreover, they display a special friendliness towards the French, who are quick to respond. England has reason to regard the Presbyterians as the best of her colonists.

The Church of England, with its 681,000, comes next in importance. It would seem not to have found in Canada a soil quite suited to its development. Among Protestants it is relatively strongest in the provinces of Quebec and British Columbia; in Ontario, it is left far behind by the Non-conformists. As in England, it includes two branches of very different, indeed almost opposite tendencies – the one distinctly Protestant, the other with a strong leaning towards Rome.

In other respects Anglicanism has remained very British. As in the mother country it is especially the religion of people of the world and of the poor. The latter are drawn to its churches by the pomp of its ceremonies and by the fact that no great financial demands are made of them. The former, by the effect of a long tradition, by the memory of England where the Anglican Church is that of the sovereign and the social authorities. One need not believe that this last argument is without appeal to the "society" of Toronto, Montreal, and Victoria. This "society" accords to religious ceremonies an important place among social functions. And one may sense a certain rivalry between the Anglicans, aristocratic and pretentious, and the Methodists, overflowing with money but bourgeois.

The Baptists, to the number of 292,000, have a clearly popular character. Their dogmatic narrowness, their individualism, their democratic and egalitarian sense, make them a church apart, which has its well-marked place among the Methodists, Presbyterians, and Anglicans. This is their strength, although "society" often affects to consider the Baptist form of religion as undistinguished, reserved for the lower classes, as Anglicanism is reserved for the aristocracy, Presbyterianism for the Scots, and Methodism for the commercial classes who are well on the way to success.

Complete separation from the state is the rule with all these churches. It has not been so always. According to the Constitutional Act of 1791, a seventh of the Crown lands was to be set aside for the maintenance of the Protestant clergy. At first only the Established Church enjoyed the benefit of this privilege. Gradually, after 1837, as the result of representations made by the Presbyterians, the other sects also began to have their share. But in 1854 the Catholics, combining with the democratic party of that time, had these ecclesiastical endowments abolished to the advantage of the municipalities. Since then no branch of the Protestant Church has sought or received any assistance from the government. The system of Catholic tithes still maintained in the province of Quebec is the only survival of the kind from the distant past.

To all appearance the independence of these churches in regard to the state has been absolutely established in the New World. Perhaps it would not be safe to say quite so positively that the state's independence of the churches, even the Protestant ones, is established to the same degree. The French conception of the lay state would seem never to have penetrated the Anglo-Saxon mind, and they have some difficulty in imagining a state entirely devoid of religious prepossessions. The Protestant clergy do not aim at controlling the government in the ultramontane Catholic fashion, but they do aim at informing it with their spirit. We shall have occasion to note more than once in subsequent chapters – and especially when studying education – that Canada, never having had its 1789, has no real comprehension of the theory of the neutrality of the state.

Canadian Protestants, indeed, are often incapable of imagining that one can think outside of religious forms. They leave one sect only to join the neighbouring sect, and abandon one religion only to adopt a new one. In France the outermost frontier of liberal Protestantism borders on religious free thought; and this in turn is next to a free thought which is no longer religious. The transition is cautious and gradual, at times almost insensible. In Canada there is nothing similar to this, at least so it appears. In "society" it is not elegant to be irreligious; and this is a sufficient reason why thousands of people go regularly to church. Even among the poorer classes a man is looked at somewhat askance who does not belong to some one denomination; and with the exception of certain mining districts in British Columbia in which the European tone of mind is in the ascendant, the English workmen and labourers are for the most part out-and-out Protestants. The census of 1901 records only 4,181 cases of persons declaring that they belonged to no religion, and only 3,613 professed "agnostics," this word being explained in a note as compromising "atheists, free-thinkers, infidels, sceptics, and unbelievers." The Englishman is never really at ease until he is duly catalogued.

In reality, unbelief is frequent in Canada, as everywhere else, though it is not often openly professed. You will hear it admitted in smoking-rooms after a good dinner has given tongues their freedom. The Canadian will explain to you then that he is in truth an agnostic, having put aside the beliefs of his youth, but that it is preferable to keep in touch with the church you have been connected with from childhood, and not to destroy time-honoured links for no very definite purpose. But these are remarks which one avoids making outside of fairly intimate circles. Public expression of such sentiments would be severely judged by everybody. It would constitute a scandal, that is to say a sort of revolt against the existing order of things, against British tradition, almost an act of infidelity to the Anglo-Saxon race. It would also be a grave imprudence, for one would have much to lose materially as a result of such freedom. Public opinion would show no mercy. "Society" would find the declaration inelegant. More than one institution would expel you from its midst. In several of the English-Canadian universities which depend partly for support on certain sects, a professor who should express anti-religious views would be severely reprimanded. Not that he is called upon to subscribe formally to any one creed. He is expected merely not to proclaim his agnosticism. It is the same thing in several of the provinces with the teacher who has to read prayers in the school every morning.

In truth there is here a real hyprocrisy, and some violence is done to freedom of speech. But the English do not resent this as Frenchmen would. They find it quite natural, when they belong to a hierarchy, to sacrifice certain prerogatives of their personality.

The free-thought movement, so powerful in France, is almost non-existent in Canada, at least in its outward manifestations. If an anti-religious opinion should emerge in the future, it could well be that it would spread first among the French Catholics rather than among the English Protestants. These latter do not like to break windows. The former, on the contrary, if they set out some fine day to emancipate themselves, will perhaps reject hypocrisy and its convenient capitulations. English freemasonry is distinctly deist. The last French lodge founded in Montreal, *l'Emancipation*, is on the contrary affiliated with the Grand-Orient of France. But for the moment these anti-religious manifestations are of very little importance. The only serious rivalry in Canada is not that of religion and irreligion, but that of Protestantism and Catholicism.

Against the Roman peril the various Protestant sects have felt the need of union. On the vast stage of the New World where there is room for everybody, they seem to have forgotten their mutual and traditional jealousies. Protestant public opinion no longer understands these hatreds among rival chapels which may still exist in certain corners of old Europe, but which in the New World decidedly belong to another age. Long ago, following the example of the United States, it broke away from rigorous and narrow dogmas, and it tends more and more to think that all Protestant religious beliefs are valid on condition that they are sincerely followed in practice. The sects which were once rivals of each other have almost entirely ceased their fights. Only the Anglicans live a little apart from the others, their customs and beliefs being too special. But the great Non-conformist Churches have several times studied the project of federation; people are always talking about it, and it is not impossible that the idea may be realized. In social life all Protestants co-operate fraternally. When their actions are not mingled together, they are at least parallel, their general tendency being the same. And Catholicism, the common enemy, reminds them periodically of the need for united action if not for unity.

One would be very wrong to doubt the depth of the anti-Catholic sentiment among Canadian Protestants. Manifestations of outward courtesy between the two religions do not signify much except perhaps a mutual recognition that the belligerents are respectable and worthy to cross swords with each other. In short, anti-Catholicism is much more violent in the Dominion than in Britain because the Roman Church in the colony is more sure of itself, more aggressive, more threatening, because the danger of its victory appears more possible, because, finally, the religious struggle is complicated by the struggle of the races.

Being the majority and, by right of conquest, masters of the country, the Protestants wish to preserve their supremacy. On this point they are uncompromising, and this is for them the primordial purpose. In a manner which is often roundabout and imperceptible, but which is also intransigent and tireless, they pursue this purpose, watching their rivals jealously, noting anxiously and indignantly their slightest progress in the councils of the state. It is thus that they have become accustomed to envisage the public affairs of the nation, from a point of view that is not secular or neutral but essentially confessional. Herein is to be seen a profound cause of the bitterness of the political struggles in Canada.

9: The General Conditions of the
Education Problem in Canada

In a country like Canada the school must sooner or later become to a greater degree than elsewhere the principal stake to be struggled for by the opposing forces, national and religious. Therein is the framework of the future. Catholics and Protestants, French and English, ask themselves alike with anxiety what is being made of their children. Hence the intense fierceness of the discussions bearing upon this subject: what is at issue is not merely the lot of a ministry, a party, a method of government, but the very destiny of two peoples and two civilizations.

The problem of Canadian education is one of infinite complexity, but its essential elements are easy enough to set out and to grasp. We have two separate races, living together under the same laws, but not speaking the same language or practising the same religion. Each of these two races is so strongly attached to that which constitutes its individuality that it would not sacrifice the smallest particle of it to the cause of the unity of the nation. Now the dream of unity is cherished ardently by the British majority, which bears impatiently with the survival of the vanquished race. Naturally the minority resists, but as it is not able and has no wish to secede, the adversaries are forced to live on side by side as best they can in the consciousness that separation is impossible and that their union can never be complete. Herein is the secret of a problem which doubtless will never be solved to the satisfaction of both parties.

The French policy is clearly defined. As it is essential for the future that the children should retain the tongue and the creed of their parents, our compatriots are determined that French and the doctrines of Catholicism shall be taught under their own supervision in public schools set apart for them and subsidized by the state. There must be no question of secular education in this clearly defined and homogeneous world in which there are few who are not obedient servants of the Church.

The Protestants, on the other hand, look with disfavour upon these schools, which they accuse of being at once anglophobe and clerical, and which they tolerate rather than accept. They regard with envy their neighbours in the United States, where the cosmopolitan elements are swiftly assimilated, and where public opinion frowns upon those sections which are disinclined to learn English. Above all, they detest the influence of the clergy, and cannot reconcile themselves to patronizing even indirectly a system of teaching which is in the hands of the *curés*. Their predilection is in favour of a system of "free," "compulsory" education, which if not secular shall be neutral as regards the Christian forms of belief.

It is easy to see that these two views cannot be reconciled. Wherever it is possible the English refuse to subsidize the Catholic schools. On their side, the French retain an invincible mistrust of the schools of their rivals, and seldom or never send their children to them. It was in these conditions that the Canadian legislator had to construct some kind of educational organization. Let us glance briefly at the result.

To begin with, so as to clear the ground, the state handed over to the Catholic Church or various independent bodies the duties of providing for secondary and higher education. It could not free itself in the same way in the matter of primary education, which bears more closely upon the condition of the mass of the people, and thereby on the future of the country. However, here also it compromised: a general federal law being impossible, on account of the contrasted character of the provinces and of their strong feelings in regard to self-government, educational legislation has been left an essentially local affair, though under the ultimate control of the parliament of Ottawa.

This was no solution of the problem, for racial hate and distrust are just the same in the individual provinces as in the Dominion as a whole. But at least there is one great advantage in the arrangement: different methods can be applied to different difficulties. We shall see how.

Let us take, for instance, a province which is almost entirely Anglo-Saxon, British Columbia. As the French element is almost non-existent there, the free, compulsory English school, secular to some extent but with a Protestant bias, will give rise to no objection. Just the opposite will be the case in Quebec, where separate denominational schools are almost the only possible institution, the French majority clinging to their Catholic establishments, while the Protestant minority hold aloof in theirs. In an English province like Ontario, in which there is a considerable French population, the English public school will of course boast the largest number of pupils, but our compatriots maintain their right not only to have the kind of education they require, but to have it subsidized. It is only in new regions like Manitoba, where our people are to be found in small numbers, that there will be difficulty in keeping the scales equal. The Anglo-Saxon majority, in its incurable dread of a clerical invasion, will be unable to resist the temptation to turn the schools into an implement to be used in the unifying of the colony. If the Catholics prove strong enough, they will resist, and there will be a sharp conflict.

A secret desire to blend the two races, together with an avowed fear of the power of the Church of Rome, are the dominating motives of the English in regard to the schools. They deplore the fact that our language still survives and is still taught, but recognize with their habitual good sense that it can't be helped, and that after all it is but right and just in a country in which one-third of the population is of French origin. The government sanctions, therefore, the giving of religious instruction in class after school hours by representatives of the different creeds. But it finds it hard to restrain itself when it sees the school absolutely controlled by the clergy. Unable to prevent this in so Catholic a province as Quebec, it scarcely attempts to do so. But in the West it feels that the Catholic Church should not be permitted to secure new strongholds. Thus the question, national and religious to start with, becomes a political one the moment one strong party refuses to bow the knee to ecclesiastical supremacy.

10: The French Catholic School in the Province of Quebec

The form of education approved by the Church of Rome in Canada and by the French Canadians in general is to be found most completely realized in the province of Quebec. To this province, therefore, let us go in order to study it in both theory and practice. It accords with two separate determinations – the one openly declared, the other rarely avowed, usually indeed denied, yet clearly perceptible. The first is in regard to the preservation in the school of the integrity of the race, by keeping it carefully isolated. The second is the maintenance of an attitude of deep distrust towards the state, to which the clergy refuse to cede the control of public education.

It is in this condition of mind that the clergy have contrived to have their schools separate, free, and denominational: separate, to preclude intercourse between the two races; free, because the state has lacked the power and resolution necessary to take them under its control, and above all because the Church has combated any such extension of its powers; denominational, because they hold that the Catholic religion is indispensable to the formation of French-Canadian civilization, and because in this new France no one ever seems to have desired or even conceived an undenominational school free from religious control.

Let us study these principles now in their application:[1] we shall see that they have the effect of rendering the state weak and the Church strong. The civil power has not attempted to turn education into a regular branch of administration. It has entrusted to the heads of families, Catholic and Protestant, the duty of organizing for themselves, separately, free and denominational schools. The provincial government limits itself to subsidizing the schools of both religions, proportionately to the number of pupils, and to exercising over them a more or less effective supervision.

The functions of the central power under these conditions are sufficiently circumscribed. The entire administrative part is under the control of the Department of Public Instruction, headed not by a responsible minister, but by a high permanent official, safeguarded from political influences, who is described as the Superintendent. On the other hand, side by side with the Department, or perhaps it would be more accurate to say above it, is the Superior Council of Public Instruction. Its president *ex officio* is the Superintendent, and his decisions have to be approved by a member of the cabinet, who in this instance is the Provincial Secretary or Minister of the Interior.

The Council is essentially denominational in its composition; it is divided, in fact, into two committees, corresponding with the two religions. The first includes *ex officio* the archbishops of the province, as well as a number of Catholic laymen nominated by the civil power. The second is composed of Protestant laymen, equal in number to the Catholic laymen, and also selected by the government. In conformity with the spirit of the denominational system of separation, these two sections act independently of each other, save in the rare instances of their having to deal with a mixed case. Their unity, therefore, is

[1] *Loi de l'instruction publique de la province de Québec, 1899.* Cf. Paul de Cazes (Secretary of the Department of Public Instruction), *Code Scolaire de la province de Québec*, 1899. *L'instruction public dans la province de Québec*, 1905.

factitious. It is separately that they decide all questions bearing upon organization and discipline, make allotment of the money placed at their disposal, nominate the inspectors for appointment by the government, and select the books which are to be used in the schools.

It is easily seen that by this system the Provincial Secretary is made to hold an insignificant place, while the Department is deliberately subordinated to the hegemony of the Superior Council of Public Instruction, in which – at least as far as the Catholics are concerned – the bishops predominate without effort.

Let us now come to the local municipalities. Catholics and Protestants have their respective schools in these, but they have to found them themselves. The state only grants them an annual subvention. However, this financial aid being insufficient, the heads of families have to draw upon their own resources in order to provide fully for the education of their children.

The province is divided, therefore, into districts, designated as "scholastic municipalities." In each of these, the heads of families belonging to the religion professed by a majority of the inhabitants elect for a term of three years a "scholastic committee," which has to occupy itself with all matters relating to the schools, including the nomination of teachers. To this end, the members of the committee are expressly empowered to levy special dues upon their co-religionists. They constitute, in fact, a kind of small special muncipal council with functions limited to educational affairs and within the boundaries of one Church.

The minority proceeds upon similar lines, and nominates regularly three Syndics; the school they organize has its share also of the state subvention. In Quebec, of course, the majority in these scholastic municipalities is nearly always Catholic.

In principle, the education is obligatory, and has to be paid for. In practice, however, it is free and optional: free, because the school fees are insignificant, and those who fail to pay are never excluded; optional, because although it is the rule that all children from seven to fourteen must be sent to school, there exists no effective method of exercising compulsion upon neglectful or recalcitrant parents.

The school involves a certain submission to the laws of the country, though it can be described without inaccuracy as free, separate, and denominational. It is free inasmuch as it is not subject to any control from the state and enjoys the most far-reaching rights. There are many clerical establishments, moreover, founded outside the jurisdiction of the regular organization, which solicit no subvention and which refuse to submit to any kind of supervision from the Superior Council, however benevolently disposed.

From the point of view of the relations between the French Catholics and the English Protestants, the educational system of Quebec has produced the best results: the two sets of schools co-exist without fear of conflict or dispute, because they have no points of contact. The situation is exactly that of two separate nations kept apart by a definite frontier and having as little intercourse as possible: that is the price of the peace which prevails in the schools of Quebec.

The people of Quebec take legitimate pride in this condition of things, the outcome to a great degree of their calmness and wisdom. We could share their content unreservedly except that in order to produce this state of equilibrium they have had to abdicate to the Church some of the most essential rights of the state in regard to education.

It is easy to note that the whole of this educational system has the effect of leaving everything in the hands of the clergy. None can deny that in the province of Quebec the political power is wielded by a majority regardful of the Catholic religion, yet the Church will not permit this majority to control, I will not say the whole field of public instruction but even that of primary education. Her doctrine is that the state may co-operate but cannot act in the matter independently.

In these conditions the absence of a Minister of Public Instruction ceases to appear as a simple matter of chance. "We avoid in this way the interference of politics in the school," it is explained. Yes, but in order to leave Catholic practice without any rival. That is why the Church will not have at any price a Minister of Public Instruction who might develop into a force rivalling the Superior Council, and perhaps supplanting it eventually. It prefers a mere official like the Superintendent, whom it can keep in his place. In 1899 there was question of replacing the Superintendent by a member of the cabinet. The Marchand Liberal ministry was in favour of the reform, and had embodied it in their general scheme for the remodelling of the Law of Education. The Church's opposition was brutal and decisive: a telegram from Rome called upon Marchand to abandon the idea. And the power of the Church is so strong, even with the Liberals in Canada, that the premier had to give way.

Under the actual system there can be no disputing the fact that all impulse comes from the Superior Council, dominated by the bishops. As they form half the Council, they have only to convince one or two of the lay members in order to secure a majority. Naturally they will use all their energies to resist any change calculated to alter an arrangement so favourable to them.

In the municipalities the clerical influence is not less manifest, though not officially recognized. The members of the committees are rarely elected without the approval of the *curé* of the parish. The heads of family are usually not very well educated men; they confine their activities for the most part to the discussion of expenditure and administration. The *curé*, therefore, even if he be not himself a member of the committee, becomes naturally enough the power behind it.

The selection of teachers, for instance, an all-important matter, can scarcely be attended to without him. It is the committee that nominates the teacher, but in most cases the candidate favoured by the *curé* stands the best chance, as is only logical after all, considering that the school is a Catholic one. As there is nothing in the law to impede education by religious communities, the masters and mistresses are in many cases members of various orders, without diplomas. The efforts of certain Liberal deputies to amend this archaic aspect of the educational system have been resolutely opposed by the Church.

The inspectors themselves, nominated by the Lieutenant-Governor, but appointed by the Superior Council, cannot well afford to go against the Episcopate. They constitute a body of active, intelligent, zealous men, worthy of the highest praise; their work is hard, especially when they have to make their way over wide stretches of country in the bitter colds of winter. Their provinces measured in square miles are immense, but their liberty of action is greatly circumscribed, for they are forced to represent the Church almost as much as the state.

We have shown the undeniable advantages of these schools from the point of view of general peace and quiet. From the standpoint of education pure and simple, the results perhaps are less satisfactory. They reveal a double peril – the indifference of the committees and the unprogressive spirit of the Catholic methods.

The committees give proof of indifference only too frequently. The members are most worthy, honest, well-intentioned peasants, but they do not always know what should be done, and are not always ready to make the sacrifices called for. In cases when expenditure is really needed they are all for economy, and knowing that the government cannot counteract their inertia, they pay no attention to the recommendations addressed to them. "These gentlemen don't care a straw for the authorities, and for the education laws," writes an inspector, M. Bouchard. "They don't hesitate to declare that they have no need of the government and its laws, and that they are going to conduct their educational arrangements just as seems good to them, without regard for anybody."[1] The result is that the schools are often very ill kept for lack of means, and the children are the first to suffer.

The inspectors are almost unanimous in complaining also that the teachers are underpaid. The committees seek to effect economies first by replacing masters by mistresses, then by cutting down the salaries even of these. Out of timidity in regard to the elections, the legislature has not ventured to impose a minimum salary. A minimum salary of $100 was asked for in vain. In certain municipalities the committees make a point of keeping the salaries of the women teachers below this figure. M. Vien,[2] an inspector, tells of cases in which women teachers who were audacious enough to ask for $100 were threatened that they might not be re-engaged, because they were held to have set a bad example to the others.

The level of the corps of teachers has been lowered. "The number of women teachers without diplomas," writes another inspector, M. Lévesque, "is on the increase unfortunately. Is this because there is any lack of certificated teachers? I believe not. What then is the cause? I do not hesitate to say that if an adequate salary were offered, the number of insufficiently qualified teachers would sensibly diminish."[3] In these circumstances it is not surprising that recourse should be had to nuns who require no diploma. Official reports point to this tendency. M. Guay, for instance, writes: "The idea of entrusting the management of schools to nuns is growing greatly in favour."[4]

In practice, the law produces very unsatisfactory results, therefore, as regards teachers. Out of 279 masters, 50 are without diploma; out of 5,051 women teachers, 733 are without it; while in addition to these 5,330 lay teachers there are 4,331 members of religious orders (1,499 men and 2,832 women) who

---

[1] *Rapport du surintendant de l'instruction publique de la province de Quebec pour l'année 1902-03*, p. 16.
[2] *Ibid.*, p. 104.
[3] *Ibid.*, p. 57.
[4] *Ibid.*, p. 49.

are not certificated. The guarantees of good education seem very greatly weakened by these facts. But the inspectors declare themselves to be powerless in view of the parsimony of the school committees. The state would have to intervene in some decisive fashion for the situation to be remedied, but it is to be feared that this intervention will not take place since the Church objects.

The other danger lies in the conservative tone of Catholic education. The Church is incapable of freeing itself from certain known, traditional defects in the giving or even the inspiring of instruction. Education as such never comes first with the Church: her first care is always to retain her influence. Hence her real exaggerated fear of the free use of books; hence the prominence given to the catechism in class; hence the antiquated school books she places in the hands of the children. True, there is something very charming about these little country schools of Quebec, so French in their whole aspect, with the comely Norman faces of the children, their teachers so neat and correct in demeanour, and somewhere in the vicinity their sympathetic *curé*. But they are suggestive of archaism rather than of progress. And this is not far from being unpardonable in young America.

11: The Public School of the English Provinces

While the French Canadians cling to their form of education – independent, denominational, and separate – the English, from similar motives, lean more and more towards the state school – free, compulsory, and tending towards undenominationalism.

The reasons for this are numerous and far-reaching. In the first place, the Protestants have not the Catholic mistrust of the state, and their clergy do not seek to replace the civil power. In the second place, the various sects, by reason of their divergences, are almost obliged to unite upon the basis of a certain neutrality, it being impossible for each small chapel to have an educational arrangement of its own: hence a kind of semi-secular system, which partakes of Christianity whilst excluding all dogma. Finally – at least in the more completely Anglo-Saxon provinces of the West – subsidized denominational education does not commend itself at all to the English-speaking majority, who are more anxious about the assimilating of those outside their fold than about the perpetuation of their own individuality: whence their attitude of disfavour towards the French Catholic schools.

To describe in detail the educational system of the different English provinces would be a long and difficult matter. It will suffice for our purposes to indicate its principal features, drawing attention to such local variations as call for remark.[1]

The general principles to be found underlying the whole are as follows: the state directs and controls the work of instruction, which it subsidizes by means of more or less important grants to the local authorities. The central administrative body has for its head a responsible minister, aided by a higher council, in part nominated by the government, in part elected, but of which the clergy are never members *ex officio* as in Quebec. The Departments of Education carry out their duties without any obstruction from the clergy – on the contrary, with their help.

The part played by the central administrative body remains a very limited one, however, for we are in a decentralized country. The schools are organized in the localities, on the spot. School municipalities analogous to those already described are constituted, which nominate committees – "Boards of Trustees" – whose powers are very extensive, and include the appointment of the principal, who has of course to be provided with an official diploma.

The subsidized denominational schools exist in Ontario by virtue of the British North America Act of 1867, which guarantees their safety under certain reservations. In the West, the Catholic minority retain the right to have their own schools, but generally speaking this is subject to their being conducted on secular lines and subjected to thoroughgoing inspections. In these conditions separate education loses a great deal of its significance. Recourse has had to be had to special compromises, sometimes almost illegal, to satisfy the violent appeals which have been made on this subject. In the following chapter we shall undertake a study into the complex and difficult subject of these conflicts.

The distinctive point about the attitude of the state in the English provinces is that it lays claim firmly to the right of supervision over subsidized schools of all kinds, and to that of enforcing its authority without let or hindrance from any other power. The inspectors, who are kept in hand, acquire in this a preponderating influence. Finally, the school is free and compulsory.

[1] Cf. Bourinot's *How Canada is Governed*.

To speak now of the most burning of all problems – that of religious instruction in the school. First of all, it should be noted that there is no restriction in Canada upon the teacher's freedom, and that in consequence denominational establishments have no obstacles in the way of their progress: the truth of this is contested by none. The points under discussion are somewhat different: in the first place, it is to be seen whether the provincial governments will consent to subsidize the schools of the minority, even when they are frankly denominational; secondly, whether the public schools of the majority shall officially provide for the teaching of any form of religion – in other words, whether they shall be denominational or undenominational.

The first question, as I have said, has been answered in the affirmative by the Eastern provinces, but in the West public opinion is all against the subsidizing of Catholic education.

The second question has been answered by a compromise – by the creation of a kind of semi-secular education in keeping with a very English – and quite un-French – conception of religion and neutrality.

There are, of course, orthodox Protestants, especially members of the Church of England, who do not approve of the exclusion of their dogmas from the classroom. They may be heard to condemn the godless school as passionately as the Catholics, for they refuse to recognize the independent existence of profane knowledge. But these devout malcontents are few in number and wield very little influence. The majority of the Protestant heads of families, taking a practical view of the problem, realize that it is a difficult matter to establish a basis of religious beliefs such as will satisfy all sects. They know, too, that child and pastor may find opportunities of meeting out of class hours, either at home or in the church, or even in the school itself. In short, they treat the matter as one of fact and convenience, and not as one of principle, as do the Catholics. They do not hesitate, therefore, to exclude from their system all kinds of dogmatic instruction. And this first part of their reasoning leads them towards secularism.

But they stop en route. They have shown their willingness to ignore the difference of creeds. According to them, the schools should be undenominational – that is, as far removed from Baptist teaching as from Presbyterian, from Methodism as from the tenets of the Church of England. But what they aim at is not a secular system, for they wish to retain a Christian character – Protestant up to a certain point – in the teaching. In the West, this religious veneer is almost altogether dispensed with; but it remains in general use, and responds to the desires of parents who wish to have their children brought up in such an atmosphere. It would, therefore, be an exaggeration to speak of secularism in reference to English Canada. The word "unde-nominational" which in appearance is synonymous with our word "laïque" has not at all the same sense.

In order to impart to the school this Protestant-Christian tone, without the intrusion of dogma, recourse is had almost invariably to the same methods. In Ontario the class begins and ends each day with a prayer and a reading from the Bible without explanation or commentary. Catholic children attending the school need not be present at these proceedings. Ecclesiastical doctrines do not form part of the school course, but the general principles of Christianity are brought into the scheme of instruction. Imperceptibly the influence of religion is thus introduced,[2] and that is what the parents wish. In addition, ministers of religion are free to gather together in the schoolroom, after the classes are over, the children of any parents who so desire.

In Manitoba the prayer is said only once a day at the end of class, and then only if a majority of the trustees so decide. Readings from the Bible are limited to certain passages indicated by the Higher Council of Public Instruction. After 3.30 p.m. the schoolrooms are open to members of the clergy of all denominations. In British Columbia matters are simplified still further. There the teacher is at liberty, if he wishes, to recite the Lord's Prayer every morning and evening.

Thus the English-Canadian school aims at secularization, but does not attain to it completely. As I have said before, the English rarely understand the meaning of secularization. They think it "respectable" to make some show of deference towards Christianity, which is the religion of most Anglo-Saxons. Not that they would hurt anyone's susceptibilities! None could have more respect than they for private convictions. Only it is bad form to fly in the face of the general feeling. It is a matter of good breeding – something to be regulated by one's British instincts.

And, in practice, things always arrange themselves, and there are not many troublesome protests from the conscientious

---

[2] "The doctrines of no Church are taught, but the principles of Christianity form an essential feature of the daily exercises." John Millar, deputy minister of education, *The Educational System of the Province of Ontario*, p. 4.

individual. "What would happen," I once asked a school inspector in Ontario, "if a teacher refused to read the Bible on the ground that he did not believe in it?" The reply was very English. "We should say to him, 'You are not asked to believe in it, you are only asked to read it.' " Obviously, in ninety-nine cases out of a hundred the teacher, even though a sceptic, will agree to read.

Another characteristic of the English school is the very keen national spirit that flourishes in it. Public opinion (by a majority if not unanimously) decides that the boys shall have instilled in them a thoroughgoing Anglo-Saxon British patriotism. In the United States the teacher is an active agent in the work of assimilation. The English Canadians are aware of this, and are not less anxious than their neighbours to mould all the diverse types of immigrants flowing into Canada from Europe into a single racial type. The future of the Dominion is at stake. This is precisely the reason why the French, who do not wish at any price to be absorbed, have so deep a distrust of the distinctively English public school.

We are now in a position to compare the school systems of both races. They have one point in common, but only one: both are national in spirit. That is to say, that the one seeks to produce French Canadians, the other English Canadians. So long as the two races continue to represent two separate currents that will not converge, it is to be foreseen that all efforts to bring about mixed education are bound to fail.

Both schools also are permeated by religion. But here the apparent analogy covers a profound difference. The English school is really not denominational, while the French school clearly is. Education in the English school is not in the hands of the clergy. Individual ministers of religion are permitted at certain hours to enter the classrooms, but their calling gives them no privilege, no place in the educational hierarchy. They are neither rivals nor opponents of the civil power.

12: The Conflicts Over the Schools

The educational problem has provoked some of the most bitter conflicts Canada has known. The school question in Manitoba in 1896 and the school question in the Northwest Territories in 1905 stand out in the history of the Dominion as two very perilous episodes, and serve to remind all those who are prone to forget it that the unity of the colony is continually endangered by racial and religious rivalries which show no sign of being moderated by the march of time.

A mixed province, but with a great Protestant majority, Manitoba could boast until 1890 of a very liberal system of education. Catholics and Protestants had each their own separate and subsidized schools as in Quebec. State control existed only in theory. The heads of families were able, therefore, with the help of governmental grants in aid, to see that their children were educated according to their ideas.

The Protestants of Manitoba came to have strong feelings in regard to the frankly clerical tone of the French schools. Their ambition was to bring about the racial unity of their province, to make of it a distinctively Anglo-Saxon country, by assimilating all the foreign elements as quickly as possible. Consequently they experienced a growing disinclination to protect even indirectly a form of education which tended in the opposite direction.

It was in this spirit of intolerance that the law was passed in 1890 which entirely transformed the system then in operation. A Department of Education was created, and all the public schools were placed under its strict control; the books in use were made a matter for effective supervision; finally, religious instruction was rigorously confined to certain hours of the day and ceased to be compulsory, the denominational character of the schools thus vanishing altogether. The Catholics retained their right to keep their own schools going separately, but failing their acceptance of the provisions of the new law, they ceased to be subsidized. This was a direct blow at the Church, and thus at the French race, which rallied sturdily round its priests.

There was intense excitement naturally amongst the French Catholics, and the conflict assumed its veritable character – that of a racial and religious war. Threatened in the very stronghold of their power, the French clergy put themselves at the head of the resistance, and began an ardent, persistent, untiring campaign.

They contested first of all the legality of the new law. The Manitoba Act by which Manitoba became part of Confederation (1870) forbade the provincial legislature to bring in any measure prejudicial to the rights or privileges of the denominational schools existing legally or *de facto* at the moment of the Union. This provision was invoked before the Canadian tribunals, then by way of appeal before the Privy Council of England. But this final court confirmed the constitutional character of the law of 1890, declaring that the Manitoba Act had not been violated, inasmuch as the actual existence of the schools was not menaced, but only their subvention.

In this first passage of arms the Protestants triumphed, but their adversaries did not admit themselves beaten. The Manitoba Act establishes the right of appeal to the Governor-General in Council against any act or decision of the legislature prejudicial to the rights or privileges of the Protestant or Catholic minorities in regard to education.[1] They made use of this, and this time the justice of their contention was recognized; but the Manitoba legislature absolutely refused to submit. It became necessary for the federal government to recall the fact that by paragraph 3 of Article 22 of the Manitoba Act they had the power to bring before the federal parliament a remedial bill by which the federal authority substituted itself for the refractory province. This law was proposed by the Conservative ministry in power in 1896. But the House of Commons, having come to the end of its mandate, had to be dissolved before it was put to a vote, and the general elections came on at this stage, in the midst of great excitement.

The positions taken up by either side were curiously confused. The one thing that stood out clearly was the violent, passionate, implacable antagonism aroused between Catholics and Protestants: the former saw themselves deprived of their subvention, and no promise of minor concessions could appease them; the latter gave themselves up once again to the familiar anti-Catholic and anti-clerical campaign, declaring angrily that the Confederation should be Protestant or nothing.

But the two parties, as usual, managed to confuse the issues. In order to curry favour with the many adherents they believed themselves to have in the French portions of the colony, the Conservative government had attempted the solution of the question by means of the remedial bill, and in consequence the Catholic clergy supported it to a man. The Liberals took up a different position, that of loyalty to the principle of provincial autonomy; but as they must somehow manage to get the Catholic vote, they argued that through the mediation of their leader, M. Laurier, they would secure by means of diplomacy what the Conservatives would assuredly never secure by recourse to the clumsy expedient of action by the federal government.

[1] Manitoba Act, 1870.

Stale from their long exercise of power and compromised by the excess of zeal shown by the bishops on their behalf, the Conservatives were beaten, and the first care of the new Liberal government was to enter into unofficial negotiations with the Manitoba ministry with a view to terminating this conflict by means of compromise. The personal prestige of M. Laurier, the prime minister, won the Catholics a solution which probably no other man could have secured them. Without being rescinded (the Manitoba government would not have consented to this), the law of 1890 was cleverly attenuated and its spirit entirely changed. This was brought about by the Laurier amendment, of which the following were the chief points:

1. In each school district the parents were to nominate three trustees, who in their turn were to select a teacher from the candidates provided with diplomas from the government.
2. The study of English to be obligatory, but French also to be taught if there are ten children of French origin in the school, and if their parents express their wish to this effect.
3. The school to be neutral in regard to religion, but to be open after 3.30 p.m. to the priest if it contains at least ten Catholic children (twenty-five in the towns), and if the parents wish it.
4. Finally (a concession not made until a later date), one of the inspectors as a conciliatory measure to be chosen from among the French Catholics.

This amendment of the law of 1890 was a magnificent diplomatic victory for the Liberal leader. Thanks to him, the Catholics have secured conditions which their official champions, the Conservatives, could not have won for them. If their independent schools have not been restored in Manitoba by law, they have been almost restored in practice: it is the parents (which means the *curé*) who appoint the teacher; the teaching of French is guaranteed; the *curé* has right of entry to the school every day. Finally, the supervision by the state is no longer unsympathetic, being no longer entrusted to an English Protestant.

The French generally are satisfied with this compromise. Their clergy, however, continue to protest on the ground of principle: our denominational schools have not been given back to us, they object. We wish to have the right to adhere to our practice of recourse to prayer at all times of the day, and we cannot admit that any form of education is independent that is subjected to close supervision by the state. Monseigneur Langevin, Archbishop of St. Boniface, spoke out more strongly still. "We are being treated like the Irish or the Russians," he exclaimed. "What we demand is (1) the control of our schools, (2) school *administration* everywhere, (3) Catholic history books and readers, (4) Catholic inspectors, (5) Catholic teachers selected by us; (6) we pay our own school tax, and are liable to no taxation for schools not our own."[2]

But in spite of such protestations the clergy, as a matter of fact, accommodated themselves to the new situation, especially since Leo XIII, while reserving the question of doctrine, unofficially recommended peace. They resign themselves, therefore, to an opportunist policy, which in the long run is not wholly unfavourable to them. A priest of Winnipeg made to me privately the following avowal: "After all, we are able to exercise our influence sufficiently, for the government has become conciliatory. We should be almost satisfied if we could only feel secure about the future." So this long and dangerous question has been settled by a compromise – we dare not say by a solution.

It was inevitable that a similar crisis should be produced some day in the Northwest Territories, where may be found the same mixture of creeds and races. The entry of Alberta and Saskatchewan into the Union as autonomous provinces in 1905 was almost bound to bring about this new crisis, because in giving a constitution to the two new provinces the federal parliament was called upon to provide for the rights of minorities in regard to education.

On February 20, 1905, Sir Wilfrid Laurier submitted to the Ottawa House of Commons bills giving their constitutions respectively to Alberta and Saskatchewan.[3] A Frenchman and a Catholic, entirely free from the intolerance that marks the English Protestant, anxious above all for a peaceful solution of the difficulty, he showed a strong disposition to provide generously for the rights of the Catholic minority. Article 16 of his bill, referring back to the federal Act of 1875, which had provisionally established the government of the Northwest Territories (the region included in the two new provinces), reserved to the Catholics the right to have their separate schools throughout. The prime minister defended this arrangement by recalling the fact that the British North America Act had guaranteed to the minorities the confirmation of the educational rights and privi-

---

[2] Cited in Lavisse and Rambaud's *Histoire Générale*, vol. XII, p. 112.
[3] An Act to establish and provide for the government of the province of Alberta. An Act to establish and provide for the government of the province of Saskatchewan.

leges of which they were possessed at the moment of their entry into Confederation. According to him, the law of 1875 should therefore be final. "Parliament," he said in his speech of February 22, 1905, "having introduced in 1875 the system of the separate school, it is introduced for ever. The question is not to be raised to-day whether the system be good or bad. It is the law." The bills and these remarks gave entire satisfaction to the Catholics. As for the Protestants, they did not realize at first the full extent of the favours involved in the prime minister's interpretation, and even his English colleagues did not protest at the time of the introduction of the bills.

However, Sir Wilfrid Laurier seemed to overlook an important fact which was to prove decisive: the law of 1875 had been replaced by the "ordinances"[4] of 1892 and 1901, which had established quite a different system of education – a normal school submitting all its teachers to an identical training; close supervision of the school books in use; effective inspection; above all, complete secularization of the school from 8 a.m. to 3.30 p.m. The separate school was allowed to survive, but it was no longer either denominational or independent. The legality of these enactments had been contested, but in vain. They had therefore definitely become law.

Thus Laurier's bills would have resulted merely in reviving the old school régime of twenty years before. When the English Canadians realized this, they rose against them as one man. Mr. Sifton, Minister of the Interior, an influential leader of the English-speaking Liberals of the West, gave in his resignation at once, and Mr. Fielding, Minister of Finance, threatened to do the same. Immediately the question assumed its real importance, and conflict broke out again violently between Catholics and Protestants. The Liberal party was shaken to its foundations, to such a point that in order to avert a crisis which would have disorganized the whole political life of the colony, the government was forced to modify the first interpretation that had been given of its system.

On March 20, 1905, the prime minister himself brought forward an amendment to his own bill. The new reading proposed for the first paragraph of his new Article 16 went as follows: "Nothing in any such law shall prejudicially affect any right or privilege with respect to Separate Schools which any

---

[4] In the Northwest Territories the Acts of the legislature were thus designated.

class of persons have at the passing of this Act, under the terms of Chapters 29 and 30 of the Ordinances of the Northwest Territories passed in the year 1901."

The meaning of this amendment is quite clear. It guarantees to the Catholic minority only the separate schools as recognized by the law of 1901. The ministers who had objected to the first form of this article agreed to support it as thus amended. The period of acute strife was over, and the government found its action approved by 140 votes against 59.

It was, however, far indeed from having achieved a victory. The lack of unity in the Liberal party was manifest to all, and it was only a similar lack in the Opposition that saved the cabinet from downfall. The persistence of racial and religious rivalry had asserted itself in disquieting fashion. In the midst of calm, within a few months after a magnificent triumph at the polls, it was enough for the old question of the schools to be raised for the whole Protestant population to rise in arms against the Catholic Church. Confederation remains at the mercy of these violent storms, and it is to demonstrate the all but impossibility of finding organic and definitive solutions to Canadian educational problems that I have sought to describe these two grave conflicts in Manitoba and the Northwest.

13: Secondary and Higher Education

In the colleges and universities in which the ruling classes of Canada get their training we shall find the same methods, the same tendencies, and the same motives at work as in the primary schools. We shall see, too, on a more restricted field, the same passionate defence on the part of the two races of their forms of civilization and views of life and ideals. Thus secondary and higher education in Canada is the reverse of a unifying institution. The two currents are indeed so distinct in regard to them that there may be said to be no conflict, for the reason that there is no contact. Let us study in turn the two forms of establishment in which the character of the two kinds of Canadian youth is given its shape.

In the French parts of Canada the state has made no effort to take in hand the management of secondary education. It has handed over this duty to the Catholic Church, which has of course accepted it as one of its natural functions, and would have strongly opposed its being undertaken by the civil power.

For the moment the Church has it entirely in her hands. The 19 French colleges in the province of Quebec are all denominational, and lay teachers are in a very small minority, numbering only 32 as compared with 527 clerical or monastic.[1] The French public approves of this entirely, regarding members of the priesthood and the religious orders as the best qualified educators of youth. This being so, naturally the politicians do not attempt to burden themselves with a task for which they admit themselves ill equipped. As the immense majority of girls also are educated in convents, the Church has full command of the avenues of the future.

The colleges provide two forms of education – classical and commercial. The former includes instruction in the dead languages. In this the Church has always excelled. The parents set great store by these literary studies, for they give access for their sons to the medical and legal professions, which are well thought of in Canada. In 1903, out of 6174 pupils, 3757 followed the classical course, while 2147 were content with the commercial, which corresponds rather with our *cycle moderne*. This shows how much attached the French Canadians are to our time-honoured educational methods.

Secondary education in Quebec impresses one chiefly, indeed, by its fidelity to somewhat antiquated traditions. Its colleges recall our Catholic institutions of former days: their outward aspect is the same, the arrangement of the classes is the same, there is the same indescribable atmosphere of *la vieille France*. Some of the buildings are superb. You can see that there is no lack of money and that you are in the midst of a wealthy world. But the whole impression you derive is that of clericalism.

I was much impressed, for instance, when attending on the 29th of November the Sainte-Marie College in Montreal, on the occasion of the fiftieth anniversary of the proclamation of the Dogma of the Immaculate Conception. The Jesuits, who manage this college, had organized the most imposing of ceremonies. The Apostolic Delegate from the Vatican was to be seen in the centre of a great concourse, surrounded by many important political personages. The programme, inscribed with the words "*Gloire à l'Immaculée*," consisted almost entirely of religious compositions, hymns, recitations, dialogues, pieces prepared for the occasion, etc.[2] I heard the "sects of Mahomet and Luther"

[1] *Rapport du surintendant de l'instruction publique de la Province de Québec pour l'année 1902-03.*

[2] Séance jubilaire offerte par le collège Sainte-Marie (Montréal) à Son Excellence Mgr. Sbaretti, délegué apostolique, le 29 Nov. 1904.

come in for condemnation, and "the two great Catholic poets of the nineteenth century, Verlaine and Coppée," for praise. All but obedient disciples were out of place at such a festival, and it is thus that a material and moral discipline almost necessarily inclines the youth of Canada towards the views to which the Church directs them.

Higher education is not less confessional in its character. It is principally represented by Laval University at Quebec and by its branch establishment at Montreal. In 1663, Monseigneur de Laval, the first Bishop of Quebec, established in the capital the "grand séminaire," to which five years later he added the "petit séminaire." It was from this that Laval University took its origin in 1852. At this date, by royal charter, the British government recognized officially the new establishment of higher education, to which Pius IX accorded by the Bull *Inter varias sollicitudines,* "l'érection canonique solennelle avec les privilèges les plus étendus." By virtue of this Bull, the university had for patron at the Vatican the Cardinal Prefect of the Propaganda. The duty of supervising matters of doctrine and discipline is entrusted to a Higher Council, composed of the Episcopate of the province of Quebec, under the presidency of the archbishop. According to the royal charter, the archbishop is a permanent visitor of the university, with a voice on all regulations and all appointments, while the duties of rector belong *ex officio* to the head of the "grand séminaire." The branch university at Montreal, inaugurated in 1878, is almost independent of the parent institution, but its organization is built up on a similar plan.

As is evident, then, the great French-Canadian university is under the supervision of the Church, of which it is in reality an integral part since it can rightly be considered as a simple development of the two seminaries of Quebec. It is only natural, therefore, that from the outset it should have been placed "under the special protection of the Blessed Virgin and have chosen for its *fête patronale* the Feast of the Immaculate Conception." Nor is it a matter for surprise that in 1873 it should have been "consecrated solemnly to the Sacred Heart of Jesus." In its strictly Catholic character it exactly meets the needs of the inhabitants of the province. If, therefore, we are to judge it impartially, it is important not to separate it from its environment.

Fully to appreciate, indeed, the charm of this ancient institution, you must have visited the historic buildings of the grand séminaire towering aloft from the rock of Quebec, dominating the whole city and the wide reaches of the St. Lawrence. You must have made your way along its dark interminable corridors, lit up here and there by narrow windows through which you catch sudden glimpses of the wonderful waterway with its background of distant mountains. You must have seen passing through its ante-chambers and sombre, old-world classrooms the long processions of clerical-looking students, in their curious old-fashioned uniforms – long blue frock-coats, with emerald-green scarves. Above all, you must have conversed in their neat and cosy little cell-like studies with the clerical teachers themselves, so French in their utterance yet so typically Canadian, so intensely Catholic and yet so far removed from the catholicity of our present-day France. Only thus can you divine, as from the personality of the whole place, the strength of those traditions in which this race is so steeped that it would feel orphaned were it bereft of the protecting arms of Rome.

The instruction given at Laval University is comprised chiefly in the three faculties of theology, law, and medicine. A polytechnic school is attached to the University of Montreal. As to the Faculty of Arts, that exists only in an embryonic stage. Disinterested study for study's sake can scarcely flourish in Canada, not because the French Canadians are incapable of it but because they cannot afford to devote several years of their life to the acquisition of a culture which can be of no immediate use to them. Though well-to-do as a rule, they are not rich. Forced for the most part to earn their own livelihood, they make haste to take up some career. Therefore, very wisely, the university aims principally at turning out practical men – lawyers, physicians, engineers, merchants.

However, as the teachers are under the influence of tradition, at once classical and Catholic, they find it difficult to free themselves from an exaggerated respect for the dead languages and out-worn methods. The consequence is that, without being able to pretend to real distinction in literature or science, they do not succeed in giving their students the really practical education of which the Anglo-Saxon youth has the advantage, and which they themselves are the first to declare essential to the progress of the French-Canadian race.

This is the weak point in their methods, and we can appreciate the weakness all the more that we have had to reproach ourselves on the same head. Granted that Laval University can turn out good lawyers and doctors, it must be admitted that it is less successful in regard to men of business. Now it is in this respect above all that our race calls for development in Canada, under pain of being left behind by rivals better equipped and with more energy and money. To abandon the scientific teaching of agricultural and industrial knowledge to the English universities in Canada would be equivalent to throwing up the sponge. France is ready to second the French Canadians in the pacific contest so essential to their welfare. Why do they not profit more by the assistance our Minister of Public Instruction has so often offered them, and is always so ready to accord?

With its work of instruction Laval University combines a work of education in the strict meaning of the word. The Church makes a special point of watching over the students entrusted to its care, not least those who have passed through Laval. It is conscious to the full of the strength of the imprint left upon the young men who to-morrow will be the pilots of their race, priests entrusted with the charges of parishes, physicians "co-operating with the priests in works of charity,"[3] lawyers, journalists, politicians, perhaps even statesmen. It realizes the importance of moulding the rising generation and making of it a generation loyally French and faithful to its clergy.

A stern system of discipline is the outstanding characteristic of university education at Quebec and Montreal. And this discipline is, it must be noted, distinctively Catholic. Its object is not merely to produce *men*, but to produce Catholics, Catholic doctors, Catholic lawyers, Catholic men of business. This is the logical end and aim of a system of education utterly at variance with that in practice under lay management.

Only naturally, therefore, the students are called upon to fulfil regularly their religious duties. "The rector is free to institute the giving of religious lectures to the Catholic students whenever he thinks well. All must attend these lectures regularly." It is natural also that their reading should be strictly supervised. "The students having at their disposal in the university library the books they require, must not subscribe to any other. They must not frequent the reading-rooms of the town, in which they would be tempted to waste their time and neglect their studies."[4] The university, it will be seen, proclaims and exercises a stern control over its inmates.

The critical spirit has never been in favour with the Catholic Church: it has its dogmas which it teaches and which are not to be discussed. That this should be the spirit of the teaching in the "grand séminaire" itself goes without saying, but it

[3] *Annuaire de l'Université Laval pour l'année académique, 1904-05.*
[4] *Annuaire de l'Université Laval, 1904-05.*

penetrates also into the university system generally. The study of philosophy may be said to be mixed up with that of theology: it is done in Latin, according to the old practice, and on absolutely dogmatic lines. At the Catholic College of Winnipeg, an establishment of higher secondary education, for instance, I had the following conversation with one of the Jesuit masters:

Q. Do you teach philosophy in Latin?
A. Certainly, that is the practice.
Q. What kind of philosophy do you teach?
A. Aristotle, St. Thomas.
Q. Don't you include any more modern philosophers, such as Descartes or Spinoza?
A. We only speak of them to refute them. They are contrary to the doctrines of the Church.

These words illustrate how French-Canadian education insists upon complete acceptance of the dogmas of the Church of Rome. The university in Canada, instead of being a centre for new ideas and the evolution of the future, is a potent instrument of conservatism. There is something venerable and poetic about Laval, which is invested with a charm for the French visitor, but it has to be admitted that for signs of progress we must look elsewhere.

In English-speaking Canada secondary and higher education are very different in character. Here we are confronted with Protestantism and Anglo-Saxon methods. The contrast is very striking.

While the Catholic Church fights against secularism with all its force, the Protestant Church accommodates itself to it quite well. In most cases it retains a kind of diffused influence over the educational establishments within its sphere; the maintenance of certain religious forms and tendencies is all it requires. It does not seek to infuse itself into every branch of study. Therefore, while complete freedom of thought is made impossible by the mere fact of this incompleteness of its secular system, it may be said that Protestant interference is not a direct menace to the independence of either teacher or student: this is the first and the really important difference between the Protestant and Catholic systems.

As to the Anglo-Saxon influence, that manifests itself openly in two forms – English and American. The English ideas are of course more tinged with the colour of the past. The American tends towards perpetual change, towards the pursuit of what is better or at least new. Left to itself, higher education in French Canada tends to remain where it is – it needs the energy of some exceptional personality among its directors to introduce organic and far-reaching reforms. In Protestant Canada, on the contrary, it is carried along by the tumultuous current of the United States and subjected to unceasing modification. Every change is not an improvement, but at least there are signs of life and movement.

In the French provinces we have seen all the colleges in the hands of the clergy. In the English provinces secondary education seems like a natural continuation of primary education. Denominational and independent colleges exist, but they are the exception. As to institutions subsidized by the state (high schools, collegiate institutes), they are run on the semi-secular lines already described; the teachers are laymen, but the general tone of the education is vaguely Christian. Public opinion clings to this religious atmosphere, which at the same time satisfies the conscience of the clergy.

The tone of this school world is Anglo-American—more often American than English, but always Anglo-Saxon. In the colleges that come under the influence of the neighbouring republic the life is more easy-going, and there is less of discipline and formality. In those which get their inspiration from England – notably Upper Canada College of Toronto – you note the desire of the authorities to anglicize their pupils, or one might almost say, to imperialize them. In strong contrast with the democratic, happy-go-lucky ways tolerated in the young American students is the Draconian discipline here maintained; in some colleges resort has even been had to corporal punishment, as in England. Their entire management recalls Eton and Rugby, which have manifestly been taken as models; games are held in high honour, especially those which are exclusively British, like cricket, as distinguished from American games, like baseball and basket-ball. In the school curriculum an important place is given to classics and mathematics, as in the mother country. Finally, though Catholics are admitted, it is unmistakably the Protestant spirit that permeates the whole establishment.

Higher education in English-speaking Canada is principally represented by the University of Toronto and McGill University of Montreal.

Founded in 1837 by the government of Ontario, the University of Toronto is absolutely secular; but it is surrounded by a network of affiliated colleges belonging to the different sects. Thus there are colleges for the Methodists, the Presbyterians, the Episcopalians, the Catholics, etc. Degrees are conferred by the university only, but instruction is carried on concurrently by the university and the colleges.

McGill University, called after its founder, who bequeathed it lands of considerable value, came into being in 1811, although its charter dates only from 1837. It is Protestant, but not confined to any one sect, the Governor-General being *ex officio* a visitor. The very numerous and very wealthy colleges affiliated to it make of it a centre of culture of the very highest importance.

The material and intellectual management of these two great institutions is of the first order. Thanks to their very large financial resources, it has been possible for them to create every kind of course; medicine, chemistry, physics, mechanics, are taught with a wealth of accessories, laboratories, etc., scarcely surpassed by the great universities of the United States. They provide everything the Canadian youth can want for his progress. Students flock to them, therefore, from all parts of the Dominion. Practical studies are given even more attention in them than theoretical, and they turn out first-rate engineers and expert chemists. Thus it is that the English, whose tastes, whose past, whose traditions are towards industry and business, are furnished with the means of equipping themselves effectively for work, and are enabled to maintain that condition of economic supremacy which renders them indisputably the dominant race in Canada.

From these two universities radiate Anglo-Saxon influences that serve to intensify the British character of the Dominion. If the French-Canadian race continues to lag behind, if it neglects to renovate its methods and ideas, they will prove a more deadly enemy to it than would be an army fitted out with the most perfected type of rifles.

There is a real battle in progress between the two groups of youths whose characters are being formed side by side. The French youths are more brilliant, better endowed doubtless from the literary point of view, but why do they always seem to confine themselves to a small number of careers which will never permit them to dominate the country? The English youths, less cultivated, but better sustained by a rich past, by an environment abounding in wealth, by their own methods of initiative, seem bound to take and keep the lead in the country. If the French do not follow this lead it is to be feared that they will be out-distanced. Their educators will be chiefly responsible for that future.

III—NATIONAL SENTIMENTS

14: The French Canadians and Britain

It is not easy to analyse clearly the feelings of the French in Canada in regard to the English. To say simply that they do not like them, even that in their inmost hearts they detest them, would not be inaccurate, but it would be too simple a characterization of a complex state of mind to describe which one should have recourse to fine shades of expression. Moreover, the term "English" has not the same unity of meaning in Canada that it has with us. The French Canadians have learned to distinguish widely between the English of the Dominion and the English of England. In dealing with the question under consideration this distinction must be kept well in mind.

When the French of Canada speak of the English, they think chiefly of the English in the provinces of Quebec and Ontario, side by side with whom they have had to pass their existence. After a hundred and fifty years of life in common as neighbours, under the same laws and the same flag, they remain foreigners, and in most cases adversaries. The two races have no more love for each other now than they had at the beginning, and it is easy to see that we are face to face with one of those deep and lasting antipathies against which all efforts of conciliators are vain.

The fusion not having proved practicable at the time of the conquest, many causes have served to perpetuate the feelings of jealousy and hostility then conceived. A conquered race (for it is only right to state the fact plainly), the French suffer more than is commonly supposed from the attitude of the victors. In truth, for all the euphemisms employed in official language, the English treat them too often as inferiors and aliens, whose slightest progress they look at askance as menacing the security of the state. In these conditions the conqueror is not England herself, distant and invisible, but the English Canadian who lives on the spot and profits in his insolent way by the victory of his ancestors. The real hostility is not between Quebec and London, but between Quebec and Ontario. To-day no less than fifty years ago this traditional and, one may say, incurable rivalry reveals one of the chief currents in Canadian political life.

However, like brothers that hate each other, French and English have to dwell under one roof. If the rural inhabitants of the two races do not come together, the townsfolk in such cites as Quebec and Montreal are naturally in frequent contact, meeting in the same offices and political gatherings. The result of these personal and daily relationships is that the separation of the two races is notably less complete at their respective frontiers, and that a series of little concordats tends ceaselessly to soften the sharpness of a rivalry which is only too real.

In this way have come about many pleasant acquaintance-ships. If the Irishman, though Catholic, shows little disposition to favour his French co-religionists, the Englishmen and still more the Scotsmen bear themselves in business affairs in such a way as to win regard. Sometimes even everyday intercourse ripens into intimate friendship. However, generally speaking, intimate relations between French and English are the exception.

Sometimes a measure of that union which racial feeling prevents is brought about by that inevitable product of British civilization – snobbishness. English "society" possesses an extra-ordinary power of fascination – one might almost say an extraordinary power of corruption. It is so convinced of its own superiority, and affirms it so boldly as an indisputable fact, that it is not disputed. Many of the members of the French bour-geoisie in Canada render homage to this mundane hegemony, and are flattered when admitted into its elegant and exclusive circles. From the standpoint of our race there is danger in this – the temptation to weak-minded persons to gain the level of their hosts by renouncing the traditions of their origin. There are French renegades who are thus moved to affect anglomania. Fortunately they are rare.

The visitor to Canada will often see French and English together, seated round the same tables, even consorting together in clubs and drawing-rooms. Anxious to emphasize the signifi-cance of these *rencontres*, Canadians – French and English alike – will boast of the perfect relations between the two bodies; they will tell you of strong ties of friendship contracted between individuals on either side; they will insist on the fact that the two political parties are mixed and not national. "There is no race supremacy among us," declared Sir Wilfrid Laurier, for instance, in Paris, in 1897. "We have learned to respect and love those against whom we fought in the past, and we have made them respect and love us. The old enmities have ceased to exist, and now there is nothing more than a spirit of emulation."[1]

[1] Sir W. Laurier's speech at the Banquet given by the British Chamber of Commerce in honour of the Colonial ministers.

It would be a mistake to be carried away by this kind of deliberate optimism. Responsible statesmen strive gallantly to keep up the fiction of an *entente cordiale*. They are able to exercise enough control over their supporters to prevent the use too openly of violent expressions of feeling, but the great public does not wax enthusiastic over their peaceful sentiments, and the irresponsible politician who is bent only on success knows how to win applause. There are oratorical effects which are always to be relied on. If the leaders do not have recourse to them, the smaller fry have no hesitation in doing so.

In the French-Canadian attitude, then, there is an outward seeming and a true inwardness. The outward seeming is artificially kept up – you might go through entire collections of official speeches without ever lighting on a phrase expressive of popular feeling – and the consistency and thoroughness of this policy are matter for admiration. It may be pursued for a long time with satisfactory results; but it is vain to ignore the fact that its tendency is misleading and that any serious mistake will suffice to set up the two peoples in arms against each other: their mutual animosity is too instinctive for any complete understanding to be possible between them.

Towards England the French Canadians feel quite differently. With the exception of a few of their leaders, they have never been in personal touch with it, and there have, in consequence, been few occasions for friction. In theory, England has nothing to do with local strifes in the Dominion, or if she intervenes at all, only in such a way that the fact escapes notice. Although this wise tradition has not been adhered to altogether during the administration of the Conservatives – or imperialist party – the English government still enjoys prestige as the distant, supreme arbiter to whom appeal is not always to be made in vain. Therefore there is no feeling of hatred towards England; on the other hand, there is no feeling of affection. When English armies are defeated upon the battlefield, as in the South African War, the French Canadians experience no extravagant grief. They even rejoice quite openly, but that is to rile their Ontario neighbours and to enjoy the diversion of treading a little on the lion's tail; it is a taste of revenge in which they indulge their injured *amour propre*. In reality they have not the least desire to see Great Britain reduced to nothing.

In truth, the point of view changes entirely when we turn from mere manifestations of popular feeling to the wise outlook of the statesmen of French Canada. In the realm of statecraft the French Canadians exhibit the most perfect *sang froid*, and it is by a veritable system of profit and loss that they reckon up in minute detail what they get from Britain and what they would lose in escaping from it.

From this balance-sheet the word "sentiment" should be entirely banished; the leaders will never admit it, of course – it would not be the thing for them to do so; but men like M. Henri Bourassa, who are not less representative of the race and who enjoy a position of greater freedom and less responsibility, do not hesitate to proclaim it openly. "We are the subjects," writes M. Bourassa, "of a power which for centuries has been the foe of the land of our origin. We owe political allegiance to a nation which we can esteem, with which we have been able to make a *mariage de raison*, but for which we cannot have that spontaneous love which makes a joy of life in common and mutual sacrifice: the atavism of the blood and all our traditions stand in the way. . . . Our loyalty to England can only be, and should only be, a matter of reason."[2]

These words from the pen of a man accustomed to speaking out, express faithfully the general feeling. For the real word *interêt* Sir Wilfrid Laurier prefers to substitute *honneur* and *loyauté* and *devoir*; but he has never gone so far as to speak of the love of the French Canadians for England; the note even in his most eloquent orations would have sounded false.

Thus our kinsmen in Canada ask themselves the simple question, "Is it to our advantage to remain under British rule?" And their unanimous answer is in the affirmative. England has given them what no other power could or would have given them – the fullest, most complete, most paradoxical liberty. There is no need for us to discuss whether she gave it with a good grace. She has given it, and so long as she does not renounce her traditional liberalism she can be sure that her French subjects on their side will not fall away from the loyalty they show her – the same loyalty they would exhibit in the execution of a contract. As one of them – a man of note, Sir Etienne Pascal Taché – was able to declare in this sense, in a phrase which has become famous, "The last shot fired on American soil in defence of the British flag would be fired by a French Canadian."

We may take it as certain that the French Canadians are satisfied with the rule under which they live. M. Bourassa says

[2] Henri Bourassa, *Le Patriotisme canadien français*.

so explicitly in an article in the *Monthly Review*:[3] "The present feeling of the French Canadian is one of contentment. He is satisfied with his lot." And it is not to the English alone that this truth is confided. As much has been said quite frankly to us Frenchmen of France. Sometimes, it will be added, with a touch of playful malice: "Very likely we should not be so well off under you!"

We have seen that this loyalism which is displayed so voluntarily never quite rises to affection. It has, however, produced among the most distinguished of French-Canadian public men a sense of profound admiration for England. Certainly most of the politicians of our race in Canada are American in spirit and customs, thinking and acting usually in the fashion of Washington congressmen. But the best of the French leaders seek their models in London. Brought up from infancy under a British constitution, they acquire and preserve for the rest of their life a British conception of government. Convinced parliamentarians, they cannot but look to the classic country of parliamentarianism; and Westminster to their eyes is clothed in an infinite prestige.

This is particularly striking in the case of Sir Wilfrid Laurier. He is undoubtedly French, and very French, both by temperament and training; but when it comes to political affairs, France to him is merely a brilliant nation in whose footsteps it would be perilous to follow; England seems to him a very much safer guide, and there is the ring of sincerity in his professions of deep devotion to the institutions of Great Britain. "Whilst remaining French," he exclaimed once, "we are profoundly attached to British institutions." On another occasion he went so far as to declare – perhaps the words escaped him: "I am British to the core."[4]

It is true that in the province of Quebec M. Laurier is sometimes accused of being too much of an anglomaniac. But M. Bourassa, who may be regarded as an uncompromising French nationalist, is scarcely less English by his political and parliamentary education. The Liberal party of Gladstone and Bright is much more to his taste than our radical or opportunist parties. "I am a Liberal of the British school," he says himself.[5] "I am a disciple of Burke, Fox, Bright, Gladstone and of the

[3] *Monthly Review*, "The French Canadian in the British Empire," October 1902, p. 20.
[4] Speech of Sir Wilfrid Laurier at the Lord Mayor's Banquet at the Mansion House, July 1, 1897.
[5] Speech in the House of Commons at Ottawa, March 13, 1900.

other Little Englanders who made Great Britain and her possessions what they are." The political life of England inspires in
him an admiration he has no desire to conceal, at the same time
that his sensitively Canadian standpoint arouses the indignation
of the jingoes: "The more I have analysed the vital parts and
the solid limbs of that splendid body politic, its strong nerves
and its rich blood, the wider has grown my admiration for Great
Britain. I used to be a contented British subject, as most of my
countrymen are; I feel now the full pride of Birtish citizenship."[6]

From the very fact of having been uprooted, the French
Canadians are naturally liable to this kind of double nature.
Placed by destiny upon a new stage with their role cut out for
them, it is natural that they should take pride in declaring that
the stage is a fine one, and the company to which they now
belong illustrious. That is why the British constitution has
among them such sincere admirers.

But we must not forget that this admiration is exceptional
and limited. For all their reasoned loyalty to England, the mass
of the French Canadians will never love the English.

15: The French Canadians and France

The French Canadians seem to have been fated by history
to find themselves in complex conditions and to have complex
feelings. In studying their attitude towards France we shall be
obliged to have recourse to refinements and differentiations just
as in studying their attitude towards England. Their racial
patriotism is not purely French; it is not even purely Canadian.
We must distinguish.

To begin with, it is incontestable that they love France. For
them, France is still and in spite of everything *la patrie*; it is the
old country whence came their forefathers, and whose creed and
speech and habits they still retain; it is the nation under whose
standard those forefathers fought on many a battlefield, and
which, for all the divergence in their destinies, continues to be
to them a beloved and sacred memory. There is not one of them
who does not cherish deep down in his heart this passionate
fidelity to the memory of France, who does not rejoice over her
triumphs and mourn over her defeats. No question here of
interest or reasoning or compromise — no need for discussion.

[6] Speech in the House of Commons, March 12, 1901.

Love lives on in these souls that cannot forget. It lives and needs no discussion.

The poet Fréchette, himself a son of the province of Quebec, has succeeded in reaching us with the sincere and passionate accents of that superb book of his in which he sings of the moving history of his people and of his own undying affection for the land of his fathers. He recites the poetic memories of Canada's early days, the epic grandeur of her wars, the sadness of her abandonment by us; and then the bitter battle of a new generation for their rights as citizens. He describes the subtle and disturbing problem of the Canadian conscience, divided between two flags, under a foreign domination which is loyally accepted, no doubt, but which is never loved. And finally he recalls the enthusiasm over the renewed relations with France, when for the first time since the treaty of Paris in 1763, a French vessel, *La Capricieuse*, came in 1855 to show our colours along the banks of the St. Lawrence.

> *Je ne suis pas très vieux, pourtant j'ai souvenance*
> *Du jour où notre fleuve, après un siècle entier,*
> *Pour la première fois vit un vaisseau de France*
> *Mirer dans ses flots clairs son étendard altier.*
>
> *Ce jour-là, de nos bords – bonheur trop éphémère –*
> *Montait un cri de joie immense et triomphant:*
> *C'était l'enfant perdu qui retrouvait sa mère;*
> *C'était la mère en pleurs embrassant son enfant!*
>
> *Nos poètes chantaient la France revenue;*
> *Et le père, à l'enfant qu'étonnait tout cela,*
> *Disait – Ce pavillon qui brille dans la nue,*
> *Incline-toi, mon fils! – c'est à nous celui-là!*[1]

It is not in poetry alone that we shall find such sentiments expressed. At the time of his visit to Paris in 1897, Sir Wilfrid Laurier had resort to language in which to speak out his love for France very different from anything ever heard from him in London. "Separated though we have been from France," he declared, "we have ever followed her career with passionate interest, taking our part in her glories and her triumphs, in her rejoicings and in her sorrowings – in her sorrowing most of all. Alas, we never knew perhaps how dear she was to us until the

[1] Louis Fréchette, *La Légende d'un peuple*, p. 285.

day of her misfortune. On that day, if you suffered, we suffered not less than you."[2]

So the affection of the French Canadian for his old mother country is lively, sincere and lasting. It has the poetry of faithful memory; it has also its imprecise mysticism. To characterize it further, one would be obliged to recognize that it is necessarily platonic, and that it is directed perhaps towards the France of old rather than that of to-day.

We have been transformed since 1763, while our brothers of the St. Lawrence remain faithful to many of the ideas of our *ancien régime*. Drawn into the orbit of another empire and another civilization, they became almost strangers to that new France which, in the name of a revolution they cannot approve, radically changed its principles, institutions and flag. There has thus been a sort of trench dug between the majority of Frenchmen and the French Canadians, which it would be difficult to fill in all at once. On the two sides the social ideals, the political conceptions, have evolved along different lines. We are no longer exactly the same people nor do we belong to the same era. Between us stretches the Atlantic and the French Revolution.

If, then, it is true, profoundly true, that the French Canadians love France, it is necessary to add immediately that most of them cannot unreservedly admire modern France. It does not realize their political and religious ideal. It is, first of all a revolutionary France; and that word does not sound well in a country where the entire youth is brought up by a church which has never recognized 1789. It is, secondly, a France which is partially, largely, free-thinking; and in Canada free thought is an object of almost universal reprobation. It is, finally, at least just now, a radical France; and the French Canadians are very attached to the principles of social conservatism.

The form of government which they would have wished to see us endowed with a few years back was that of a monarchy, traditional or constitutional; the Comte de Chambord found the strongest sympathies among them, and later the Comte de Paris received at Quebec and Montreal such a welcome as neither Jules Ferry nor Gambetta could ever have hoped for. However, they are too intelligent not to recognize now that the Republic is a *fait accompli*. They can but regret that it is not a Catholic Republic – perhaps the Méline ministry came nearest to winning

[2] Speech of Laurier in Paris, August 2, 1897.

their approval. For the ministries of M. Combes and M. Waldeck-Rousseau they have had nothing but words of indignation.

If the love of the French Canadians for our country survived until now merely by reason of the past, its continuance would be much imperilled. Where is now the France of Joan of Arc, of Henri IV, and of Louis XIV? The Comte de Chambord used to talk of the "flag of Arc and Ivry," but he could not raise it aloft. It is necessary, therefore, for the French Canadians to accustom themselves to modern France, or rather – and this is the solution which in their profound affection they have intuitively found – it is necessary for them to continue to love France however revolutionary, however anti-clerical, simply because she is France.

In truth, for all the divergence in their tendencies there has never been a greater feeling of cordiality between the two peoples than during the last twenty years. The leading men of French Canada and France have learned to know and appreciate each other. There has been a greater interchange of visits, and just as the French-Canadian leaders have been quick to express their appreciation of the warm reception we have given them, so our statesmen have been accorded a greeting in the Dominion such as they can never forget.

So much for the national feeling of the French Canadians in regard to France. It is now necessary to state precisely their attitude politically. "Should we be more Canadian than French?" asks M. Bourassa, "or more French than Canadian? In other words, should we be the French of Canada, or Canadians of French origin?" His answer is quite clear. "We must remain essentially Canadian."[3] They have no hankering after reunion with France; on the contrary, their desire is all the other way. Love France, yes – but only in a platonic sense. "Far be it from me," proceeds M. Bourassa, "to attempt to stifle the voice of the blood in my compatriots. Our love for France is legitimate and natural. It may continue to be, and should continue to be, deep and enduring, but it must remain platonic."[4] And he ends with a striking and decisive phrase: "Let us be French, as the Americans are English."[5]

M. Bourassa is an upright man, accustomed to considering questions clearly and to speaking out boldly. His way of dealing with this matter is a little hard, perhaps, but it is true; he it is

[3] Henri Bourassa, *Le Patriotisme canadien français*, pp. 10, 11.
[4] *Ibid.*
[5] *Ibid.*, p. 13.

who expresses the real feelings of his compatriots, and not those facile and grandiloquent orators who too often conceal the vagueness of their sentiments under the impressive sound of their phrases. The Canadians, as I have said already, feel that in having been freed from the rule of France they have been freed from some very great evils. "If the Treaty of Paris had kept us bound to France, " says M. Bourassa, "what would have become of us? Supposing we had escaped under the sanguinary Reign of Terror, it is more than probable that Napoleon would have sold us to the Americans, without even consulting us, as he did in the case of Louisiana. Had we survived the Empire, how could we have adapted ourselves to the present régime? We have been able to retain our character as Normans and Northern Frenchmen to a much greater extent than our brothers beyond the sea: all our instincts make us hate the centralization, the administrative organization, the legal militarism, and all that is involved in the essential imperialistic rule which Bonaparte gave to modern France, and which the Third Republic has maintained in all its integrity."[6]

In the mouth of a Canadian this reasoning is quite intelligible, and we must admit that it is not without good grounds. British institutions are much more to his taste than ours would be: he has learnt how to make use of them, and has made them his own. Our institutions, of which he has never had any personal knowledge or experience, must inevitably have the aspect to him of an unknown régime more to be feared than desired.

In these circumstances the love of the French Canadians for France could not possibly give umbrage to the British government. To use the simile of Prince Bülow, there is in question nothing but a *tour de valse innocent*, with nothing to provoke inevitable jealousy!

If, therefore, England continues wise enough not to disquiet herself over these manifestations of platonic emotion, and not to ask the French Canadians for a love they cannot give her in place of the prosaic loyalty they do give her already, she may safely suffer them to draw still closer their bonds with France; they will not betray her confidence. The thing is so certain that some of our Canadian kinsmen have already foreshadowed the position they would take up in the event, fortunately most improbable, of a war between France and England. "Were such a conflict confined to these two powers, the French Canadian,"

[6] *Ibid.*, p. 12.

says M. Bourassa, "could be counted on to stand loyally neutral. Should even the French navy, by the most improbable of war fortunes, attack the coast of Canada, the French Canadian could be relied upon for the defence of his country."[7] This precision of statement smooths the way for the development of our relations with Canada, as far as the British government is concerned. No obstacle can be put in our way from the stand-point of political interests.

We are now in a position to understand the dual attitude of the French Canadians, as explained by Sir Wilfrid Laurier in the speech (already cited) which he delivered in Paris on the 19th of July 1897. "We are faithful," he said, "to the great nation which gave us life. We are faithful to the great nation which gave us liberty." Is there anything difficult to understand in that? No, and this chapter will have served to prove it. To England is given the loyalty that has its origin in self-interest, for it is she who guaranteed the French of Canada their untrammelled liberty. But to France go their hearts, for the memory of the land of their forefathers cannot be taken from them.

16: The National Sentiments of the English Canadians

After the subtleties of feeling which we have just described, the state of mind of the English Canadians will seem simple, for, unlike their French rivals, they are not drawn in opposite directions by sentiment and self-interest. They have but one flag, the Union Jack, which symbolizes to them the unity of the British Empire, and if they cherish a special love for Canada herself, there is in this nothing to detract from their loyalty to England. Their position, therefore, would be exactly similar to that of the Australians, New Zealanders, and other British colonists, were it not that they are always conscious of having alongside them, tolerated with impatience, a foreign race whose destinies are inextricably involved in theirs. This could not but be a source of violent conflict and, as a consequence, of an intensified fervour of nationalism in their hearts. Their patriot-ism is made up in large measure of haughty belief in British

[7] Bourassa, "The French Canadian in the British Empire," *Monthly Review*, October 1902, p. 31.

superiority, asserted sometimes offensively, at the expense of the impliedly inferior French.

The English Canadians consider themselves the sole masters of Canada; they were not its first occupants admittedly, but it is theirs, they maintain, by right of conquest. They experience, therefore, a feeling of indignation at the sight of the defeated race persisting in their development instead of fusing or being submerged. And to the classic cry of the mother country – "No Popery!" – they add another of their own – "No French Domination!" English Protestants and French Catholics thus find themselves face to face every day in the political arena; and the English obstinately make it a point of honour not to let themselves be surpassed by adversaries whom they judge backward and inferior.

An attitude frequently adopted in Anglo-Canadian circles is that of ignoring deliberately the very presence of the French. From their whole bearing and conversation, you might suppose that the French element in Canada was quite insignificant. You might spend many weeks among the English of Montreal without anyone letting you realize that the city is two-thirds French. Many travellers never suspect this.

And if you seek to draw the attention of the English to their French fellow-citizens, they will discuss them either patronizingly and somewhat disdainfully, or else in tones of harsh severity, seldom sympathetically or without prejudice. They would have you understand that the language of the French Canadians is only a *patois*, and the whole race at least a hundred years behind the times.

This attitude of ill-will, latent or made manifest, does not, of course, prevent our kinsmen from asserting themselves and laying claim boldly to their share of the light of the sun. And, as a matter of fact, the English willy-nilly have to take them into account. At election times the English have to solicit their valuable support. It has even been necessary to choose a prime minister from amongst them!

The English generally have sense enough not to fly vainly in the face of hard facts. Therefore they made a show of accepting in a proper spirit the nomination of Sir Wilfrid Laurier. Nevertheless, it is impossible not to note the deep hurt done to the *amour propre* of certain English Conservatives of Ontario by this promotion of a Frenchman to the highest post in the state. A Frenchman, a Catholic, prime minister! Truly the humiliation was extreme! Sir Wilfrid has never been completely accepted in the great British province. He came to power in 1896; at the elections of 1900 and 1904 Ontarian public opinion has gone against him. Because of his line of policy? Yes, in some respects, without doubt. But there was always another powerful motive, expressed with brutal frankness in the admonition given by electoral agents, "Don't vote for that damn Frenchman!"

Whenever a question comes to the front in Canada involving a conflict between the races, this irreconcilable division immediately reappears. Then there rushes forth an avalanche of violent expressions going far beyond the normal sentiments of those who use them, but not to be dismissed simply as the hackneyed clichés of journalists and politicians.

Let us recall, for instance, those memorable sittings of the Canadian House of Commons when M. Bourassa animadverted severely, but in the most correct manner possible, on the participation of the Dominion in the South African War. The English Canadians would have wished to secure unanimity in this imperial, if not national, question. The reports of the sitting of June 8, 1900, are there to remind us of the insults with which the courageous French member was assailed. "Shame! Shame! No traitors here!" were among the cries repeated over and over again in the midst of mad excitement even by the leaders of British opinion themselves. From one of their own race they would doubtless have taken strong words. But that a Frenchman, a foreigner, should in their own House of Commons run counter to the Empire was more than they could stand. It was in vain that their opponent appealed to his record for unquestioned loyalty to the throne, they refused to see in him in this hour of wild emotion anything but a species of infidel mistakenly given access to the sacred temple of the British race.

We have cited this particular instance out of thousands to show the anti-French feeling which takes hold sometimes of the English in Canada. Almost always, in the heat of their passion, their insults come to a climax in the word "treason." In this very popular term their inveterate mistrust of the other race finds expression. They cannot forgive it for having survived and progressed – for being there. They profess that in bearing with it England has harboured a snake in her bosom. "Laurier, Tarte, these French Papists are, I believe, rebels in the depths of their heart."[1] More than one Ontario fanatic has that idea fixed in his narrow brain. And the English-Canadian public, amazed to see

[1] Words reported by M. Albert Métin in *Autour du Monde*, p. 238.

these aliens occupying a preponderant place in a British state, cry out in chorus, "Shame! Shame!"

Intelligent people know, of course, what account to make of these taunts. They do not suppose for a moment that M. Bourassa is going to appeal to France or that Sir Wilfrid Laurier is going to renounce allegiance to the king. It is really only a Canadian quarrel – a quarrel between the opposing elements. Sensible English Canadians know that the flag is not in danger, but they strive to maintain the supremacy of the English Protestant spirit against the pretensions of the Catholic Church. On this point there is no difference among them. Talk to any Englishman of Montreal or Ottawa or Toronto, you will always hear the same thing. He may be a warm-hearted man, enjoying excellent personal relations with the French, even praising sometimes their recognized good qualities. It is all the same. His tone will be, at bottom, that of an adversary.

In this way the constant rivalry between the two races has served to whip up Canadian patriotism, making it keener and stronger. But it does not owe its birth, of course, to this cause. Like all colonials, the English Canadians have a natural love for England. English and Scottish emigrants cherish, it is well known, a deep and lasting tenderness for the old country. The Irish as a rule carry away with them into the new countries in which they establish themselves only a feeling of hatred for their oppressors; but in Canada their attitude is somewhat exceptional, and out of jealousy of the French they are moved sometimes to take sides with the English and Scots. It may be said, then, that the mother country stands well in the affections of the British in Canada.

Naturally a more exalted patriotism is to be found in the towns in which pure-bred Britons congregate most and in those in which French rivalry makes itself most felt. Thus, such ancient garrison towns as Halifax and Victoria are famous for their jingoism. Toronto seems to imbibe from its university (in many respects a European institution) and from its innumerable Protestant churches that imperialist spirit which makes of it the true centre of the British movement. It seems that there is a direct connection between London and these cities.

But when you turn away from these traditional strongholds you find that the imperial spirit diminishes notably, or to be precise, that Canadian patriotism increases as British patriotism falls off. In the western provinces, for instance, the population is very composite. It includes, of course, many English-born settlers who never slacken in their devotion to the old country. But, alongside them, what crowds of immigrants from all parts of the world, of all races and religions – men who assuredly will become good Canadians and will be ready to take the oath of allegiance to the king, but who will have no reason to have any special regard for England. There can be no doubt as to fresh supplies of Canadian patriots being forthcoming, but the recruiting of British patriots is far from being assured.

It would be quite a mistake, indeed, to suppose that the English always meet with good will in the Dominion. As is the case with almost all the other Anglo-Saxon colonies, Canada has evolved for herself a life apart, special interests and time-honoured traditions all her own. Not for anything in the world would she consent to be merged with England. When England proposes that the political, economic, and military bonds between them should be drawn closer, she is far from acquiescing with enthusiasm, just because England is one thing and Canada is another.

In these circumstances the British subject who disembarks on the banks of the St. Lawrence, in the West, or even in Ontario, runs the risk of finding himself an exile. He will not find a Liverpool or a Birmingham in Montreal or Toronto or Winnipeg, while in Ottawa, despite certain surface aspects, it is an American political life that reigns. On the other hand, many Canadians regard England as a nation of the highest respectability, but perhaps a little behind the times, for which reason they are not always ready to accept her ideas as gospel truth. Some are influenced in their attitude by their reverence for titles and anxiety to remain in relation with the British peerage. But the mass of farmers and artisans will not suffer themselves to be treated in the way in which men of rank are apt to treat the labouring classes in England. Far from considering themselves a lower order of beings, they have borrowed from America the gift of self-esteem, together with a curious sensitiveness which makes them prone to suspect that you are laughing at them and not taking them seriously enough. Thus when an English visitor talks to them as colonials, which is as much as to say provincials, they get angry, and let out with characteristic New World freedom. How many grievances have I not heard vented in regard to the tactlessness of certain English visitors, unable to understand that Canada is no longer a mere dependency but a veritable nation!

England, then, regarded as an allied and tutelary power, is looked on with favour in the Dominion. Nevertheless, there is a gradually widening gulf between the people of old Europe and the people of young America. These are faithful to a sovereign power which does not oppress them, for which they even have affection, so long as it does not assert itself. But we shall see presently that the partisans of an imperial union are endeavouring to go up stream against a current whose force forbids it.

17: The Attitude of French and English Canadians Towards the United States

Hitherto we have only analysed the attitude of the Canadians towards two distant nations, not even belonging to the New World; in truth, there is something paradoxical in this survival of British rule and French tradition in the midst of the America of to-day. But we must now recall the fact that for a distance of several thousand miles the Dominion is divided from the United States only by a quite imaginary frontier.

Such close neighbourhood, involving as it necessarily does frequent intercourse, could not fail to produce real if not close bonds between the two countries, amounting if not to intimate friendship at least to a genuine familiarity. And so it has happened: by a sort of osmosis American ideas, habits, and tendencies have penetrated from Boston and Portland towards Saint John, from New York towards Montreal, from Buffalo towards Toronto, from St. Paul towards Winnipeg, from Seattle towards Vancouver. Thus, although they do not belong politically to the great Republic, the different provinces of Canada come within its sphere of influence. Pursuing the course of inquiry to which we have devoted our attention in the preceding three chapters, let us see now with what feelings the French and English Canadians are inspired by their great and powerful neighbour.

The feeling which rules among the French when they think of the United States is a mixture of alarm and mistrust. Personally, the Americans seem to them likeable enough, more so than their aggressive neighbours of Ontario; their social customs and mode of life are largely coloured by those of the States, and many of them indulge regularly in trips to New York, just as our provincials come to Paris. But the fusion goes no further. They return from such expeditions to their peaceful province thanking Heaven they do not live in the midst of the turmoil they have left behind them.

It is manifest, at first sight, that the idea of annexation is a source of dread to them, and not without reason. Thanks to their stubborn energies, they have secured for themselves a pleasant place in the sun in British Canada. In their remote domain of Quebec, far from the tumult of New York and Chicago and all the wild frenzy of American life, they have succeeded in constructing a life of their own, maintaining their own language and religion and traditions, and have obtained by their persevering efforts a form of government which guarantees them their autonomy. A hundred years of struggling has developed a humble group of vanquished colonists into a strong and prosperous people, talking on equal terms to their former conquerors, and multiplying so enormously in numbers that no government now is independent of their votes. In these conditions they have reason to be proud of the results achieved and to be afraid of imperilling them.

That is why they regard with fear the notion of any union with America. "Should we be obliged," they ask themselves, "to begin the same long struggle all over again? And could we be sure of victory? Would the United States sanction the official use of our language and its exclusive use in our schools? Knowing their uncompromising nationalism, their barely disguised contempt for foreign systems of civilization, could we indulge in such hope? And even if these privileges were confirmed, what would our influence amount to in this new community? Instead of being two-fifths, we should be a mere one-fortieth – reduced, that is, almost to a cipher."

The Catholic clergy, needless to say, are all of this view. I have already spoken of their loyalty to the crown and shown how their high dignitaries are among the strongest pillars of British rule. Under the Union Jack, by a tacit agreement with the government, they help to keep their flocks in contented subjection, and in return they have practically *carte blanche*, at least in the province of Quebec – controlling churches, schools, colleges, and universities.

Would they receive the same treatment from the United States? It is scarcely likely. They would be accorded their liberty, doubtless, but nothing more. The Canadian clergy thought the matter out long ago. They took up this attitude at the time of the Treaty of Paris. In 1775 and 1812 the British government had their strong support. Their conduct in similar circumstances would be the same to-day.

And their attitude is not determined exclusively by political considerations. It is their constant desire, as we have seen, to keep their flock out of the range not merely of Protestantism but also of the influence of American Catholicism, which is too liberal for their taste. The Canadian Church is right, in pursuance of this aim, to wish to maintain the status quo; for while their policy of isolation is possible under British rule, it is to be supposed that under an American régime the full flood of democracy would rush unimpeded into the calm region of the St. Lawrence, sweeping along everything with it, and the old French nationality in its Catholic form would be gravely menaced.

The fact that there are nearly a million French Canadians living in New England does not affect the situation at all, or only emphasizes the peril. These emigrants, who were not to be kept at home, seem to have been definitely separated from the bulk of their race; it is true that they continue to speak the language and to cluster round their parish priests, but they are far from forming a compact group like that in Quebec: if they constitute an important element in the states in which they live, in none can they be regarded as the predominating element; and it is quite clear that they will not do over again in the great Republic what their fathers did in the Dominion. You may resist British civilization, but American civilization submerges you every time!

Their example, therefore, does but confirm the French of Quebec in their attitude of reserve. Canadians before everything, they seek only to preserve what they have secured, or if they try to achieve more still, they wish at least to do so without change of rule. To the glory of America, in their eyes beset with danger, they prefer the simple security of their ancient Canada.

If isolation is comparatively easy for our race, it is impossible for the English Canadians. Between them and the Americans there is practically no difference in language, and the difference in race is perceptible only to the practised eye. From this it results naturally that their ways have become almost identical. The towns to the north and south of the frontier are astonishingly alike. Toronto has nothing of a British city in its aspect, and Winnipeg is a new edition of Chicago. The private life of the English Canadians is modelled to a great extent on that of their American neighbours: their occupations, recreations, tastes, prejudices, are all the same. Their business affairs are run on American lines, no single detail in their buildings and offices recalling the mother country. In short, their whole material existence has come completely under the influence of the New World.

It is only natural, therefore, to ask whether some day the adjoining countries will not be united by closer political bonds. The English Canadians have often considered the point. In these conditions of neighbourhood and similarity the thing has seemed natural, almost logical.

In the first instance it was certain provinces that, adopting a policy of bluff, threatened the Confederation that they would go over to the United States if they were not conceded certain specific privileges which they had demanded. Not perhaps officially, but by the voice of public opinion, British Columbia and Nova Scotia had recourse to these tactics, which were, however, not taken very seriously. Even in Ontario – that strong-hold of British patriotism – many English Canadians have spoken openly of secession in their moments of resentment against what they called "French domination." But one must regard such ebullitions as the outcome of mere bravado, in-tended to impress the general public, rather than of a ripe and reasoned-out determination. At bottom, by taste and tradition, the English Canadians remain very English still.

What threatens British rule more seriously is perhaps the play of economic interests. Formerly, indeed until quite recently, most of the Canadian merchants imagined that the prosperity of the country could only be achieved by dint of a close commercial union with the United States. We shall see presently how the Liberal party made itself the champion of this policy. This idea has now been temporarily abandoned, chiefly in consequence of the hostility displayed towards it by the Americans, but we must not ignore the fact that it may be revived some day and regain great favour. I am not forgetting the existence of the imperialist movement! I shall show at the end of this book how scanty in Canada are its chances of success. Besides, colonials do not relish the introduction of sentiment into business affairs.

There is therefore no insuperable obstacle in the way of an economic or even political rapprochement. Two countries so close and so alike seem destined to come together, almost to be blended in one. So Mr. Goldwin Smith, at least, has sought to demonstrate in his brilliant writings.

However, for thirty years past there has been nothing to

show in any decisive fashion that the idea of annexation is making any advance. Canada has been becoming more and more Americanized, especially in the West, but politically the Dominion remains loyal to England, and seems more than ever distrustful of her powerful neighbour. During the last ten years, above all, the whole tendency has been towards the mother country. If there are politicians who would relax the bonds of imperial rule, this is not with a view to preparing the way for secession, but simply to increase the autonomy of the colony without leaving the Empire. Talk of annexation, formerly quite common, is for the moment not heard. Professions of patriotism are in favour, and some of the separatists of yore are now ardent imperialists. You may travel from one end of the country to the other, visiting all the towns, without ever hearing the expression of any wish for a different flag.

For the present, then, the feeling of opposition against the idea of American absorption is indisputable and quite sincere. But will it last? It would be imprudent to assert that it will. The English Canadians may change their views; they may allow themselves to fall gradually under American influence so thoroughly that one fine day they will find themselves transformed unwittingly into authentic Americans. But this is a matter for the future. For the moment there are in Canada only two dominating tendencies that we need note – a steady loyalty to England, and a constant growth in purely Canadian patriotism.

The strength and growth of this purely Canadian patriotism – that is what stands out clearly before our eyes as the result of our inquiry into the national sentiments of the two races. Divided against each other by violent rivalries, they are united only when the destiny of Canada as a whole is in question. Then they succeed in almost forgetting their dissension, and take counsel together as to what they are agreed in wishing, and still more what they are agreed in not wishing. Agreed to remain faithful to the British crown and to reject all idea of annexation to the United States, they are agreed also to stand up for their autonomy against interference from London. And thus it is that the *colony* of Canada is speedily becoming a veritable *nation*.

No one has succeeded better than Sir Wilfrid Laurier in giving expression to the pride of this newly-made nation and to the love felt for her by her sons. "I love France, which has given us life," he said in Paris in 1897; "I love England, which has given us liberty; but the first place in my heart is for Canada, my fatherland, the land of my birth. . . . You will agree with me that the national sentiment of a country has no worth save in the pride with which it inspires her sons. *Eh, bien!* we Canadians, we have this pride in our country!" And in London, speaking to an exclusively British audience, the Canadian prime minister was not afraid to affirm the claim that is in the heart of all his fellow-citizens: "It has been said with truth that Canada is to-day a nation." With this quotation we may well conclude: there is no other that gives such faithful rendering to Canadian thought.

PART TWO

THE POLITICAL LIFE OF CANADA

I–THE CONSTITUTION AND ITS OPERATION

18: The Canadian Constitution and Its Operation

The constitution of Canada presents no original feature: it partakes at once of British parliamentarianism and of American federalism, but there is nothing in any of its provisions to attract attention by reason of its novelty; its chief interest lies rather in the way in which it is applied. It will suffice, therefore, to devote a brief chapter to an analysis of it. We shall give more time to a study of the practical conditions under which it works. In this way we shall get a good impression of that curious mixture of English traditions and American customs which gives the keynote to Canadian political life.

According to the British North America Act, 1867, art. 9, Canada is a kingdom of which the King of England is sovereign. But as a matter of fact its constitution is that of an almost independent federal republic. We shall see presently to what extent the Dominion is really a colony, but for the moment we can ignore this consideration and think of it as practically enjoying entire autonomy in all home affairs.

This condition of things was not the work of a day, and is not due exclusively to the benevolence of England. It has had to be struggled for, sometimes fiercely, by the Canadians themselves. Their parliamentary history, though it may lack the dramatic surprises of our own or the prestige of that of England, is none the less a splendid example of energy, courage, and determination. It may be well here to recall quite briefly some of its essential phases.

The evolution of the Canadian constitution from the time of the conquest to that of the establishment of Confederation in 1867 may be divided up into four periods, each of which, from the point of view of autonomy and liberty, constitutes a distinct advance upon the one preceding.

During the ten years that followed the Treaty of Paris – that is to say, from 1763 to 1774 – the country was placed under the most arbitrary rule. The victors had indeed guaranteed to the French Catholics, then a majority of the population, the free practice of their religion, but they kept them systematically outside the government, and barely allowed them to be represented in the Council, though this was a purely consultative body, advising the Governor.

In 1774 the Quebec Act, passed by the British Parliament, introduced some important improvements into this veritable conquerors' rule. Henceforward English and French were put on an equal footing, the use of our language was sanctioned in official documents, and the guarantees already ceded to the Catholic Church were solemnly confirmed. It is true that electoral representation in any shape was postponed, but the two races sent members to sit side by side in the Legislative Council. England gave proof of a really large-minded and tolerant spirit, and it was manifest that instead of endeavouring to subjugate her new citizens by force she was anxious to win them over by sympathy.

As a result of the American War of Independence and the great influx of loyalists which ensued, the numbers of the English in Canada were greatly increased, and it became possible to give the colony a larger measure of self-government. By the Constitutional Act of 1791, Canada was divided into two provinces, Upper and Lower Canada. A Governor-General was to reside in the French region, a Lieutenant-Governor in the English – the less important. In both provinces the law created two chambers, one to be chosen by the government, the other to be elected. The weakness of this system resided in the fact that the Ministry was not responsible to the elective Assembly and that there was a chronic rivalry between the elected members and the ministers, especially in the French province. This resulted in an open revolt in 1837, under the leadership of the celebrated patriot Papineau. It was repressed remorselessly, and for two years the French province was placed once again under despotic rule. It was then felt that some drastic reform was essential. Lord Durham, despatched to the scene as special envoy, advised the British government, in a report still famous, to grant the colony self-government without reserve.

By the Union Act of 1840 the two provinces were united and the two elective Assemblies merged in one, each of the two former provinces sending to it an equal number of members.

The French language was at first barred in the official and administrative life of the country, but later (by the Union Act Amendment Act, 1848) it was restored to its old position. Henceforth everything tended towards liberalism. From the date of Lord Elgin's tenure of office in 1847, there were no longer any but responsible ministers in Canada, in full accord with the spirit of parliamentary government. It was under the Union of 1840 that the Canadian people served its apprenticeship to constitutional life.

Twenty-seven years after the passing of the Union Act the Canadian constitution was further developed, and the Confederation after long and painful negotiations between the future parties to it was ratified by the imperial Parliament by virtue of the British North America Act of 1867. Little by little, the feeling that all the provinces of the Dominion should be united asserted itself, and in spite of the obstinate resistance of certain local interests, it was possible for unity to be born out of the most extreme diversity. Composed at first of only four provinces, Quebec (Lower Canada), Ontario (Upper Canada), New Brunswick, and Nova Scotia, the new federation added, in 1870, Manitoba and the Northwest Territories; in 1871, British Columbia; and in 1873 Prince Edward Island. Finally, so recently as 1905, the two provinces of Alberta and Saskatchewan, detached from the Northwest Territories, became autonomous members of the Union.

So, at the moment when Canada received from the mother country in 1867 its constitutional charter, under which it still lives to-day, its people were prepared by long experience for the exercise of the most extensive liberty. By a constant, if not always easy, evolution the powers of the Crown, that is of arbitrary government, had little by little been reduced and weakened. At the same time the popular will, through the action of elected assemblies, had reached the stage of controlling, not only the public income and expenditure, but also, in virtue of the responsibility of ministers, the whole conduct of government. There remained nothing to prevent a constitution, which was this time almost definitive, from handing over to the Canadian nation the almost complete power to determine its own destiny. It is this constitution of 1867 which we shall now study.

Under the constitution of 1867, the Dominion comprises two categories of government, provincial and federal.

All the provinces entering the union preserve their autonomy, with all the machinery of a true political organization.

In this sense the British North America Act has maintained a wide degree of decentralization. It has even increased the liberty of the French Canadians by separating them administratively from their old rivals of Upper Canada.

Each province has over it a lieutenant governor nominated by the Governor-General and fulfilling the duties of a functionary of the Dominion. These duties are strictly constitutional in the sense that he is not free to take part in politics; his relation to the local assembly and the responsible ministry is like that of the president of a republic. If he possesses the right to dissolve the legislature and if he exercises this right not infrequently, it is understood that he must have regard for strict impartiality in so doing.

By virtue of a now established rule, it is the elective assemblies of the provinces that are responsible for the lines of policy pursued. Chosen by what almost amounts to manhood suffrage (except in Quebec and Nova Scotia, where certain restrictions still exist), they represent that elective power of Canada which as the result of persistent conflicts has at last prevailed over the time-honoured ascendancy of the Crown and of its governors with authoritarian pretensions. If Quebec and Nova Scotia still have non-elected upper houses, everywhere else the unicameral régime prevails, a reasonable system in areas which are often thinly populated. In the Quebec legislature both the English and the French languages are official.

The provincial executives are made up of six or seven responsible ministers chosen from the parliamentary majority. The administration is carried on with the help of a body of officials entirely distinct from that of the federal government. Each province is thus complete in itself, like any great state. In some cases there is a touch of extravagance about this, but one must remember that most of the provinces, before entering into the Union were already self-governing and that they do not intend to forget it.

The British North America Act sets forth with precision the limits within which these provincial governments are free to legislate. They alone may amend their provincial constitutions, they may deal with taxation and loans, with the traffic in alcoholic liquors, with local public works, public companies, and above all with education. Their independence even in these matters is, however, not complete. The Governor-General, that is to say in fact the federal ministry, retains the power of vetoing at any time within a year any provincial law held to be un-constitutional or injurious to those rights of minorities guaranteed by the Constitution of 1867. In the case of legislation on educational matters the federal parliament is able to substitute itself for a recalcitrant province and to pass a remedial law re-establishing the rights of a minority held to have been infringed.

Thus the union of the different parts of the Confederation is a real one; for they possess autonomy without independence. But the federal government is chary of interference, for it knows that the spirit of decentralization remains strong.

The federal government is framed upon the same model as the provincial governments. The Dominion has over it a Governor-General, who resides in Ottawa, representing the British Crown. He is selected by the British government and is an imperial functionary. However, save in his relations with the home government, between which and the Canadian government he acts as an intermediary, he is really but the constitutional president of the Canadian republic. It is he who promulgates in the king's name the laws voted by the federal parliament, without the usage ever having been established that he may exercise a right of veto. Exception has, of course, to be made of those measures which affect the Empire as a whole or which are unconstitutional. All his decisions have to be counter-signed by a responsible minister. The selection of the prime minister is one of his most important prerogatives; but, as he is limited in his choice to the parliamentary majority, and as public opinion has generally pointed to some particular man, he has not much freedom in exercising it. He has the same powers as the king in regard to the dissolution of parliament.

The federal parliament is composed of two houses. The first, the Senate, contains a maximum of 84 members appointed by the government, each province being represented by a certain proportion of members. The Speaker of the Senate is not elected by his colleagues, but nominated by the government. The powers of the Senate are in principle the same as those of the lower house save in financial matters, in regard to which they cannot take any initiative and have no right of amendment. The Senate is a mere survival from the past, and plays quite a secondary role in the conduct of affairs.

The House of Commons is the real centre of legislative power. Elected by the same voters as the provincial parliaments, it contains 213 members, the province of Quebec being entitled by the British North America Act to a fixed number of 65. The other provinces are represented in proportion to their population, the division of the 148 seats varying in accordance with each decennial census. It is the House of Commons that votes the budget, makes and unmakes ministries, and carries out the line of policy accepted by the country at the elections. The two languages, French and English, are official in the Ottawa parliament, each speaker expressing himself in which he pleases, and all official documents being printed in both.

The federal government is made up regularly of fourteen cabinet ministers and sometimes several other ministers not in the cabinet. It comprises ordinarily the following posts: President of the Council (Prime Minister); Minister of Justice; Finance; Trade and Commerce; Labour; Agriculture; Secretary of State; Fisheries; Interior; Militia; Public Works; Railways and Canals; Customs; Inland Revenue; and Post Master General. Decisions are come to collectively in the name of the Governor-General, who is supposed, according to the old tradition, to be acting on the advice of his Privy Council. In reality the cabinet is absolutely free to take what action it chooses, and only consults the representative of the Crown as a mere formality. The cabinet has the entire responsibility. It is an accepted thing, moreover, that all constitutional questions are to be interpreted as liberally as possible and in the way most conformable with the spirit of parliamentary government.

Everything that concerns the Confederation in the ordinary course of events comes within the scope of the federal parliament and ministry: commerce, customs duties, navigation, fisheries, posts and telegraphs, army and navy, banks, the condition of the Indians, the criminal code, the census, questions of naturalization and immigration, sales and grants of public land, etc. As the British North America Act has specified precisely the two domains, federal and provincial, disputes in this connection are rare, and the central and local authorities are usually in complete accord.

It will be clear from this survey that in form the Canadian constitution is in the main inspired by the British parliamentary spirit. We shall see now, as we proceed to study the way in which it works, that in practice it is often applied in a purely American spirit. This mixture of influences imparts its chief interest to the political life of the Dominion. We shall discover it in the whole organization and nature of its political parties, in the character of its elections, and in the whole tone of its parliamentary existence.

19: The Role of Parties in Canadian Politics

Political activity in Canada is carried on, according to the rules of the parliamentary system, by two rival parties which, turn by turn, succeed each other in power. In this chapter we shall study their character and role.

Constituted on the British model, Canadian parties have not escaped the American contagion which more and more tends to penetrate the Dominion. From the metropolitan power they derive their names (Liberal and Conservative), their respect for British forms, certain of their traditions. From the United States, the tone of their polemics, their eye for material advantages, above all their shrewd working of the constituencies. It is a curious fact that the French influence in this field is totally non-existent. Not only do the English-speaking population not submit to it, which is natural, but the French Canadians have a fashion of conducting politics which in no way recalls our spirit or methods. They seem to have forgotten our jealous individualism, our impatience of disciplined action. Anglo-Saxon practices have become familiar to them and they have adapted themselves with an ease which would be inexplicable did not one recall that they come in great numbers from French provinces that were historically friends of hierarchical rule and were, like Normandy, akin to southern England.

Originally formed to subserve a political idea, the parties are often induced, especially when they have partially attained their goal, to place themselves above the principles that were the reason for their birth. On these occasions the pure and simple continuation of their own existence becomes their principal preoccupation and the measure of their ideals. Such is the dangerous slope on to which, as elsewhere and to a much greater degree than elsewhere, Canadian parties constantly allow themselves to be swept. Even without a programme they continue to live, still more to prosper. As the carrying out of their practical activity perverts their true nature, they tend to become chiefly agencies for the conquest of power. As for doctrines or reforms, these are put aside, distorted or transfigured according to the needs of the moment. And they frequently end by appearing to be no more than weapons, blunt or sharp, which may be taken up indifferently by either of the adversaries facing one another. During this time the organization, held in admirable marching order by skilful managers, continues its regular activity, capable of functioning without ideas, like a well-mounted piece of machinery. This is exactly where danger reveals itself. The natural form of the political party risks being corrupted into an unwholesome caricature, a machine for winning elections.

The fact that in the Dominion parties exist apart from their programmes, or even without a programme at all, frequently deprives the electoral consultations of the people of their true meaning. In the absence of ideas or doctrines to divide the voters, there remain only questions of material interest, collective or individual. Against their pressure the candidate cannot maintain his integrity, for he knows that his opponent will not show the same self-restraint. The result is that the same promises are made on both sides, following an absolutely identical conception of the meaning of power. Posed in this way, the issue of an election manifestly changes. Whoever may be the winner, everyone knows that the country will be administered in the same way, or almost the same. The only difference will be in the personnel of the government. This is the prevailing conception of politics – except when some great wave of opinion sweeps over the whole country, covering under its waters all the political pygmies. In the intervals between these crises, which are violent no doubt but at bottom healthy, even the most naive can hardly help but see that it is not the party which is at the service of the idea but the idea which is at the service of the party.

Canadian statesmen – and each generation regularly produces its crop of them – undoubtedly take higher views. However, they seem to fear great movements of opinion, and they devote themselves to weakening such movements rather than encouraging them or availing themselves of them. Thus, deliberately and not from narrowness of mind, they also help to confirm the state of things which we have just described.

The reason for this attitude is easy to understand. Canada, we know, is a country of violent oppositions. English and French, Protestant and Catholic, are jealous of each other and fear each other. The lack of ideas, programmes, convictions, is only apparent. Let a question of race or religion be raised, and you will immediately see most of the sordid preoccupations of patronage or connection disappear below the surface. The elections will become struggles of political principle, sincere and passionate. Now this is exactly what is feared by the prudent and far-sighted men who have been given the responsibility of maintaining the national equilibrium. Aware of the sharpness of certain rivalries, they know that if these are let loose without any counter-balance, the unity of the Dominion may be endangered. That is why they persistently apply themselves to prevent the formation of homogeneous parties, divided according to race, religion or class – a French party, for instance, or a Catholic party, or a Labour party. The clarity of political life suffers from this, but perhaps the existence of the federation can be preserved only at this price.

In this sense the existing parties are entirely harmless. The Liberals and the Conservatives differ very little really in their opinions upon crucial questions, and their conception of power seems almost identical. Both parties are made up of heterogeneous elements: employers and labourers, townsmen and farmers, French and English, Catholics and Protestants, are to be found alike in both. In these conditions any attempt to assume an explicit attitude towards burning questions would shatter them into atoms, and they are able to preserve their unity only by dint of extraordinary compromises. In this way they have come to regard each other without alarm: they know each other too well, and resemble each other too closely for that.

This conception of politics is no doubt prudent. One must record, however, that it indisputably tends to lower the general level of political life. In the deliberate absence of programmes, questions of material interest, of public works, take too important a place. There are certainly more burning issues; people are always thinking of these, but the leaders, prefer that they should not be talked about. The subjects which remain available for discussion are not numerous. In addition, the parties borrow one another's policies periodically, displaying a coolness in this process that would disconcert us Europeans. It happens frequently too that on the necessity of some great economic measure – the second transcontinental railway, for example – everyone is agreed. The question is not whether it shall be carried out but who shall carry it out. In such circumstances what can the names Conservative or Liberal mean? They mean nothing but government and opposition. We shall attempt later to give the characters of the Liberal and the Conservative. Let us acknowledge that we shall succeed only with difficulty; for their differences are minimal and their common points very numerous.

It might be supposed that this being so, the frontiers between the two great groups would be as elastic and indeterminate as their policies, and that politicians would pass easily from one to the other. But this is not so at all. In Canada the party is almost a sacred institution, to be forsaken only at the cost of one's reputation and career. It is held in esteem almost like one's religion, and its praises are sung in dithyrambs that are often a trifle absurd. Its members owe it absolute loyalty even in the smallest matters, and individual vagaries of opinion are sternly condemned. Oppose your party in defence of some doctrine which it formerly maintained itself but which the necessities of the moment have led it to abandon, and you will lose your reputation by your independence. Thus M. Bourassa, who separated himself from Sir Wilfrid Laurier over the question of participating in the South African War, was violently taken to task by many of his political friends. In theory you may be right, they said to him, but don't you see you are compromising the unity of the Liberal party? In the eyes of politicians the reproach was overwhelming: "Party first, Principles afterwards!" might almost have been their cry.

And you should see how the party organs treat the disloyal member who goes over to the enemy! No sarcasm, no insult, is spared him. The words, "Traitor," "Turncoat," "Knave," seem inadequate to describe the turpitude of his crime. This is somewhat ridiculous, considering that a man may change his party without changing his policies; but one has to remember that the party is a sort of club, a brotherhood, an association of men, advancing shoulder to shoulder on the way to power, and sharing good and evil fortune alike.

The reasons for which men cling to their party are indeed both intricate and numerous – sometimes they are moved by interest, sometimes by sentiment. Family feeling, tradition, good fellowship, have much to do with it. A family has been Liberal or Conservative for generations past – its members grow up in the parental faith. Later, after marching in line with their companions under the same leaders, there would be a feeling of shame at quitting the ranks; electoral campaigns gone through together, and all the memories clustering round them, serve to create an *esprit de corps* which has not much to do with programmes and doctrines, but which constitutes an extraordinarily strong connecting link. Finally, we must not forget that, in following the fortunes of one party, a man has every chance of seeing it, sooner or later, in office. It can then shove you into employment, provide you with profitable subventions, give you some advantage which you have long coveted. There is a tacit contract which the voter on his part makes it a point of honour not to break.

In ordinary times a political machine thus perfected is almost bound to work all right, but it is not possible to keep the burning questions of race and religion always in the background.

The most consummate diplomacy could not, for instance, have prevented the religious question from being raised in 1896 over the schools of Manitoba, or the race question from coming to the front in 1900 on the occasion of the South African War.

When, in spite of their efforts, the parties find themselves face to face with these disquieting realities, they can no longer turn away from them. They must declare their stand, or at least they must speak.

Several results may then follow. Under irresistible pressure the habitual structure of groups may break up, and a new distribution of men according to their views may come into operation. Or opinion may try to canalize itself into the cadres of the existing parties. Ordinarily, however, the solution is much less simple. By reason of their heterogeneous composition Canadian parties can never take a clear position on a fundamental question. In order to satisfy nearly all their members they are almost necessarily reduced to distinctions and compromises. It follows that, because the voters do not know what to do in order to make a clear choice, since the question is not clearly posed, the meaning of the vote is generally falsified in the following manner: some, not very many, vote according to their convictions against their party; others, very numerous, vote for their party against certain of their convictions. In this latter case the need to hold on to or to win power is more pressing than the need to affirm a particular policy.

Never was this complexity made manifest in a more flagrant manner than in the general election of 1900. On this occasion French Canadians, strong pro-Boers and proven anti-imperialists, were to be seen voting in large numbers for a ministry which had established the famous preferential tariff of 1897 in favour of England, despatched the Canadian volunteers to the Transvaal, and declared boldly its adhesion to the imperialistic movement. On the other hand, English voters in Ontario whose imperialism was beyond suspicion were to be seen voting against Sir Wilfrid Laurier, though in sympathy with his policy. The first disapproved of the tendencies of the ministry but wished at all costs to keep at the head of the state a man of their own race; the second could not forgive him for being a Frenchman and a Catholic. As this example shows, no voter in this great consultation of the electorate was able to express his whole opinion. Such is the generally misunderstood story of Canadian politics.

However, if the question at stake were held to be really

crucial and more important in its issues than the existence of parties, the Canadian public would find itself rent in two clear divisions, just as though these makeshift parties had never existed. For example, if the right to use the French language were called in question, all French Canadians, Liberal or Conservative, would unite together as one man in defence of what they regard as the inalienable patrimony of the race; while if the Catholic Church were attacked in regard to any of its essential instruments, all the faithful independently of their race or party would rally on her side.

Fortunately for Canada, there would seem to be little danger of such conflicts. In a new country of wide extent and great prosperity material questions are apt to take precedence of all others. The immediate need is to people the newly opened territories and turn them to account, to construct railroads and waterways. The country has to be made to pay. To this end the methods to be adopted are not much in dispute. The only thing disputable is by which party these enterprises shall be brought to a successful issue. For a nation divided in so many other respects it is a guarantee of quiet that on this one point everyone is agreed!

20: The Elections – The Party Organizations

There can be few countries in the world in which elections – whatever the questions at issue – arouse more fury and enthusiasm than in Canada; there can be none in which political contests are entered on with greater gusto. At election-time the public life of the Dominion is to be studied in one of its most curious and characteristic manifestations.

The life of a parliament is in principle five years, but ordinarily a dissolution takes place soon after the conclusion of the fourth.[1] The voting is in single-member constituencies, and takes place everywhere on the same day;[2] there is no second poll, and the first is always decisive, even if there has been no absolute majority. In accordance with the English system, candidates who have no declared opponents seven days before the election become members "by acclamation," as it is styled. The suffrage varies in the different provinces, and is not universal in all. One

---

[1] Since 1867 the general elections have taken place in 1872, 1874, 1878, 1882, 1887, 1891, 1896, 1900, 1904.

[2] There are some unimportant exceptions to this rule.

person can vote in more than one constituency. These rules, for the most part, have their source in England. We shall see, however, that in practice the United States' influence is to be seen.

It is the strong two-party organization which characterizes and dominates Canadian elections. These are principally – uniquely, one might say – a duel between Liberals and Conservatives, and there is hardly a place for any independents. Everything contributes to discourage them. In effect the law favours concentrations of votes. A provision that is hardly democratic obliges candidates to deposit a sum of $200, which is confiscated if they do not win half of the number of votes cast for the elected candidate. There is not only no second ballot, but it is not well thought of by those who know its real character. Does it not tend to facilitate the birth of new parties, by encouraging differences of opinion on the first ballot? This is enough to make the party leaders, guardians of discipline, declare without hesitation that they fear it greatly. What they would prefer is precisely the disappearance of dissidents, whoever they may be. "Our parliamentary régime," said one of them to me, "is fitted for two parties, no more. In the name of principle, then, we oppose the formation of secondary groups, and consequently the second ballot which might provoke them."

It is not difficult, then, to understand the weight of authority appertaining to each party. To a far greater extent than its members taken individually, it is the party that fights, talks, and promises. The programme imposes itself morally and almost materially as well upon those whom it takes under its wing. The semi-anarchy which marks our political contests in France, in which everyone is left to himself, makes it hard for us to form any idea of the rigour with which the Canadians enforce obedience in electoral matters.

It is the party, a veritable moral person, that treats with the great forces whose support it requires – railway companies, the Catholic clergy, industrial and commercial companies, etc. Large followings depend on these powerful organizations. The elections are expensive affairs, and money must be got for them somehow. These essentials are generally already dealt with over the heads of the candidates by the time the campaign begins.

The central organization of each party is reduced to a minimum. It may be said to consist in the one case of the prime minister, in the other of the leader of the opposition, each of whom indicates the general lines to be taken. There is, properly speaking, no organizing body dealing with the whole of the

Dominion. Matters are seen to in each province on the spot, under the direction of some influential politician, who with a large and elaborately constituted staff conducts all the operations like a regular chief-of-staff. Canada being very much decentralized by reason of its immense extent, the freedom left to each of its provinces is considerable. They all take their cue, however, from the leader of the party, and each party hangs together well.

The provincial leaders have a tremendous task to get through, having to superintend sometimes as many as fifty or sixty elections. First of all they have to make sure that there shall not be more than one of their party candidates for each seat, for a splitting of votes would be fatal. They have to keep an eye upon every phase of the canvassing, to be in constant communication with the newspapers, distributing all the election literature, despatching speakers to all the public meetings. A hundred other details require their attention, whilst they must contrive all the time to keep the whole field of battle in sight.

Let us glance now at the actual proceedings in a single constituency. These differ, of course, in different provinces, especially according to whether the constituency be in a town or in the country, but there are certain traditions and customs that prevail throughout and that justify certain generalizations.

Five or six weeks before the voting-day the candidates are nominated by a local convention held in each constituency. The siege of the masses has already taken place. What has still to be done – and it is no small matter – is to hold on to friends and to make sure of doubtful voters. In this work Canadian politicians are dangerously expert, with their combination of Norman shrewdness and Yankee realism.

In each local centre the candidate chooses four or five influential men, who are known in the French districts as chiefs; according to the amount of money at his disposal, he hands them sums of $20, $40, or $60, which it is understood that they are to expend in the interest of the cause. Naturally a portion of this money stops en route. The candidate is aware of this, but he shuts his eyes, having need of the co-operation of people of importance whose opinions are listened to. Besides, when these have their pockets well lined with dollars, they carry themselves with more assurance and have more go in them. Having more confidence in themselves, they inspire more confidence in others. Their bearing indicates that the party's coffers are full, and their suggestion of opulence wins many adherents.

The first action of these chiefs is to hire a place which shall serve as the headquarters of the party organization, where they stock all the pamphlets, posters, announcements, etc., as well as portraits of the candidate, and the provincial or federal leaders. Here they establish their offices, and welcome all comers with the utmost cordiality and amiability. It would seem as though they were haunted by the fear of not being sufficiently gracious. Nothing is more curious, especially in the English districts, than the difference between the reception that one receives in a business office and in a political committee-room. In addition to the expenses involved in all this, there are other items, more or less justifiable, of which the candidate is not supposed to take cognizance. Canadian public opinion is very tolerant in regard to these.

These first preparations having been seen to, the candidate takes a carriage, a sledge, or a train, and begins a round of visits and meetings. In the country districts – especially in the French ones – he goes from locality to locality, following certain traditional methods, visiting the smaller villages during the week, and keeping the Sunday for the more populous centres. It is in these, in the open space in front of the church, that he delivers his most important addresses. In most of these open spaces in the province of Quebec there are small wooden tribunes for use on such occasions. In fine weather everything goes off perfectly, but even if it rains or snows the meeting is not abandoned. Umbrellas go up, and those who are cold stamp their feet, while the orator's voice gives out the flowing periods, prefaced always with the words, "Messieurs les Electeurs!"

In the cities there is a different order of procedure. The mass of voters assemble together at monster meetings for a general exposition of the party programme, a public debate, and a visit by some personage of distinction; while smaller meetings are held in different quarters of the town, or for each separate profession.

But public meetings are not enough in themselves. House-to-house canvassing, as the English call it, is also essential. In the French districts the canvassers begin usually with the priest, unless his displeasure has been incurred, which is a grave matter, though not necessarily fatal. Then one proceeds to make the rounds of adherents and opponents, evading dangerous discussion with the latter, and talking rather of the weather, unless some one particular topic should appeal to them. All these ceremonies are carried out most politely, for the country-bred French Canadian is a lover of forms.

Visits of this kind are more difficult in the urban centres. In some of the Western cities, for instance, there are entire quarters inhabited by foreigners who only know a little English, and who are not to be reached by the ordinary posters or addresses. Special posters are made out for their benefit in their own languages, but they are scarcely to be won over otherwise than by personal visits, backed up by promises and presents. These foreigners constitute very important bands of voters, whose presence sometimes dangerously warps the meaning of appeals to the voters.

Meanwhile the great forces whose interests have been solicited and secured are not being inactive. Their co-operation is the result of the negotiations made before the party programme was completed. In return for the promise of a tariff or the withdrawal of some threatened parliamentary bill, the business men make money contributions, the Church puts into play the power of its propaganda.

The Canadian government, not having the Napoleonic bureaucracy at its back, is not able to exercise its influence after the fashion of ours. Its influence is called into action rather by its office-holders, who hold out promises in its name. "Vote for the government, and you shall have such and such a subvention, new railway, or appointment." These are the words you will hear uttered by the ministerialists – no attempt to disguise the nature of the market transaction (as with us). The Opposition, instead of protesting, retaliate with promises of what they will do for their supporters should they come into office. Thus both sides call into play the powers of the state in order to catch votes.

In a country in which the entire population belongs to one or other of two religions, it is inevitable that the voice of the clergy should count for much. It must be said, however, that the Protestant parsons and ministers do not as a rule take an active part in the elections. If they intervene, it is to plead for new laws in defence of morality or to combat existing laws which violate their Protestant idea of morals. They rarely take up a position as a body on the side of either party. As we have seen already, it is quite otherwise with the Catholic clergy.

But the predominant influence, which if a party is bent on victory must be either secured or rendered neutral, is that of the great commercial, industrial, and financial concerns. The resources of the government are to be assessed in money, whether they take the form of office, subventions, or public works. Now, the great concerns are well equipped for a contest with it upon this ground, having great armies of voters dependent upon them, besides having certain public bodies under their control. You hear of gas, water, and electric companies forcing a municipality to carry out their demands; of some huge industrial company, employing thousands of hands, dictating its wishes to a provincial ministry, to whom its support is necessary; of some director of a railway through some region with no other line of communication treating on equal terms with members of the federal government, and sometimes as master of some of its ministers.

It is only natural in these circumstances that there should be bargaining. The railway companies especially require to come to terms with the government, for a session never passes in which some new bills affecting their welfare have not to be passed. It is essential to them to have a majority on their side, and if possible a minister to bring the bills forward in their interest.

The entire history of Canada is full of these bargains between financial powers and the political parties. In 1872, for instance, Sir Hugh Allan, promoter of the Canadian Pacific, gave more than $300,000 to the Conservative party for their campaign. In 1887 a sum of more than $100,000 came out of the funds of several great companies eager for concessions and subventions for distribution in twenty-two constituencies of the province of Quebec. In 1891 the promoters of a huge dock enterprise supplied nearly $120,000 for campaign funds.[3] In 1904 it is notorious – without it being possible to know the exact figures – that the Canadian Pacific Railway and the Grand Trunk Railway scattered money about lavishly – the former among the Conservatives, the latter among the Liberals, both with a view to controlling the second transcontinental line that was being sanctioned. No doubt cynicism goes too far sometimes, as in 1872 and 1891, and there is a scandal, and ministers themselves are injured. But normally it is considered quite the thing that contributions should be made to the party funds in this spirit, and without them both parties would be at a loss how to conduct their campaigns.

We come now to the voting-day. The chiefs have studied the register carefully and made an estimate of the probable number of votes. In the towns, naturally, the unforeseen has a wide margin. In the country, where everyone is known individually, it is a case merely of bringing one's adherents up to the ballot box and keeping them out of reach of the foe.

On the morning of the great day all available conveyances

[3] Willison, *Sir Wilfrid Laurier and the Liberal Party*, II, 18.

have been hired, often at exorbitant prices, a practice which reveals a characteristic form of corruption. The chief organizers, taking up a central position, keep in constant touch with the progress of the voting: in such a village, things go well; in such another, electors resident some distance off have failed to record their vote – a carriage is despatched to the scene at once to bring them in. Sometimes just the opposite manœuvre is resorted to with equal success: by some ingenious stratagem the adversary's electors are kept away from the polling booth. A Conservative railway company, for example, despatches Liberal workers miles away to execute some quite unnecessary piece of work!

At the end of the day the excitement has reached its utmost limit. Old men, invalids, cripples, are roped in. Sometimes these just turn the scales, the election being won by 40 or 50 votes out of 3,000 or 4,000. The victory can only go to a party which is perfectly organized. But it can be seen from our remarks that organization is capable of being carried to excess.

21: The Elections – Their General Character and Tone

The electoral campaigns in Canada, with their curious mixture of old British forms and new American free-and-easy practices, may be characterized as distinctively colonial. By the use of this word, so full of meaning to English ears, I mean to class Canada as belonging to that group of Anglo-Saxon peoples which out-do England herself, if not also the United States, in the extraordinary realism of their political life.

The charge of vulgarity is one of those brought most frequently by the English against their colonial fellow-subjects. The Canadians are not proof against this accusation in their public life. It is not that they are particularly violent: during the elections of 1904, which I followed closely, I did not hear many downright insults, and the vocabulary of the candidates struck me as containing comparatively few outrageous expressions. Without having recourse to unseemly language, however, they have a way in the Dominion of making terrible accusations in the simplest, most direct fashion, that go beyond our most violent outbursts of low abuse. The thickness of the Anglo-Saxon skin renders possible the use of certain forms of words that with us would call forth hot protests and duels. In the calmest, most unimpassioned way you hear politicians regularly accused of putting money in their pockets, without anyone, even the man against whom the charge is brought, seeming in the least shocked. The thing is of too common occurrence. This cold-blooded attitude baffles one's understanding, and one would almost prefer to witness a little violence. In the same way in parliament quite important personages may be heard to talk of the "stupidity" and "ignorance" of their "honourable friends." In France such remarks would lead to angry outbursts. In Canada the members thus alluded to hardly frown.

We must keep in mind this marked difference in temperament in order to understand the way in which the Canadians deplore our violence, while we in our turn look on astonished at their brutal frankness of speech. Charges of corruption and peculation are bandied about from start to finish in their elections, and are really too prevalent altogether. Such charges are not unknown with us, but what marks them in Canada is the fact that they are not made in the heat of the moment – they owe their introduction to a plan of campaign prepared in advance, quite deliberately. By whom? Irresponsible journalists, you will surmise, calumniators by profession. Not at all. By the official agents of the great parties, who place quite circumstantial accusations against some of their opponents, with names and details, in the forefront of their campaign literature.

A pamphlet, for instance, which was distributed broadcast in 1904 by the Conservative party under the title *Facts for Liberals and Conservatives*, contained three caricatures, inscribed "Proofs of Prosperity," which were quite simply defamatory. In the first (to cite only the one, for the others were of similar character) one of the members of Laurier's ministry is represented, with a huge diamond pin in his tie and rings on all his fingers, standing between a hut and a palace. Smiling with self-satisfaction, he points to the hut and says, "I had to live in that a few years ago," and then pointing to the palace, he goes on, "After a period of Liberal government, I have this to live in now." The caricaturist asks in large lettering, "Where does the money come from?" Note that the minister's name is given in full.

The Liberal camp is not behindhand, and replies with other accusations. The illustrated pamphlets, published and circulated by the party, contain suggestive images. One represents an English flag, beneath which can be read this exhortation: "Keep both hands on the Union Jack – but not as the Tories did it before!" What does this signify? The drawing makes it clear.

On the red portion of the flag may be seen the marks of two dirty hands, and from these marks stand out certain significant words which are meant to recall to the voter the scandals of the Conservative administration: "Scandal, Debt, Extravagance, Steals, Corruption, Boodle, Fraud, Langevin, McGreevy!"

In another cartoon of the same collection Mr. Borden, leader of the opposition, is seen followed by his shadow and exclaiming: "If I could only get rid of this shadow!" On the shadow we can read the unpleasant words: "Pacific Scandal – Send me another $10,000. Rykert Timber Limit Scandal – Something for my old age. Langevin-McGreevy Scandal – $700,000. Senecal's Commissions – $50,000. Curran Bridge Scandal – $270,000. Levis Graving Dock Scandal – $174,787. Esquimalt Dock Scandal. . . ." And so on, filling a whole page!

This exchange of accusations habitually plays a principal part, at times when one or other party has had a long lease of power. Naturally it is not ministers alone who are attacked. Ordinary members and candidates come in for their share and take their part in it. And as the expenses and resources of most persons are a matter of general knowledge in this vast but thinly populated country, there is ample scope for insinuations. Where did such and such a politician suddenly get the means to build that new house of his in the fashionable quarter? And this other, with the extravagant wife and daughters, how does he manage to live in such expensive style? What service was it that made the railway company place that *char-palais* (parlour-car) at the disposal of a third? This is the kind of thing you find set out in plain print, without extenuation of any kind. The unimpressionable English temperament makes it all possible, and to the easy-going colonial it all seems quite natural and to be taken as a matter of course.

The tone of the public meetings in Canada benefits also from this British phlegm. They are almost always quiet and orderly. The speakers are listened to, and discussion is possible. In the French parts, however, while the same conditions exist to a great extent, there are essential points of difference.

In the English parts of Canada set debates have become the exception at election-time. The parties are apt not to agree as to the lines upon which the debate should be conducted. The usual thing is for each candidate to convoke his own meeting, inviting opponents to be present as well as allies, but running the whole show himself. The meeting takes place in some large hall or theatre, and all the local leaders appear on the platform or stage beside the candidate. There is much enthusiasm and shouting and a great show of English flags, and the walls are hung with all kinds of inscriptions and symbolical decorations.

But in spite of all these trappings, which pall after the first time you see them, the English political meetings are generally extremely dull. Eloquence is rare at them, and, characteristically, does not seem to be called for. The audience arrives ready to applaud their champions and to listen patiently to their interminable discourses, largely made up of figures. Two hours of this experience (brevity is not a British characteristic) seems to tire them a little, but they come to life again presently, when the inevitable jovial Scotsman takes the stage and begins telling them stories, addressing them as "friends" or "boys," and succeeding in making them laugh. Sometimes, of course, the tone is raised by an eloquent speech or by the outburst of some dissension. The jingoes, for instance, express themselves vigorously. The two chief characteristics of these gatherings are distinctively British – patriotic sentiments and commercial statistics.

Very different is the aspect of the meetings in the French districts. They often take the form of debates, in which the French Canadian seems to find a quite passionate enjoyment. Their love of oratory is indeed extraordinary: neither distance nor rain nor snow has effect to keep them away when there is a speech to be heard. And you should see the tense way in which they listen in absolute silence, not just the passive silence of the English, but the sensitive silence of the subtle Norman, appreciative of fine shades of meaning, and wonderfully responsive to delicate flashes of wit and gleams of humour.

The speakers themselves are equally unlike those you hear in the English gatherings. They really understand the art of public speech. Not that they are invariably eloquent, or even well trained, but they have life and "go" in them. They wake their listeners up, or at least do not let them go to sleep. They indulge in lively repartee, seasoned with Norman salt. It is not always the most highly educated who speak best, for the less cultured are often more racy of the soil. The man of learning is sometimes apt to form himself too much on classical models, and the oratorical methods of Cicero and Lamartine are a bit out of place in his string of platitudes. But this is the exception, for heartiness and delicacy are the true characteristics of the French Canadian.

It should be added that without losing their natural qualities the French in Canada have adapted themselves surprisingly to the rules and regulations governing the British form of debate. Their discussions are carried on in as serious a spirit and as decorously and methodically as is the case in the most sensible parts of England. No education could have been more desirable for them. It has enabled them to take an excellent place in the political life of the Dominion.

If physical violence is absent from Canadian elections, corruption, as I have shown already, is to be met with in diverse forms. There has been a great improvement during the last twenty years, but alcohol, money, and fraudulent elections are still far from having lost their harmful influence.

To begin with, there are the inevitable drinks which are offered by the election agents or by the candidate himself, and which have for purpose and effect merely the putting of the electors into good humour. But the actual purchasing of votes is the really serious thing. Naturally, this is carried out on a large scale only in certain districts, but there are many in which the margin between the two parties is so fine that it is all important to get hold of the doubtful voters by hook or by crook. In some constituencies in Quebec, Ontario, and Manitoba, votes are to be bought not merely from the poor people but from well-to-do farmers. Sometimes appearances are saved by the device of letting out a conveyance for the polling-day at an exorbitant price, but often the transaction is put through quite simply and shamelessly. A public man in Manitoba told me how at the close of one of his meetings a number of electors approached him to barter with him there and then for their votes.

Then there are yet other constituencies, traditionally corrupt, where the cynicism of electoral agents knows no bounds, the lists of voters and voting papers being tampered with. At an election in October 1903 at Sault Ste. Marie (Ontario) the results of the poll were thus falsified. Bogus electors were imported from the neighbouring part of the United States and given their board and lodging and generous payment in return for handing in illegal voting papers to certain venal individuals similarly remunerated who had been installed as officials in the polling booths. An appeal was made against the election with 213 charges of specific corruption. At the sixteenth case investigated the court declared themselves satisfied with the evidence already produced, and invalidated the election.[1]

Such flagrant cases as this are of course rare, but the influence of the American "machine" has permeated the whole

[1] See *Mail and Empire*, Toronto, Sept. 17, 1904.

colony, and there are Canadian experts who have carried the science of handling votes to a dangerous perfection. Both parties warn their followers against the wiles of these people. As an illustration of what is done, let us study the pages of a pamphlet officially published by the Liberal party *à propos* of the general election of 1904, in which are set forth certain methods of falsifying the voting papers – methods naturally attributed in this case to the Conservatives. It contains a wealth of new and suggestive expressions: *slipping*, for instance, is involved in the ascribing to Conservatives votes given for Liberals: *switching* means the mixing up of voting papers in such a way as to profit by the confusion; *stuffing* is the fraudulent recording of votes by impersonation of the dead or absent; *spoiling* is the invalidating of the voting papers of the other side by surreptitiously marking it on the outside.[2]

The author of this brochure would have us believe that the Conservatives enjoy a monopoly of these fraudulent tactics, but the Conservative leaders address precisely the same warnings[3] to their followers, and it is scarcely credible that all the virtue is on one side and all the vice on the other. Both parties wind up by crying, "Vote for our candidates if you would put an end to these abuses." And it remains a matter for astonishment that they do not disappear!

From all that we have said, it will be gathered that election expenses in Canada are very high. The normal and legitimate outlay is considerable to start with, and when we come to the more dubious items we have to reckon up in thousands of dollars. In a very interesting article in *La Patrie*, M. Tarte, who knows both parties through having belonged to each in turn, estimates as follows the cost of the campaign in Montreal in 1904. He writes:

A general election is a cause of legitimate expenditure on the part of the leaders of political parties and of those members who are prepared to buy the honours they solicit. Let us pass in quick review the electoral divisions of our city.

Saint-Antoine. *Both candidates are men of means, large means. How much will they disburse through the medium of their election agents? Will it be less than $20,000 or $25,000 apiece? There have been previous elections in which the happy (!) candidate had to hand out more.*

[2] *Seven Years of Liberal Administration*, 1904.
[3] *Facts for Liberals and Conservatives*, 1904.

Sainte-Anne. *This division is less expensive than that of Saint-Antoine. Oh! things are not done by prayer. We believe that each candidate will keep within $10,000 or $12,000 just at first.*

Saint-Louis *and* Saint-Laurent. *Ask the treasurers of both organizations, if you know them, what was the legitimate expenditure of the candidates.* La Patrie *does not pretend to exact information. We suspect, however, that without an available sum of $15,000 ready money no candidature would stand much chance.*

Before we come to the centre of the city – that is to say, Saint-Jacques *and* Sainte-Marie *– let us glance discreetly at* Maisonneuve. *Here we have a minister as candidate. A minister is a man who is supposed to have power and plenty of money. If Monsieur P. meets with an opponent of weight, can he expect to get off at less than $25,000 to $30,000? You are either a minister or you are not! His adversary, who pleads poverty because he is of the opposition, must provide himself with at least $10,000. The opposition spends less, but it must spend. All these figures are approximate. They represent $160,000 in round numbers. In electoral expenses the numbers are always round!*[4]

Even if these figures be patently an exaggeration, even if we reduce them by a half or a fourth, they serve to indicate the really deplorable power exercised by money. Such expenditure is not only dangerous in its demoralizing influence upon the electorate, but also in the crippling effect it may have upon the resources of the elected member, who runs a risk of debt on his entering parliament.

We must not, however, conclude that these financial misdemeanours form the basis of the Canadian elections. That would be a great mistake. We must remember the saying of Rousseau: "The people are never corrupted, but often they are deceived." When the margin between the parties is very narrow in a constituency, bribery and corruption may serve to turn the scale. But, generally speaking, great currents of public opinion are not to be turned aside by the force of the dollar. In the chapter which follows we shall see what are the arguments that really weigh with the Canadian electorate.

[4] Article of M. Tarte in *La Patrie*, reproduced by *La Verité*, Oct. 15, 1904.

22: The Elections – The Arguments that Tell

In all electioneering programmes there are certain points upon which the politicians lay stress, instinctively as it were, because they know them to be calculated to impress public opinion; and nothing throws more light upon the real spirit of a constituency than the kind of language addressed to it by the candidates, its licensed flatterers. In this chapter we shall study the arguments of a general character which the Canadian election organizers are most given to invoking, and which ensure victory to their party when they can make out their claim with sufficient plausibility. They are four in number: the defence of one of the two races or of one of the two religions against the other; the prosperity of the country; the promise of public works or material local advantages; and the personal prestige of the party leader.

The appeal to racial exclusiveness combined with religious bigotry is the first and last cartridge of the politicians of the Dominion. Before thinking of any other reason, or after all other reasons have been exhausted, they come to or return to this, feeling themselves here upon solid ground from which they can at will stir up the passions of the populace. I have already explained that Canadian statesmen worthy to be so called in contradistinction to the ordinary politicians hesitate in their generous solicitude for the peace of the country to let loose the currents of mistrust and hatred which they would be unable later to control. They are, however, sometimes forced to remember that there are in Canada two jealous peoples, having in many respects interests apart, and they also cannot always refrain at certain opportune moments from playing a little racial politics. Sir Wilfrid Laurier, habitually an apostle of union, has not hesitated, on various occasions, to remind his fellow-citizens of Quebec of all the advantage to be derived by them from having one of their own number as federal prime minister. "Do not forget," he said to them at Montreal in 1896, "that if there is a Liberal ministry at Ottawa, it is a Frenchman who will be at its head."[1] This was an appeal, discreet but quite undisguised, to the sentiment which has ever since accorded him the faithful and enthusiastic support of almost all the French Canadians.

If the leaders cannot avoid these racial appeals altogether, it may be guessed that the smaller fry make use of them recklessly. In the region of the Lower St. Lawrence the affirmation of the

[1] Cited by A. Métin in *Autour du Monde*, p. 238.

rights and claims of the French race forms the *leitmotif* of every campaign. Purely racial arguments never fail here of their effect, and the number of politicians who do not have recourse to them, openly or otherwise, is small indeed.

The English of Ontario are still more sensitive to racial and religious prejudices. The presence of our race in Canada is a perpetual subject of irritation to them, and at bottom they resign themselves to it only with difficulty. You should hear the tone in which they speak of "French domination," "the French-speaking prime minister," "these French papists" who are "rebels at the bottom of their hearts." In the elections of 1900 they selected as their scapegoat M. Tarte, Minister of Public Works, guilty (among a hundred other misdeeds) of having delivered franco-phil speeches in Paris at the Universal Exhibition. Their dia-tribes against him, repeated *ad nauseam*, soon became the stock refrain, and the great newspapers let themselves go on the sub-ject with truly deplorable violence. "If we wish to remain faith-ful to the Queen and the flag in the hour of peril, how can we safely allow a Tarte to control our destinies? If Tarte were free to act as he liked, the English flag would not be floating over Toronto to-day. . . . Are we going to have Tarte to rule over us? Vote for British liberty, for a stronger Empire, for industrial stability and progress. Vote against absolutism, robbery, race prejudice, against treason and Tarte."[2]

The effect of this agitation was so strong in Ontario that the Conservatives won 11 seats: the number of their successful candidates went up from 44 to 55, while that of the Liberals, the followers of Laurier and Tarte, went down from 48 to 37. In Quebec, for analogous reasons, the opposite result was brought about, and the Liberal ministry carried 58 constituencies out of 65. Manifestly the French province had voted for Laurier be-cause he was French; the predominantly English province had voted against him because he was not English.

Fortunately, though the opposition between the two races is always latent, it does not always manifest itself in these out-breaks of anger. In the intervals, material interests resume the preponderant place natural to them in all countries, but above all in new countries. The national prosperity, indeed, seems to affect people much more closely in Canada than in France. In France so many people are in receipt of fixed incomes, which are scarcely touched by the ebb and flow of economic life. In America, on the contrary, the great majority of the population

[2] *Mail and Empire*, Nov. 5 and 7, 1900.

are directly or indirectly engaged in commerce, industry, or agriculture, so that no one, so to speak, escapes the fluctuations of the general fortune. The result is that, in Canada as in the United States, when business goes well everything goes well. People have money, high spirits, good humour. They spend, they build, they amuse themselves; they hope to spend, build, and amuse themselves still further. No one is indifferent to the general situation, which profits everyone and the cessation of which would be a public misfortune.

In these circumstances the party which can invoke in its favour the argument of prosperity has in its hands a weapon of the first importance. If it is able with any show of truth to say to the electors, "Renew our lease of power and the existing prosperity will continue," it is sure to touch a responsive chord. If, on the contrary, it is a time of commercial crisis, it is the cue of the opposition to put all the responsibility for it upon the government, and to cry from the housetops, "Put us in, and all this shall be changed!" With a few variations, this is the tune taken up regularly by either side at each federal election: the singers change but the song remains the same.

The elections of 1904 were fought out very largely, almost entirely, upon this basis. The Liberals took to themselves all the credit for the prosperity of the country, and compared it with the financial "slump" which had marked the closing years of the Conservative term of office before 1896. Here are the words, lacking assuredly in impartiality, in which one of their pamphlets set forth the question:

A DEPLORABLE SITUATION! BEFORE 1896

What was the situation during the last years of the Conservative Administration? As almost all Canadians know, business was stagnant, little or no progress was being made, the country was moribund, people were emigrating in thousands. . . . Confidence in the government was destroyed. These were some of the results of the last years of Tory rule. Truly the country needed a doctor to attend to it. Those were dark days; fortunately the clouds have passed.

HAPPIER DAYS! FROM 1896 TO 1904

Let us now turn over the page and look at the present state of things and at the situation during the last few years. It is undeniable that since 1896 the country has been completely prosperous, that all kinds of businesses are in progress and flourishing, that work is abundant, that every honest and active man is able to find suitable employment. . . . The tide of prosperity seems to have turned our way just at the moment when the Liberals assumed office. It has risen still higher regularly year by year ever since! . . . The vexation and despair of 1896 have given place to enthusiasm, energy, and pride. Canadians show that they are conscious of belonging henceforward to a great nation. National pride is their dominating sentiment. . . . The only class of people really dissatisfied is that of the Conservative politicians.[3]

It is not hard indeed to understand that the latter would not be wholly delighted over a state of prosperity so invaluable to the cause of their opponents. They endeavour by a complicated system of reasoning to show that in reality this prosperity is their doing, but their attitude lacks elegance. "If a man puts money into a business," they say, somewhat ill-humouredly, "if he adopts a wise plan in his management of it, provides for it the most up-to-date machines, and establishes agencies to ensure its commercial success, then if he goes away leaving his successors a fortune in process of formation, should the credit be given to the inheritors or to the real founder? . . . A great wave of prosperity passes over the world. Canada equipped by the Conservatives is qualified to profit by it. The Liberals, taking on our policy ready-made, install themselves in power, and have nothing to do except record the inevitable prosperity brought about by the Conservatives. They proclaim to all the world that Canada (equipped by the Conservatives) is prosperous. To whom belongs the credit? To the man who made the plans or to the man who inherited them? Intelligent people will reply that it belongs to the man who made the plans – to the inventor, organizer, and constructor."[4]

Although there is not lacking some truth in this plausible reasoning, one finds it easy to guess that bitter recriminations of the kind produce no good effect, but the reverse. The elector loves success and simple statements, and finds more to his taste the illustrated pamphlets in which the Liberal party demonstrates to him by means of suggestive and convincing illustrations the satisfactory way in which things are going. Let us take, for instance, some typical pictures from a series of pamphlets entitled "Laurier Does Things." A big farmer, freshly shaved and looking very pleased with himself, meets Mr. Borden,

[3] *Seven Years of Liberal Administration*, 1904.
[4] *Conservative Policy, the Policy for Canadian Development*, 1904.

Leader of the Opposition, who seeks to convert him to sane Conservative ideas. But the elector, shrewd and skeptical, replies, "Give me one good reason, Mr. Borden, just one, why I should put an end to such excellent management!" Mr. Borden, perplexed, has no reply to make. On another page, two groups of persons are represented. In the first, Mr. Fielding, Minister of Finance, holds out an enormous bag representing his surplus to Jack Canuck (the Canadian John Bull), who dances with delight at receiving it. In the second, Mr. Borden, in mourning, is sobbing out, "Alas! alas!" while by his side a decrepit old man, the Tory party, raises his arms to heaven and exclaims, "The country is going to the dogs!" On yet another page, we see a chorus of four personages, a farmer, a manufacturer, a workman, and a consumer, all in new clothes and good spirits, intoning together the praises of the ministry and rejoicing in their good fortune.

By dint of repeating to the Canadian public in this way that it is rich, happy, and prosperous – all which, indeed, is in large measure true – they end by carrying conviction. From this it is an easy step to satisfy the electors that a continuation of such a state of affairs is dependent upon the maintenance of the Liberal party in power. And it ends by the majority hearkening to the appeal, "Vote for Laurier and Prosperity!"

It is not enough, of course, merely to establish the fact of success. It is necessary to guarantee its continuation by new promises. Public works are what colonials demand most of all; they know that by the construction of roads, bridges, canals, and above all railways, the natural riches of the country are made exploitable and the value of land, and hence all other values, increased. Thus provinces, municipalities, and individuals are all united in soliciting from the government as much in the way of public works as possible. The minister who has the distributing of them is a great electoral power; sometimes even this distribution becomes an essentially political question, and then it is the prime minister who takes it in hand himself. It needs very remarkable adroitness to succeed in giving satisfaction in one direction without causing dissatisfaction in another, and the whole parcelling out of public favours is a work calling for diplomatic gifts, and not to be delegated to an understudy.

In 1904, for instance, the Laurier ministry had put in hand a marvellous programme from an electoral point of view – namely, the construction of a second transcontinental railway. The projected line was to traverse all the provinces, from Nova Scotia to British Columbia, and it was possible to call up a vision to electors of tremendous advantages; millions were to be expended, there was to be work for thousands of labourers, there were to be greater transport facilities, reduced tariffs, increased immigration, rise in value of land, reclamation of immense regions as yet uncultivated – in one word, a really strong impetus given to the whole economic life of the Dominion.

As may be imagined, with so alluring a programme in their hands, the ministerial candidates did not hesitate to make something out of it officially in their election addresses: "Vote for the government, and you will have this railway"; "Vote for me, who am in with the ministry, and you will have that branch line that would be so useful to you"; "Vote for me, I have influence at Ottawa, and if you do, a lot of money will be spent in the constituency. If you don't, the constitutency will suffer."

These arguments may seem like old friends. Is there a single ministerialist deputy in France who has never had recourse to them? It must be admitted, however, that at home a sort of modesty forces those who use them to cover them over a little and blur their contours. This art of understatement seems to be totally ignored in Canada. Thus at Winnipeg, on the 29th of October 1904, at a public meeting organized in Selkirk Hall in favour of the Liberal candidate, Mr. Bole, the following inscription adorned the walls:

THE WEST WANTS COMPETITION ON RAILWAYS!
LAURIER, BOLE, AND PROSPERITY!
THE GRAND TRUNK MEANS 125 MILLIONS FOR WINNIPEG!
PROSPERITY – DO YOU FEEL IT IN YOUR POCKETS?
VOTE FOR THREE YEARS MORE OF PROSPERITY!
VOTE FOR BOLE AND YOUR OWN WELFARE!
VOTE FOR THE GRAND TRUNK AND HIGH WAGES!

Mr. Bole was elected by a big majority against two opponents – one a Conservative, the other a working man. He had found the argument that told!

Now for another instance of the same kind of appeal to self-interest – half ingenuous, half cynical – in a smaller sphere. This is how a local correspondent of *Le Canada* defends the member for Saint-Jérôme (province of Quebec) : "The Conservatives are doing their utmost to decry the ministerial candidate, but they can't succeed. . . . The reproach Dr. Desjardins with not having been a great orator in parliament. That is a very paltry charge. . . . Fortunately, Dr. Desjardins has something better than fine words to his credit, and his record of work done since he became a member – that is, during the last sixteen months – is the best reply to his censors. Dr. Desjardins has secured for his county in sixteen months more than the Conservatives gave it in eighteen years. That represents in all the pretty figure of $175,000, made up as follows. . . ."

This kind of language, innocent of any kind of disguise, is held in all the constituencies without giving rise to serious protest, for it is really from this standpoint of profit and loss that the Canadian public regards its parliamentary system. All they ask of their representatives is to take up the same point of view. Whether it be a question of a local subsidy or of a railway through the length of the Dominion, the latter must not forget that they are elected to pursue the policy of results!

Not, of course, that the Canadian electors are absorbed exclusively by their local or individual interests. They are conscious that an attitude of unity and consistency is essential to the conduct of a great colony, almost as independent as a nation. Admirers, like the English, of strong individualities, they love to put in the place of honour a man of authority and prestige. Their commercial idea of credit, which they carry into politics, makes them feel that their reputation cannot fail to be strengthened if they have at their head a personage of distinction, calculated to impress people with a sense of his worth.

That is why it is of the first importance to the success of a party that it should be led by someone who inspires confidence, and whose mere name is a programme in itself. As long as the Conservatives had Macdonald for their leader, they voted for him rather than for the party. So it is with Laurier and the Liberals of to-day. If Laurier disappeared, the Liberals would perhaps find that they had lost the real secret of their victories. Thus, in accordance with the Anglo-Saxon habit, the Canadians attach themselves rather to the concrete reality than to the abstract principle. They vote as much for the man who symbolizes the policy as for the policy itself.

So much, then, for the four principal arguments which are most effective in rousing Canadian public opinion. According to the provinces and the circumstances, they vary in their efficacy, but they have always to be used, and when a party is at a loss for any one of them its cause cannot fail to suffer thereby. It is not difficult to conclude that the parliamentary life which is the outcome of such elections must reproduce their chief characteristics. This is what I propose to show in the following chapter.

23: The Parliamentary Life of Canada

The parliamentary life of Canada is inspired at once by the influence of British traditions from afar and by the influence of American customs close at hand. Beneath forms borrowed almost entirely from England, a political activity goes on which belongs even more to the New World than to the Old: the "properties" are English, but the piece is American, and those who take part in it are, as someone has well said, American actors on an English stage. From this curious mixture of the Capitol and Westminster we get a complicated creation which it is almost impossible to define in precise terms, owing to the contrasts it presents.

The form, let us agree, is English. Although the Dominion is a confederation, we know from a study of the constitution of 1867 that its régime is a faithful copy of the parliamentary system of the mother country. A faint reflection of the Crown, the Governor-General (like the provincial lieutenant-general) is merely a decorative personage, to whom respect is due, but who is carefully placed outside the arena of parties. The ministry is not responsible to him, but only to parliament. Parliament alone has the control of the general administration of public affairs, of which from election to election it is the real centre.

The respect manifested for parliament is a very British sentiment. Its members are really proud of belonging to it, and like to think of themselves as younger brothers of the M.P.s of Westminster. I have never known them to compare themselves with the congressmen at Washington, who for that matter are held in but scant esteem, even in their own country. In respect to the prestige enjoyed by their representative assemblies, Canada resembles England rather than the United States.

The English House of Commons is the model to which reference is most often made at Ottawa. Its forms have been minutely copied; the Commons chamber is a reproduction of the famous House at Westminster; the seats are not arranged in the shape of an amphitheatre as in Paris, but facing each other; and a Speaker, dignified and formal, seated on a kind of throne between the two parties, has on his right the ministerialists and on his left the opposition. The ministers occupy the first row of the seats of their party, forming a "treasury bench." On the other side are concentrated their opponents in a parallel row of seats, their leader and his principal lieutenants; this is the "front bench" of the opposition.

The opening and closing of the session are carried out, just as they are in London, with an antiquated ceremony somewhat out of keeping with the simplicity of this colonial *milieu*, but to which the Canadians of all races and all classes are tenaciously attached. As to the debates, they partake of that curious mixture of discipline and *laisser-aller* which characterizes all English gatherings from which women are excluded. Members wear their hats while seated, and lounging attitudes are allowed – are even considered to be a sign of elegant nonchalance; one remembers that such men of note as Disraeli and Balfour have affected this negligence and air of unconcern. When a member rises to speak, he takes off his hat, and without moving from his place addresses himself to the Speaker, not to his fellow-members. Members refer to each other not by their own names, but by that of the constituency represented. This often produces a quaintly exotic effect in the French-Canadian language, such as the following exordium: "Monsieur l'orateur, l'honorable membre pour Québec a dit. . . ." Approbation is signified by sonorous, guttural cries of "Hear! Hear!" The whole impression is thoroughly British.

The work of the House is carried on in accordance with the methods in use in Westminster. The Speaker's authority is considerable in regard to questions of procedure, but it is understood that in regard to all political questions he must remain absolutely impartial – very different in this respect from the Speaker of the American Congress, who is a veritable "Leader of the House." The individual rights of members are very carefully safeguarded. The French minority, in particular, has the privilege, by provision of the constitution, of free use of French. All the official documents, indeed, are printed in both languages. Speeches may be made in either, being afterwards translated for the official reports, also printed in both. In practice, however, the French are almost always obliged to speak in English, for otherwise they would not be properly understood, and their speeches would make no impression. Most of the speeches of Sir Wilfrid Laurier and M. Bourassa have been made in the language which is not theirs. It should be noted that the French Canadians are the first to show their respect for British traditions. At heart they are very proud of being in some way affiliated to the venerable *Mater Parliamentorum*.

This almost religious admiration of English parliamentary usages strikes everyone who gets a near view of the political world of Ottawa. What is more curious still is that it is observable in certain provincial legislatures, such as that of Quebec, where the procedure I have described is followed in the most serious way by Frenchmen – Frenchmen almost exclusively, as a rule. The simplicity of tone and demeanour is perfect, but they are careful to maintain all the due forms, thus giving proof of a form of anglomania which is very intelligible in view of the acknowledged supremacy of the English in such matters.

The parliamentary régime is carried on, then, in Canada in the usual way. The parties and their leaders make a point of constitutional correctness, citing ancient precedents which often have been long forgotten. Just as the Americans are given to invoking the shade of Washington or Jefferson, the Canadians invoke the authority of Pitt or Peel or Gladstone, thus professing themselves political disciples of these great men.

Such is the outward aspect of the Dominion parliament. If now we look below the surface, we find ideas and methods which are colonial or American, but not in the least English. In truth, it is impossible for an elective chamber to differ much from the body of voters who have chosen it. Is it not there for the purpose of representing it? Now the Canadian electorate is very American, as we have seen, in its aims, its customs, and its ideas. We shall find many of its elected representatives marked with the same imprint.

We have noted the arguments which tell with the electorate; those which tell in parliament are not fundamentally different. Perhaps the rivalries between races and religions are less fierce at Ottawa from the fact that they are discussed by men of greater education, knowing each other better and standing in greater fear of the consequences of violence. They produce a crisis, however, every now and again – sometimes most alarming in its character. The South African War provoked the fiercest storm of this kind that the colony has every known since the now distant days of Papineau.

But in ordinary times economic considerations preponderate, the deputies being expected above all to think of the general prosperity. The same interest holds sway in all colonial parliaments, for nothing is more essential to a young colony than its agricultural, industrial, and commercial life. An important difference is to be noticed, however, as between Canada and Australia. In Australia the democracies have generally shown active hostility to what we in France have agreed to designate as *la féodalité financière*. The Dominion, on the contrary, following the example of the United States, has generally organized its development in accordance with, and by means of, this *féodalité*. The material results have been magnificent, but from the point of view of the character of public life this has resulted in a peril which serious-minded Canadians are the first to deplore: the legitimate policy of interests tends sometimes to become a less legitimate policy of business. In the light of the preceding chapters there is in this no cause for surprise.

It is believed, in truth, that the financial influences so powerful during the elections do not stop outside the doors of Parliament. It is not enough to have helped towards the victory of a party – it is necessary to go on and secure from it this or that new bill or concession or tariff or subsidy. In the great majority of cases the parliament only thinks of the general interests of Canada, but there are particular interests which know well how to look after themselves. In order to secure favours, the great railway companies and the great industrial and commercial establishments find it necessary as well as quite natural to employ special agents in the lobbies. In America these intermediaries, whose transactions are not necessarily incorrect, go by the name of lobbyists.

This custom, imported from the United States, indicates an undisguised and to say the least too intimate connection between business and politics. The leaders have a place apart and are above suspicion, but this could not be said of certain politicians who do not hold themselves as responsible as they should to their conscience and their constituency. Too often their election expenses are in part defrayed by a big company with some new enterprise on hand; and in consequence they do not take their seats as absolutely free men, some of them, holding perhaps important parliamentary posts, being no better really than the accredited agents of some great group of capitalists. These men are of course exceptions to the general rule, and there are also many admirable examples to be seen of party loyalty and sincere disinterestedness. But truth compels us to state that side by side with them are men who are engaged in business as well as in politics and for whom, in accordance with a conception which is too American, politics itself is a form of business.

The danger of financial influence, which is real in Ottawa, is not less real in the provinces, where the legislative bodies are smaller and a few votes are enough to turn the scales. On the other hand, it is easier to know the record of each individual member, and therefore to exercise pressure upon anyone when necessary. It is a fact known to all that certain great companies sometimes acquire such power over the local assemblies that they can rely upon securing the decision they may want in regard to almost everything in which they are interested.

In short, Canada has suffered the power of finance to invade her politics, instead of crushing it down like New Zealand. Thus financial scandals are frequent in her political history. Doubtless this is inevitable in countries of rapid growth which are obliged to give special attention to questions of business.

Do we conclude, then, by assimilating the habitual tone of the parliament at Ottawa with that of American legislatures? By no means. The rivalries of race and religion which so profoundly divide the colony have at least this advantage, that in their way they raise the character of Canadian political struggles and from time to time inject some passion to displace the discussion of material interests, giving the orators an opportunity to fight for ideas in the European fashion, which some of them do with incomparable brilliance. Thus the celebrated crises of the Manitoba schools, of the South African War, of the schools in the Northwest, gave rise to really superb debates such as the American Congress never knows, and as the British House of Commons itself seldom experiences. One understands that in these conditions the Canadians may be proud of their parliament. In spite of some weaknesses it fully deserves their pride.

The political personnel of the Dominion is as diverse in character as the varied aspects of political life at which we have been looking. At its head there are men of the highest calibre, who get their inspiration direct from the highest English traditions, and who would not be out of place in any assembly in the world; taken as a whole, it may be said to comprise a large number of mediocrities of a type similar to that in the United States. There is no one characterization that would describe it.

As there is no aristocracy in Canada and hardly any leisured class, the federal House of Commons is inevitably composed of men who follow some profession or who are closely interested in the work of the nation – especially lawyers, businessmen, doctors, journalists, and farmers. Hence payment of members was found to be an absolute necessity, involving a departure from the aristocratic English traditions. Members are paid $2,500 a year, and by a recent enactment a yearly stipend of $3,500 is accorded to ministers who have been more than five years in office, while the Leader of the Opposition is paid $7,000. There is probably no other country in which such a functionary is officially remunerated. The idea is an ingenious one, and proves that the two parties are disinclined to favour new groupings, and on the contrary recognize openly their use to one another.

These conditions allow of political life becoming a career and means of livelihood. In Canada it is often a career in the best sense of the word. Many members of the best families are proud to represent their fellow-citizens in parliament. The difficulty and variety of the problems awaiting solution seem to have called forth a class of public men in the Dominion distinctly superior to that possessed by Australia or New Zealand. The names of Macdonald and Laurier belong to the general history of the world, and their country is naturally proud not only of having produced them but of having known how to appreciate them.

With such leaders, giving themselves up entirely to their country and their party, Canadian political life, despite its vulgar element, assumes at times a breadth and elevation worthy of the utmost respect. Taking it as a whole, then, and in spite of the defects I have pointed out, one may say that the Dominion has been well served by the confederation of 1867.

II–THE PARTIES, THEIR PSYCHOLOGY AND PROGRAMMES

24. The Liberal Party – Its Domestic Policy

We have seen how the working of the parliamentary system in Canada rests essentially upon the existence of two parties, which come alternately into power. Let us now make a study of the psychology and the programmes of each.

It is only since Confederation in 1867 that Liberals and Conservatives have come to define their real tendencies and, so to speak, take stock of themselves. But we must go back to 1840, the date of the establishment in Canada of a genuinely parliamentary constitution, in order to discover the origin of the various groups whose coalitions later were to result in the formation of the two great federal parties.

At this epoch – a very important epoch in the evolution of the country – two currents of opinion manifest themselves. The Liberals, mostly French, ask that the new liberties shall be made available in a loyal and generous spirit; the Conservatives, mostly English, are disposed to appeal to governmental authority rather than to parliament. The Liberals, or Bleus, have a left wing, composed of Democrats, or Rouges, who keep up the radical tradition of Papineau. The Conservatives have a rearguard in the Tories, uncompromisingly English, and a vanguard in the Grits, recruited chiefly among the Scottish Presbyterians and representing the more advanced element in the British population.

These first combinations have nothing stable about them, and it is not long, therefore, before they become transformed. The moderate Liberals, the Bleus, are naturally led to ally themselves with the Conservatives, and end by blending with them into a mixed Anglo-French party, which assumes the name of "Liberal-Conservative," or more frequently of "Conservative" alone. On the other hand, some Bleus remain faithful to their old alliance, and the Rouges and the Grits unite to form a remodelled Liberal party. When Confederation has become a *fait accompli*, towards 1870, it may be said that the assimilation of the groups and sub-groups is more or less complete; there remain, it is true, many surviving features of the recent past, but there are in reality only two great parties – those we know to-day.

The Rouges and the Grits were relatively advanced in their notions. Papineau and his disciples had the radical temperament; above all, they were not disposed to allow themselves to be dominated by the Church, and there were even anti-clericals among them – a nuance now very rare in the Dominion. Influenced, apparently, by the Revolution of 1848, the younger and more ardent among them gave themselves up to ideas which were very advanced for the Canada of this period; in their journal, *L'Avenir*, they demanded, for instance, among other reforms, the extension of public education, decentralization, the election of the Governor, of the Upper House, of the magistracy, of the high officials, universal suffrage, the abolition of the seigniorial rights and of clergy reserves; and they spoke freely of the independence of Canada and of annexation to the United States.[1] The Grits had a similar programme, and the union of the two groups seemed clearly enough foreshadowed; together they might be expected to form a party no longer merely Liberal, but radical and democratic.

It is not hard to realize the disquiet aroused by such ideas in a country for the most part so conservative as Canada, and especially the strong hostility they could not fail in calling forth from the Catholic clergy. The Rouges became at once an object of fierce hate to the Church of Rome, and it has taken the present Liberal party nearly half a century, though so much more moderate in their aims, to secure the neutrality, I dare not say the support, of the clerical authorities. It took them nearly as long to convince the public at large that they were not revolutionaries, anarchists, fomenters of trouble and disorder.

The heritage bequeathed by the Rouges was, indeed, of a compromising character. It had therefore to be an early and constant preoccupation of the young Liberal leaders of the time of Confederation to declare themselves resolutely moderate. The editors of *L'Avenir*, pupils of Papineau, deserved in some respects the designation of Radicals, and they turned their eyes towards the men and the principles of the European continent. M. Laurier, on the contrary, from the time of his election to the local legislature of Quebec in 1871 and to the federal parliament in 1874, has made a point of repudiating French radicalism and declaring himself a votary of the liberalism of Gladstone.[2]

[1] *L'Avenir*, May 21, 1851.
[2] See M. Laurier's first speech in the local Assembly at Quebec, November 10, 1871, and his first speech in the Ottawa House of Commons, April 1, 1874.

And as the years have passed, this tendency on the part of the Liberals of Canada has developed: they seek more and more to hide all traces of their Rouge origin and become more and more wedded to moderate ideas. That is the note of a famous declaration of policy given forth at Quebec by M. Laurier in 1877. "I know," he declared in the course of a prudent, almost timid, exordium, "that, for a great many of my fellow-country-men, the Liberal party is a party composed of men holding perverse doctrines, with dangerous tendencies, and knowingly and deliberately progressing towards revolution. I know that, in the opinion of a portion of our fellow-countrymen, the Liberal party is made up of men of good intentions, perhaps, but men none the less dupes of their principles, by which they are unconsciously but fatally led to revolution. I know that, for yet another portion, not the least numerous, liberalism is a new form of evil, in other words a heresy, carrying with it its own condemnation." On the morrow of the Commune, as in 1848, radicalism and even liberalism evoked visions of anarchy in Canada. It is interesting to note, therefore, the decisive tones in which the speaker proceeds to dissociate himself from the French radicals. "There exists in Europe," he goes on, "in France, Italy, and Germany, a class of men who have nothing liberal about them beyond the name, and who are the most dangerous of men. They are not liberals, they are revolution-aries; they are so exalted in their principles that they aspire to nothing less than the destruction of modern society. With these men we have nothing in common. But it suits the tactics of our opponents always to compare us with them."[3]

Clever tactics they were, for the Canadians are at heart an order-loving people. The Liberals of to-day know this well, and we need no other explanation for the preference they have given to the liberalism of the British type.

Moreover, the English Liberal party presented the model with the highest prestige. M. Laurier has always taken its prac-tices as a criterion. A photograph in which he is represented on Mr. Gladstone's arm has found its way all over the colony; portraits of the English parliamentary leaders are to be seen in all the political clubs. Those of Jules Ferry or Waldeck-Rousseau would be sought for in vain, not because their merits are under-valued by our Canadian compatriots, but because they would not for anything be indebted to the founder of the lay school

[3] Speech on Political Liberalism at Quebec, June 26, 1877.

or the author of the law on religious societies. They prefer to sing (and with what conviction!) the praises of English liberalism. "What could be more beautiful," proceeds M. Laurier, in the speech just cited, "than the history of the great English Liberal party in this century? First we have Fox – Fox, the wise and generous, the defender of the oppressed, wherever the oppressed are to be found. A little later, it is O'Connell we see demanding and securing for his co-religionists the rights and privileges of British subjects. . . . Then come in succession the abolition of the governmental oligarchy, the repeal of the Corn Laws, the extension of the franchise to the working classes. . . . Liberals of the province of Quebec, these are our models, these are our principles, this is our party."[4]

Of the French Revolution, of the rights of man and of the citizen, you hear never a word! Reference to them would sound ill in Canada. Those French Canadians who have attempted to evoke our democratic tradition have discovered that their words fell flat. Canada, as I have shown already, does not pass a favourable judgment on 1789 and 1793; 1848 alarmed it, and the Revolution of the Third Republic, radical and anti-clerical, seems to it a misfortune. That is why M. Laurier, in his interesting considerations on political liberalism, insists so much on the differences between it and French radicalism. The welcome accorded to his speeches by his own partisans shows how necessary were his categorical declarations to reassure a section of the Canadian public. "Now at last we know," wrote a journalist, "the road we are taking. It leads us no longer to revolutionary excesses. Liberalism has been divested of its wild garb and of its anti-social and anti-religious character. . . ."[5]

Nearly thirty years have passed since this remarkable profession of faith and there is no sign of any weakening in the Liberal attitude then taken up. Quite recently, one of the most distinguished of Sir Wilfrid Laurier's lieutenants, M. Rodolphe Lemieux, Solicitor-General of Canada, re-echoed in a speech at Montreal, at a banquet given by the National Club, March 1904, what his chief had said in 1877. "We are no longer," he said, "fomenters of anarchy, thank God! We wish, on the contrary, to strengthen the institutions of our country. We are no longer the descendants of Voltaire, as a Conservative leader used to assert. Our political thought takes its inspiration from

[4] Cited in Mr. J. S. Willison's *Sir Wilfrid Laurier and the Liberal Party*.
[5] Cited by J. S. Willison, *op. cit.*, I, 331.

the great English school of liberalism. We are no longer apostles of a new religion. We are disciples of the old, true religion. . . . We are no longer fierce sectarians, wild-eyed votaries of the Convention. We are constitutionalists and moderates."[6]

Do not these words recall the phrase of Thiers: "The Republic will be conservative or there will be no Republic"? The terror of Rouge ideas seems indeed firmly implanted in the minds of those who are still designated "Rouges" in Quebec. In their dread of seeming too advanced, they have succeeded so well in convincing the world of their moderation that it is not easy now to discover in what points their political doctrines distinguish them from their Conservative opponents.

But if the Liberal party found it difficult to reassure the timid and the moderate, they have found it more difficult still to overcome the prejudice of the Church. Until after 1896, the date when they established themselves in power for so long, they had to bear the burden of the anti-clerical reputation which belonged to the Rouges of 1848. The clergy persisted in identifying them with these predecessors of theirs and in regarding them as representatives of the Revolution in all that word conveyed to Catholic minds of what was impious and terrible.

It was in vain that in 1867 and afterwards they repudiated their compromising extreme left, already half ignored. The Church objected to the term liberalism in itself. Rome has condemned Catholic liberalism, it maintained, therefore it cannot approve of political liberalism. More than ever, committed to ultramontanism since the Syllabus and the Vatican Council, the Canadian ecclesiastical authorities affirmed these two propositions with a precision which could leave no room for doubt in the minds of their flocks:

1. Liberalism is a form of error, a heresy already virtually condemned by the Head of the Church.
2. A Catholic cannot be a Liberal.[7]

In thus seeking to confuse liberalism in politics with liberalism in religion the Church overreached itself, for this resulted in making the recording of votes a matter of conscience in which it claimed the right to intervene. Accustomed to speak authoritatively, the bishops scarcely condescended to discuss: they ordained. Thus it was that on the occasion of the elections of 1878, Monseigneur Bourget, Archbishop of Montreal, wrote as

---

[6] Speech at Montreal, March 8, 1904.
[7] Résumé of Catholic objections to liberalism made by M. Laurier in his speech on *Le Libéralisme politique*.

follows: "Our Holy Father the Pope, and after him the archbishop and bishops of this province, have declared that liberal
Catholicism is a thing which must be regarded with horror, like
the pestilence. No Catholic is allowed to call himself a liberal,
even a moderate liberal. In consequence, a Liberal, even when a
moderate, must not be elected by Catholics as their representative. The entire clergy held the same language, sometimes more
emphatically still. "The Church only condemns what is evil," a
curé declared to his flock about this time. "If liberalism has been
condemned, that is because it is an evil thing. You must not
therefore vote for a Liberal."

Twenty years later the question of the Manitoba schools
served to show that the Church had not relaxed in her hostility
to the Liberals. In less extravagant terms, perhaps, but still in
the most absolute way, the entire episcopate, backed by the
entire priesthood, declared against M. Laurier and his party with
a violence that the Canadian public has not yet forgotten. They
were beaten, but after compromising themselves completely
with the Conservatives and by virtue of a policy consistently
followed by them for half a century.

The uniformly unbending and almost aggressive attitude
maintained by the Church towards the Liberal party imposed on
the latter the line it should take in self-defence: it had to become
a party of resistance against the excessive pretensions of the
power of Rome. Not an anti-clerical party, be it understood; for,
once the generation of the Rouges of 1848 had vanished, their
successors had hastened to abandon everything in their methods
that tended to violence or to godlessness, or even to anti-clericalism, and became respectful Catholics again, with wives who
were submissive to the priests and children educated by them.
Most of them deplored a conflict which was really painful to
them, but they were forced to defend themselves against the
undue provocations of the Church. In this spirit the Liberal
leaders, abstaining from such a line of opposition as would have
hurt them among the French populace, began by making public
profession of their reverence for religion and the Church. But at
the same time they claimed for Canadian citizens the right to
vote, and for the civil power the right to manage its own affairs,
without episcopal direction. This was not an affirmation of the
theory that the state was above the church – they dared not go
so far as that – but only of the view that church and state were
independent of each other.

No one maintained this doctrine with more elevation than

M. Laurier. No one contrived in so dignified a manner to demand for the elector, the deputy, or the minister, the right to consider public questions from a standpoint not narrowly denominational, but broadly Canadian. To this proud claim he devoted one of his greatest speeches, delivered on the 3rd of March 1896 in the House of Commons at Ottawa, on the occasion of the crisis in Manitoba. "I am here," he said, "the acknowledged leader of a great party, composed of Roman Catholics and Protestants as well, in which Protestants are in the majority, as Protestants must be in the majority in every part of Canada. Am I to be told, I, occupying such a position, that I am to be dictated in the course I am to take in this House, by reasons that can appeal to the consciences of my fellow Catholic members, but which do not appeal as well to the consciences of my Protestant colleagues? No. So long as I have a seat in this House, so long as I occupy the position I do now, whenever it shall become my duty to take a stand upon any question whatever, that stand I will take not upon grounds of Roman Catholicism, not upon grounds of Protestantism, but upon grounds which can appeal to the conscience of all men, irrespective of their particular faith, upon grounds which can be occupied by all men who love justice, freedom, and toleration."

These noble words, truly liberal in the highest sense of the word, nevertheless gave rise to vehement Catholic protests. The Bishop of Trois-Rivières condemned them explicitly from the pulpit (May 17, 1896). "This," he declared, "is the most open affirmation of the liberalism condemned by the Church I have ever known to be made in any legislative assembly in our country. The man who speaks thus is a rationalist liberal. He formulates a doctrine entirely opposed to Catholic teaching. He practically asserts that a Catholic is not obliged to be a Catholic in public life. This is a fundamental error, and can only lead to deplorable results."

These words might well have provoked even the most moderate of opponents into violent rejoinders. The English Liberals of Ontario did in truth lose their cool heads, and had recourse to all the classical cries of British anti-clericalism. But they did not carry with them the Liberal party as a whole. On the contrary, with fine logic, at the very moment when the clergy were contesting his right of conscience in regard to politics, M. Laurier made a point of standing by the liberal declarations which he had given out twenty years before upon the priest's right to express freely his opinions like any other citizen. "In the name of what principles," he asked, "could the friends of liberty deny to the priest his right to take part in public affairs? In the name of what principles could they deny him the right to have political opinions and to express them – the right to approve or disapprove of public men and of their acts, and to teach the people what they believe to be their duty? . . . No! let the priest speak and preach without restraint, it is his right! Never shall the Liberal party contest this right."[8]

Thus in this battle the Liberals scarcely joined in the attack. After a strenuous struggle with the Church for the Catholic elector's freedom of conscience, they went no farther, ready to respect the positions acquired by their adversary, asking only that it should claim no more. Their wish in reality was to secure an understanding with Rome upon some fairly acceptable basis. And this they succeeded in achieving on the morrow of their brilliant victory in 1896.

The Church, recognizing that the Liberal party was in power for a long time to come, was the less disposed to persist in a useless opposition since there was no question at the time of any fresh campaign. It was conscious, too, of the profound change that the party had undergone since the distant days of the Rouges, and it knew that it could boast of a great number of the faithful in its ranks.

The reconciliation was not official, but it was real. The priests ceased their violent interferences, while retaining in their hearts an instinctive sympathy for the Conservatives. At the elections of 1900 and 1904 clerical intervention was inappreciable. The new ministry, for its part, did not make use of its success, won in spite of the clergy, to indulge in reprisals. Anxious before all things for an understanding, it only sought for peace. Since 1896 the bishops acknowledge that they are no more disquieted under Liberal rule than under Conservative.

By a long evolution, lasting over half a century, the Liberal party has succeeded then almost completely in dissociating itself from the radical and anti-clerical programme of the Rouges of 1848. If anti-clericalism and socialism wish to manifest themselves in the Dominion, they must do so outside the ranks of official Liberalism. Thanks to this transformation, the Liberals have achieved office. We must admit that they have lost something of their individuality in so doing! Are not they themselves the first to admit that between them and the Conservatives the difference has come at times to be imperceptible?

[8] Speech on Political Liberalism, 1877.

25: The Liberal Party – Its Economic Policy

We cannot appreciate to the full the character of the Liberal party of Canada after a study of its purely political aspect only; for that, we must know something of its economic programme. In this field it has as a traditional platform a commercial liberalism which favours treaties of commerce, whilst its Conservative opponents are the accredited champions of a protectionist policy which sometimes goes as far as prohibition. So much for principles. In practice, naturally, we shall find many exceptions to the rule.

Should negotiations be entered into with the United States for a reciprocal reduction of tariffs, and even a customs union, so as to open the immense American market to Canadian products? Or should Canada meet the Yankee provocations with reprisals, and following the American example deliberately protect her industries? Should Canada enter upon such negotiations with other powers also – the mother country first of all – or should she rather defend herself against them? These are the problems which have always served most to divide the Canadian parties. Without going farther back than the establishment of Confederation, let us study first the attitude towards them taken up by the Liberal party when in opposition – that is to say (save for a brief interruption), from 1867 to 1896. Then we can examine the position it has adopted since its accession to power in 1896.

During this period of nearly twenty years we find both parties striving at all the general elections to define their principles as clearly as possible. Under Macdonald the Conservatives proclaim noisily their national and protectionist policy. The Liberals are not so downright in their declarations, for if protection is a simple, straightforward idea (or very nearly so), economic liberalism is multiform in its aspects. Are they free traders or advocates of a complete customs union with the United States, or only of treaties of commerce? It is not easy to make out just at first.

In theory, the Liberal leaders of the Cartwright and Laurier type are free traders. Their strong British traditions explain this; considering themselves the disciples of the English Liberals, they find it quite natural to accept the doctrines of their masters and to employ their arguments in favour of commercial liberty. Thus in their speeches they talk of "free trade as in England." At the Liberal convention of 1893 we find M. Laurier, in his capacity as leader of the party, holding forth as follows: "Our policy should be a policy of free trade as in England. It is to be regretted that the present position of the country does not make this practicable to the letter, but I propose that we should at least accept the principle upon which it is based."

It will be noticed that the speaker, having professed free trade, immediately goes on to say that its application to Canada is impossible. The balance of the federal budget depends indeed principally upon the customs receipts, and no politician assuredly would dare to place the finances of the colony upon other bases. In these circumstances the maintenance of a tariff, a purely fiscal tariff at least, is inevitable. The Liberal leaders do not fail to admit this, and thus the rigour of their free trade undergoes a first and important attenuation: if they continue to repudiate protection, they nevertheless acquiesce in the maintenance of certain customs duties, but according to the phrase used in their programme, "for revenue only."

Economic liberalism in Canada gives up, then, the pursuit of an unrealizable free trade to become in practice a policy of treaties of commerce. With whom? With all powers disposed to enter into them, but above all with the United States, for everything is dominated by the fact of the presence of this enormous neighbour.

Supposing that Washington is ready to negotiate, what would Ottawa propose, with the Liberals in power? A treaty of reciprocity, of course. But what kind of treaty: limited reciprocity or unlimited – complete customs union? The question is complex and delicate, for it suggests, if it does not actually involve, the problem of the annexation of Canada.

A customs union – the extreme solution – would have the look, and not without reason, of a blow aimed at Great Britain. It is in vain that its advocates affirm – sincerely or otherwise – their loyalty to the British Crown; they cannot carry conviction. Public opinion persists in regarding them as separatists, virtually if not wittingly. Although, then, they are numerous in the Liberal party, the party itself, whilst adopting many of their ideas, avoids declaring openly or officially in their favour, feeling that they are compromising allies. In spite of this reserve, the Conservatives do not hesitate to denounce the "veiled treason" of their adversaries. It is a sheer calumny, for the Liberals are not traitors. Yet one may be allowed to remark that during their long period of opposition they were scarcely Anglophil, and that they look more willingly towards the United States than towards England. And have they not had as leaders, first an Irishman, Mr. Blake, and then a Frenchman, M. Laurier?

Such is the state of mind, at once daring and timid, that characterizes their attitude at the general elections of 1891 and 1896. They reject officially the idea of a customs union with the United States as being dangerous politically, and fall back upon that of as wide a form of reciprocity as possible. The more ardent, who seem in the ascendant in 1891, advocate unrestricted reciprocity – that is to say, continental free trade for the whole of North America. The more moderate, who seem to have got the upper hand after 1893, are content with a limited reciprocity – that is to say, a more or less complete treaty of commerce.

In 1891, M. Laurier thus expresses himself in an election address: "The reform suggested is absolute reciprocal freedom of trade between Canada and the United States."[9] This is nothing else than continental free trade. The country finds it difficult to distinguish from a complete customs union and takes fright at it, and the Liberals are easily beaten by the nationalist protection policy of Sir John Macdonald.

The Liberal party now realizes the absolute necessity of reassuring the public, and, starting from 1893, they begin to diminish the range of their programme. At their convention in 1893 they still employ the sacred word "free trade," but they talk more willingly still of freer trade, which after all implies the abandonment of undiluted Cobdenism. They fly no longer the flag of continental free trade, and only ask for a treaty of commerce. "Having regard to the prosperity of Canada and the United States as adjoining countries, with many mutual interests, it is desirable that there should be the most friendly relations and broad and liberal trade intercourse between them. . . . The first step towards obtaining the end in view is to place a party in power who are sincerely desirous of promoting a treaty on terms honourable to both countries. A fair and liberal reciprocity treaty would develop the great natural resources of Canada. . . . The Liberal party is prepared to enter into negotiations with a view to obtaining such a treaty."[10]

Thus the Liberal party, on the eve of coming into power, has gradually evolved a programme which is moderate and realizable. Shaking itself free from its extreme left, it concentrates upon a policy of treaties of commerce which while applying above all to the United States can apply also, in its opinion,

[9] J. S. Willison, *op. cit.*, II, 162.
[10] Platform of the Liberal Convention at Ottawa, June 1893.

to other nations. On the other hand, it not only declares itself ready to maintain a fiscal tariff, but its leaders, in their private conversations, and even in letters which are not marked "confidential," do not hesitate to calm the anxieties of manufacturers by promising them that if there should be any customs reforms they will be gradually and considerately introduced. All this foreshadows the retention by the Liberals when they shall come to power of a great part of the protectionist policy of their predecessors.

At the elections of 1896, the Conservative party, crippled by the death of Sir John Macdonald, made stale by their too long lease of office, are completely beaten, and M. Laurier becomes prime minister. He at once shows himself ready to negotiate with Washington on the lines indicated in the programme of 1893. But McKinley has just been elected president, and a strong protectionist revival is manifesting itself in the United States. The new ministry, therefore, has its shoulder against a door hermetically closed, and long before the debate on the Dingley Bill it realizes that the Americans will do nothing, and that the hopes raised during President Cleveland's term of office must be entirely abandoned. Thus the dream of an entire Liberal generation vanishes away in the face of the manifest and seemingly lasting hostility of the American government.

It is at this point that, with a very colonial casualness, the Liberal party changes its ground completely and adopts in part the programme of its adversaries. "If our American friends wish to make a treaty with us," says Mr. Fielding, Minister of Finance, in the House of Commons, April 22, 1897, "we are willing to meet them and treat on fair and equitable terms. If it shall not please them to do that" (and Mr. Fielding knows well that such is the case) "we shall in one way regret the fact, but shall nevertheless go on our way rejoicing, and find other markets to build up the prosperity of Canada independent of the American people." The meaning of these words is perfectly clear. From the moment the United States reject our advances, we cease to make any more, but let it not be imagined that we have no other string to our bow! We Liberals have always advocated a rapprochement with our great neighbour, but if they give us the cold shoulder what is there to prevent us from turning in the other direction to negotiate a commercial understanding with the mother country, for instance? In thus acting we claim to be remaining faithful to our economic creed, for we are ready – upon an acceptable basis, it is true – to conclude treaties of commerce with all such powers as show themselves willing.

From this mode of reasoning resulted the celebrated Fielding tariff of April 22, 1897, establishing preferential duties in favour of England. It left the Americans cold, it is true, but it filled the English with immense enthusiasm; they were determined to see in it a decisive step towards imperial union, and at once classed M. Laurier in the first rank of Mr. Chamberlain's lieutenants. Such are the little ironies of politics, for assuredly M. Laurier's past was in no way that of an imperialist. The Conservatives of Canada raged at the Liberal leader (the word is not too strong), and could not forgive him for having taken their programme and applied it with success. Was it not Sir John Macdonald and Sir Charles Tupper who were the first to launch the idea of a differential tariff in favour of England? And here were M. Laurier and Mr. Fielding carrying it out! Was it not Sir John Macdonald and Sir Charles Tupper who in 1891 had been able with some show of justice to accuse the Liberals of neglecting the mother country? And it was these same Liberals who were now being exalted in London as the most admirable British patriots! It was a piquant situation, and the Liberals who had not foreseen it were themselves somewhat astonished, though the new move had their entire approval, inasmuch as it increased tenfold their strength as a party.

The customs legislation of 1897 includes some reductions of duties, but on the whole it is distinctly protectionist, and this Mr. Fielding himself does not deny. "That tariff," he said in the House of Commons, June 7, 1904, "has proved a good revenue tariff. . . . It has included a considerable measure of incidental protection, and in that respect it will command the admiration perhaps of some honourable gentlemen opposite, who are more anxious for protection than some of us on this side of the House." In truth, the preference of 33 per cent accorded to England leaves us still far from imperial free trade. The economic liberalism of the Laurier ministry seems to us then toned down; its members seem even to have lost the habit of singing the praises of free trade; anxious guardians of the important and legitimate interests acquired by protection, they would hesitate to withdraw from the manufacturers the precious and sometimes indispensable support of the state. Thus, while remaining advocates more than ever of treaties of commerce, they think of them only on a basis of a sufficient measure of protection.

Such, for instance, is their attitude towards England. They declare themselves ready to negotiate with her on condition that she, adopting protection, should cede to Canadian products advantages over her own market. But let there be no mistake about it: there is no question of a complete customs union or of imperial free trade. The Canadian Liberals would not dream of doing to-day, even for the mother country, what the Conservatives refused to do in the past for the United States: they stand too much in fear of British industrial competition. Their economic policy in regard to England may, in short, be accurately enough described by an expression now some fifteen years old – that of "limited reciprocity."

But this limited reciprocity is not reserved exclusively for England. Other powers are free to propose it to the Canadian government, which seems disposed to regard such proposals favourably. That, at least, would appear to be the meaning of a declaration made by Mr. Fielding on June 7, 1904. "I think," he said in the course of the budget speech in the House of Commons, "it would be well for us to have a maximum general tariff and a minimum general tariff, and the British tariff below that as we have it to-day. The maximum tariff would only be applied to those countries which pursue, if I may call it so, a hostile policy. . . . They cannot complain if we have a maximum tariff, and we would be justified in saying that this tariff should be materially higher than the tariff which we are willing to extend to other countries which are willing to trade with us on fair and reasonable terms. . . . So we would have a maximum tariff, as we have the German tariff to-day, to apply to such countries as do not manifest a disposition to trade with us. We would have a minimum general tariff to apply to countries that are disposed to trade with us. And then below that we would have the British preferential tariff to apply to the mother country and to such colonies of the Empire as it may be expedient to extend the benefit of that tariff to."

Even if these minimum and preferential tariffs be fundamentally protectionist (and this it is to be feared is the case), it remains none the less true that the fact of Canada's wishing to create several different categories of duties shows that she does not propose to shut herself up behind a policy of prohibition.

As the outcome of the long process of evolution described in this chapter, the Liberal party has then ceased to be a free trade party, to become simply the more moderate of the two protectionist parties.

26: The Conservative Party

In studying the constitution, programme, and evolution of the Liberal party we have defined by implication the position of the Conservative party. Without undertaking to sketch out the history of the latter, let us try to trace its guiding principles and the significance of the changes it has undergone.

It was the outcome of the union effected about 1854 between the Bleus of Quebec and the Tories of Ontario. The Bleus were the moderate Liberals, who parted company with the Rouges, just as the Tories parted company with the Grits. Together they formed an Anglo-French Conservative party, benefiting by the support of the Church of Rome, which for nearly half a century brought the mass of French Canadians into their ranks. In these years preceding Confederation the party had already formed its individuality, and shaped its programme, and secured all the real elements in its strength.

In presence of the hostility shown by the United States to the idea of commercial reciprocity, it declares itself protectionist. In its dread of annexation, it shows a tendency to draw closer to the mother country. Above all, it can boast a real leader, adroit, stirring, of great reputation, in Sir John Macdonald, a statesman of farreaching intelligence, who will be able to keep it for a long period in office by the authority of his name, the largeness of his ideas, and the remarkable practical skill displayed by him in his electoral and parliamentary tactics.

Confederation came about in 1867, and from 1867 to 1896, with an interval of five years, it is the Conservative party that rules Canada. Its defeat in 1873, caused by financial scandals, is not of a political character. A brief storm has been unable to change the deep current of opinion, and in 1878 the country returns faithfully to Sir John Macdonald.

Quebec is the great stronghold of the Conservatives at this period, and sends them solid majorities regularly to the Ottawa House of Commons. Here is a table showing how Quebec Province is represented therein:

	Liberals	Conservatives
Election of 1867	20	45
" 1872	27	38
" 1874	33	32
" 1878	20	45
" 1882	17	48
" 1887	29	36

Ontario wavers between the two parties. It does not become sincerely and profoundly Conservative until Quebec assures power to the Frenchman Laurier.

In the course of its long years of success the main strength of the Conservatives consisted in their having a real leader who knew how to take up popular causes and make them his own. Thus it was that they carried out the gigantic enterprise of the Canadian Pacific Railway, provided the Dominion with a system of customs duties which in its broad lines still exists, and prepared the Canadian people for the blossoming of that imperialist movement which was to have its hour of immense popularity at the time of the Queen's Diamond Jubilee in 1897.

The Canadian Pacific is indubitably the result of the Conservative policy. When the Conservatives of to-day looking backwards boast of having done more than anyone else to equip the colony and render possible its remarkable economic development, and claim to have ensured the unity of Confederation by the construction of this immense railway, they but assert an incontestable truth. For this great work Canada owes them real gratitude.

The establishment of a transcontinental railway had been promised to British Columbia with a view to persuading it to enter into Confederation. The efforts of the first Macdonald ministry to put it into execution had been stopped in 1873 by terrible financial scandals in the political world. Under the Liberal Mackenzie ministry the project made no advance. Thus, when the Conservatives returned to power in 1878, the railway being still delayed, British Columbia allowed it to be understood that she would withdraw from the Union unless she obtained prompt satisfaction. Macdonald, understanding that the work must be got through at all costs, put it in hand at once. In 1880, supported by Sir Charles Tupper, he entered into negotiations with a great English company; the following year the project received the sanction of the British Parliament; then the Canadian government pushed matters on so quickly that on the 26th of June 1886 the first train started from Montreal for Vancouver – five years earlier than had been anticipated. By the realization of this grandiose conception, which at first had seemed to many people impossible, the Conservatives earned for themselves a reputation as a party of vast enterprises, with the great interests of the nation profoundly at heart.

Whilst thus helping to consolidate the unity of Canada, the Conservative party devoted attention to securing the economic personality of the colony through the medium of a resolutely protectionist policy. They had made efforts in this direction on various occasions already even before Confederation. But it is about 1878 that we find Sir John Macdonald and his friends, on their return to power, putting on foot the national and protectionist programme which has since been the chief feature of the party policy.

The whole of Canada was suffering at this time from a deep economic depression. Wages were low, manufactories were coming to a standstill, commerce was in a state of deplorable insecurity. Agriculture was no less affected, owing to a depressed home market and the extremely low prices reigning abroad. Governmental income collapsed. It was a time of crisis in the full sense of the word. As usual, the public blamed the government, and called upon it to *do* something—to draft a programme of reforms and discover a remedy for the situation. Like a certain type of invalid, the country clamoured for a prescription at any price. The Liberal party, committed by its traditions to free trade, or at least to anti-protectionism, would not hear of the establishment of high tariffs against foreign competition, and it had no panacea calculated to attract the public. In a word, it was impotent.

Sir John Macdonald, who in opposition had been biding his time, saw that the hour had come for him, and that the best possible policy – the necessary, inevitable policy – was that of protection regarded "not as a temporary expedient, but as a national policy." He started out on his electoral campaign in 1878 to the cry of "Canada for the Canadians," followed by enthusiastic adherents who felt they were being led to victory.

It was not an ordinary victory – it was a veritable triumph; the Conservatives regained power for a period of eighteen years. Strong in its success, the Macdonald ministry set to work at once on the carrying out of its programme, and brought forward a distinctly protectionist tariff bill, which was accepted on the spot. Since then, under the Liberals as under the Conservatives, the same economic policy has prevailed. The tariff has undergone numerous modifications, but, taken as a whole, it has remained a protective tariff, never becoming that tariff "for revenue only" of which the Canadian free traders were so fond of talking. In this sense, it may be said that it was the Conservative party that established and regulated the customs régime of Canada.

In describing his programme as "National," Sir John Macdonald sought to pose as the champion of Canadian integrity. In this way he flattered not only a number of great interests but also the patriotic sentiments of the English Canadians, and thus prepared the way for imperialism. The Conservatives began indeed at this period to aim at a closer union with the mother country. They took this course the more readily that they were able not without some truth to accuse their Liberal opponents of treating with the United States and of hiding thoughts of annexation beneath their adherence to diverse and sometimes dubious forms of commercial reciprocity.

Towards 1891 patriotism had become one of the most effective planks in the Conservative platform. Sir John Macdonald turned it to account with consummate art. "As for myself," he said in the election of 1891, "my course is clear. A British subject I was born – a British subject I will die. With my utmost, with my latest breath, will I oppose this 'veiled treason' which attempts, by sordid means and mercenary proffers, to lure our people from their allegiance. During my long public service of nearly half a century, I have been true to my country and its best interests, and I appeal with equal confidence to the men who have trusted me in the past, and to the young hope of the country, with whom rest its destinies for the future, to give me their united and strenuous aid in this my last effort for the unity of the Empire and the preservation of our commercial and political freedom."

Such an appeal is, in the true sense of the word, nationalist. And at this period, when the party was at its zenith, the Conservatives were nationalists essentially. Their most effective weapon against the Liberals, suspected of favouring annexation despite their disclaimers, lay in their affirmation of British patriotism.

This attitude led naturally towards imperialism. Sir John Macdonald, as a principal founder of Confederation, and as prime mover in the matter of the Canadian Pacific, had been throughout his career in close relationship with England, where he was held in high esteem. In the course of the different negotiations which he had carried through, he had met the great English ministers, Disraeli and Gladstone. Disraeli especially had charmed him, and he felt himself in sympathy with the renowned founder of imperialism. Closer bonds still had attached him to England; he had had bestowed upon him by the Queen the high distinction of the Order of the Bath, and he had been appointed a member of the Privy Council. In one word, he was a genuine British citizen, and to a far greater extent than the

Irishman Blake or the Frenchman Laurier, successive leaders of the Liberal party, he was disposed to steer his course in accordance with imperial policy.

He did so with conviction, but at the same time with a strong sense of reality. At a period when many Canadians considered quite calmly the possibility of separation, he affirmed staunchly and openly his wish to draw still closer the bond of union with the mother country. Not that he was ready to forego the least atom of colonial autonomy: he was conscious that this was out of the question and not very desirable. But at the moment when it was necessary to stimulate public opinion in one direction or the other, he declared clearly alike in his speeches and in his correspondence for unity with the Empire.[1]

If his political imperialism remained inevitably in a phase so indeterminate that no British statesman has ever been able to analyse it, his economic imperialism very soon assumed a more definite shape. His conception of protectionism directed above all against the United States, his desire for new markets, open largely to Canadian products, made him turn naturally towards England. He was thus led to conceive, something after the style of a precursor, the policy of preferential tariffs.

Already in 1879, in concert with his ministers, Sir Leonard Tilley and Sir Charles Tupper, he had made overtures in this sense to England: an interesting but unsuccessful proposition, for at that period no English leader would have dared to become responsible for a project involving the acceptance by England of the principle of protection.[2] He had come back again and again to this idea, which he had gone into closely and which he cherished. Here, for instance, is what he wrote in 1891 to Mr. W. H. Smith, First Lord of the Treasury and leader of the House of Commons in Lord Salisbury's ministry: "Canada has undertaken the development of her resources on so large a scale that she must have revenue, and from various causes can only look to customs and excise for it. While, therefore, she cannot promise a reduction of her customs duties, she will be quite ready to give British goods a preference of 5 or even 10 per cent in our markets if our products receive a corresponding preference in England. The United States are the chief rivals of English

---

[1] See his correspondence with Disraeli, for example, the letter of Oct. 7, 1879, cited by Joseph Pope in his biography of Sir John Macdonald.

[2] This fact is recorded in a letter from Sir John Macdonald to Mr. J. S. Helmcken, March 30, 1891. Cf. Mr. Pope's biography of Sir J. Macdonald, II, 219.

manufacturers with us at present; with such a differential scale as I suggest, all that we do not make ourselves would be supplied by the mother country."[3]

We must admit that this programme was not ill planned, for once they were installed in office the Liberals appropriated it. They have introduced the preferential tariff, without discarding the protectionist system; and in the course of two colonial conferences in London, in 1897 and 1902, they have adopted the principle of commercial reciprocity within the Empire. How came it that the Conservative party, so powerful in 1891, allowed itself to be supplanted by its rivals and to lose the benefits of so popular a programme and so brilliant a past? That is what I must explain now in bringing this chapter to a close.

The star of the Conservatives began to pale. To begin with, Sir John Macdonald died in May of that year – a severe blow to the party, for the personality of the leader counts for so much in Canada. He was not replaced, or at least not adequately. In less than five years the Conservative staff is decimated and four prime ministers in succession disappear: Sir John Abbott and Sir John Thompson die; Sir Mackenzie Bowell is overthrown by an intrigue on the part of his own lieutenants; Sir Charles Tupper remains on, to be beaten in the elections of 1896. There are divisions in the party, and it loses its prestige as well as its unity. With unheard-of rapidity, all its services are forgotten; the normal working of the Canadian Pacific has become such a matter of course that no one thinks of giving the credit for it to those who made it a possibility. The Conservative party has grown old!

It still retains its protectionist programme, to which may be added that of imperialism. But at the moment when it most needs to be able to thunder against the "veiled treason" of the advocates of annexation or of a customs union, the Liberal party with a rare skill has achieved a transformation which has made it acceptable even to those by whom in the past it was most feared.

In 1896, now completely freed from the compromising patronage of the Rouges, the Liberals have ceased entirely to be anti-clerical, even if it should be admitted that they could ever be so described. They are still to be engaged in a terrible fight with the Church over the Manitoba schools, but this will be the final outburst of hostility; reconciliation will follow easily, which will prove lasting. It must be borne in mind that since 1885 or

[3] See Mr. Pope's biography, II, 218.

thereabouts, under the influence of men like Count Mercier, premier of the province of Quebec, the French Liberals of Canada have been undergoing a notable change: they are as Catholic as they can be, and their French nationalism has the air of being purer than that of their Conservative compatriots, who are forced by the necessities of power and their alliance with Sir John Macdonald to acquiesce in perpetual compromises. Owing to this fact, the latter lose many votes in the French province, which in 1891 even gives a small majority to their adversaries. Let but a popular leader of their own race be proposed for the first place in the ministry, and nothing else will be needed to induce the mass of French Canadians, from national feeling, to turn completely round.

On the other hand, the Liberal leaders when they feel that they are on the threshold of power, tone down considerably their free trade professions; on the eve of the 1896 elections they reassure the Protectionist interests by means of explicit declarations. There is now nothing to prevent them from taking up the government of the country.

Finally, after the Liberal victory of 1896, the Conservative party receives a really stunning blow by seeing its adversaries actually adopting its imperialist programme, carrying out its old project of preferential duties, and strengthening the bonds with England to the sound of a flourish of trumpets. Sir Charles Tupper and his friends are unable to contain themselves at the sight of Sir Wilfrid Laurier and Mr. Fielding reaping all the glory and applause. Feeling they must offer some resistance to measures of which in their hearts they cannot disapprove, they are reduced to complaining that England has been given too much – nothing has been asked from her in exchange for the preference she has been given. By a curious irony, their imperialism is thus made to look less generous than the imperialism of their fortunate rivals.

From this moment, the Conservative party falls more and more into confusion: it is beaten in 1900, and again in 1904. Its programme has lost almost all its efficacy. Protection is a useless weapon now that the Liberals have become protectionists. Imperialism remains more serviceable to them, inasmuch as Sir Wilfrid Laurier is not altogether a disciple of Mr. Chamberlain's, though a clever enough diplomatist to be in some degree an imperialist. Thus baffled, the Conservatives have to fall back on violent jingoism. As Quebec has failed them completely, they are now almost entirely English. Out of jealousy at French success, Ontario has come back to them, and this time almost completely. In 1900 their electoral campaign is carried out to the tune of "Down with French domination!" But it was in vain. The other provinces combine to govern without Ontario and without the Conservatives.

They have even ceased to be regarded as the party of great enterprises. In 1904, Sir Wilfrid Laurier takes in hand the project of the Grand Trunk Pacific, and the opposition fight him so maladroitly that they give the public the impression that they do not want to have a second transcontinental railway. As the country is strongly attached to the scheme, it votes more than ever for the ministry in power.

Thus Sir John Macdonald's successors end by having no programme of their own. What is the explanation of it? Simply that in view of the similarity of the principles of Liberals and Conservatives to-day there is no longer question of any contest in the political arena of Canada except between a government and an opposition, or between two parties equally Conservative. Anything may arise out of such a situation.

27: The Absence of a Third Party

In studying the programme and the following of the Liberals and the Conservatives, we have alluded to numerous interests of various kinds, national, religious, commercial, industrial. We have inquired as to whether the electors were French or English, Catholic or Protestant, free traders or protectionists. But it has never been necessary for us to know the social class of the members of either party. The reason is that the question of class until now has held but a quite insignificant place in the public life of Canada. Why is this so? Will this state of things last? Or would it be possible for a Labour party to be formed in British America? That is the problem into which we have now to inquire.

In spite of its growing industrial wealth, the Dominion still remains above all an agricultural country. It is to-day more or less what the United States were thirty or forty years ago, before a movement of expansion beyond all precedent made of them one of the leading manufacturing nations in the world. Consequently the artisan element is infinitely less numerous than the agricultural element.

There are, indeed, very important centres of industrial production, but they are scattered and far apart. First of all, we have in the east of the colony the group of Maritime Provinces, in which the steel works of Sydney (Cape Breton) stand out for notice. In the provinces of Quebec and Ontario must be mentioned the manufacturing regions of Montreal, Toronto, Hamilton, Kingston, and Quebec. It is in these localities that the great manufactories and the great industrial agglomerations are to be found. Proceeding westward, and leaving Sault Ste. Marie on one side, there is nothing to mark this side of the Rocky Mountains except the great camp of Winnipeg, an unfinished city, always in a state of reconstruction and fermentation and marvellous growth – a great agricultural centre, railway junction, and shop – the place whither the immigrants come and whence they go on again: in short, a new Chicago. Then at the other extremity of the continent, on the far side of the mountains, British Columbia, a land apart, distant, out of the way, almost self-governing – a land of fisheries, mines, and forests, with its half Canadian, half Californian mining centres of Crows' Nest Pass (coal), Rossland (iron and copper), Nanaimo, Cumberland, Ladysmith (coal). We must not forget finally an industry that is more important than any and that extends all over the surface of the colony – the vital, essential railway industry which affords employment to a considerable section of the working population.

By reason of this dispersion of a relatively small number of artisans over an enormous expanse of territory, by reason still more of their striking differences of origin, language, and character, there really does not exist, properly speaking, any working class in Canada. Moreover, there is not so wide a gulf between the industrial artisan and the agricultural labourer as exists with us – the distance between them is easily bridged. Thus no one ventures to talk of the "Canadian workman," for this expression does not convey any precise meaning, covering as it does many different types of men with nothing in common but the name.

In the Maritime provinces the industrial workman is generally a native of the country, though the Sydney steel manufactories have imported a good deal of American skilled labour. In this part of the colony, which stands somewhat to one side, the working population is mostly British, stolid, and somewhat slow-going. The more active elements are tempted, as everywhere in America, to go West.

If we pass to the French province, the contrast is remarkable. The French-Canadian artisan is usually a peasant attracted to the factory by the bait of regular wages. He provides an inferior kind of manual labour not exacting high wages, just as is the case in the great factories in New England. The psychology of the Quebec countryman turned artisan undergoes little change. He remains entirely under the control of the clergy, and his new role effaces in no way his national character. Many strikes have been stopped through the influence of the priests, and in many cases the workmen have accepted terms which otherwise they would have rejected, simply because the priests counselled submission. The Church does all it can to keep the French workmen apart from the English – this separation being essential, she feels, to the preservation of their race. Montreal, it should be mentioned, presents an exceptional state of things: the time is perhaps not far distant when the working class of this great city will become emancipated.

In Ontario we find workmen of a more purely Canadian kind. The Toronto artisan, akin to the artisan of the United States, but educated and trained in a very British atmosphere, is pre-eminently Canadian. If one could speak at all of the "Canadian workman," it is certainly in the great English province that it would be necessary to seek the type.

In the West – Manitoba, Alberta, Saskatchewan – American influence is very strong, the number of American immigrants being so considerable. The still greater number of European immigrants of all kinds when assimilated to their surroundings produce a type of workmen very different from those of Eastern Canada.

The province which has become most Americanized is British Columbia. With the exception of Victoria, which is a very English city, the whole of this region resembles most strikingly the neighbouring states of Washington, Idaho, Montana, and Oregon – themselves neighbouring states to California. Indeed, in spite of the Canadian Pacific Railway, British Columbia has more intimate connection with the American Northwest than with Eastern Canada. To the north as to the south of the frontier, you find mushroom cities springing up suddenly in the midst of a wonderful country, with a composite population of British, Americans, Europeans of all kinds, Chinese and Japanese; small wooden shanties, as many bars as dwelling-houses, on one side the trim residences of respectable folk, on the other whole streets given over to prostitution, swarming hives of Chinamen, such is the character of these Western cities, which have nothing in common, not merely with the cities of the East, but even with Winnipeg, Regina, or Calgary. You feel that the everlasting "boom" of California is not far distant.

The rates of wages in Canada vary in accordance with the variety of conditions. In the Maritime provinces and in Quebec they are about 25 per cent lower than in the corresponding regions of the United States. In the great manufacturing centres the workman earns $2.50 to the $3.00 he would be earning in America; but in general the level is lower, the proportion of skilled workmen being small. In Ontario wages are higher, and are about equal to the wages earned in New York. In the West, manual labour being comparatively scarce, wages rise rapidly – the skilled workman earning $3.00 a day easily, and sometimes more. This is the case also on the Pacific coast, where the conditions are the same as those in the American Northwest.[1]

Such are the natural and normal conditions determining the levels of wages. They are modified by artificial relations between employers and workers. Let us see what these relations are in Canada. First of all, employers have not a very well-defined attitude toward their employees. Some are ready to recognize the unions, others take their stand openly for resistance. It would seem that the Canadian working class are not yet sufficiently self-conscious to awaken the fears of the rich. The rich are at the stage where they declare themselves to have at heart the welfare of the workers, while preferring that these should not go too thoroughly into the question for themselves. In this respect the Liberal employers do not seem to differ appreciably from the Conservative.

The workers have begun the work of organizing themselves according to American methods, but have been retarded greatly by all their differences of race, language, moral and material conditions. In imitation of what has been done in the United States, they have established in most of the towns special trade unions for each trade; the different trade unions in each locality take part frequently in Trades and Labour Councils. There is a general federation of these for the whole of Canada, known as the Trades and Labour Congress, which holds a general convention every year. The majority of the unions belonging to this Congress are affiliated to the American Federation of Labor. The word "general" which I have used is not quite accurate, however, for Nova Scotia, Prince Edward Island, and British

[1] Consult the excellent study by M. Albert Métin *Le Travail au Canada* (Memoires et documents du *Musée social*, Mars, 1905).

Columbia have remained the centres of separate organizations.

These unions have until now devoted themselves principally to professional ends – the securing of higher wages, the reduction of the hours of labour, the improving of the conditions of employment either through their own action or by means of amicable negotiations with employers or through the mediation of the state. However, they have lately shown a tendency to take a larger part in politics, if not actually by asserting themselves at elections, at least in a general sense. The tendency of the Trades and Labour Congress is undoubtedly to exercise influence over the social legislation of the country.[2] Some of the unions, chiefly in British Columbia, are of a distinctly socialistic character, but these are the exception. The others in their manifestoes are content to employ vague formulas by which they do not commit themselves.

The state has now begun, as a matter of fact, to display a certain activity in regard to labour questions. Social legislation, it is provided by the B.N.A. Act of 1867, is a matter for the provincial legislatures; a number of different protective laws have been voted by them during the last twenty years – during the last ten years especially. As for the federal parliament, its powers are more limited. Nevertheless, by a clever development of the prerogatives belonging to it through its control over the railways, it has not only established a system of conciliation and arbitration (not compulsory) in regard to strikes, but also a Department of Labour, charged with the task of collecting statistics and publishing them every month in an official periodical, the *Labour Gazette*. Under the direction of a distinguished manager, Mr. Mackenzie King, the Department of Labour is carrying out a work of the highest interest.

Coming now to the political side of the matter, we find that the Canadian workers, in spite of some isolated victories at the polls, have not yet succeeded in constituting themselves a third party. The organization of such a group involves, in truth, numerous difficulties. The agricultural predominance, the scattered condition of manufacturing industries, the absence of marked differences between the social classes, have all combined to prevent the growth of any real class feeling. If such a feeling exists in British Columbia and shows signs of coming into existence in Montreal, it cannot be said to be evident elsewhere. In a new country, prospering and developing rapidly, the gen-

---

[2] Verbatim Report of the Proceedings of the Trades and Labour Congress, 1904.

eral interests of all classes are too interlaced and interdependent for it to be easy to organize a class policy; the policy of national prosperity comes before all else.

The conditions of the parliamentary system, moreover, make it difficult for a third party to come into being. The lack of a second ballot serves to discourage the workmen from any effort to get in a candidate of their own, for if they are a mere minority they know that in this way they merely waste their voting power. On the other hand, the two great parties are so strongly organized and so well disciplined not only at the elections but also in parliament that it is almost hopeless to elect candidates against them, and that even if some independents are sent to the Commons they are isolated, lost, practically reduced to impotence whatever their talent. If then the workers must want to get something done – as is almost always the case – they must enter into an understanding with either the Conservatives or the Liberals, in order to negotiate the conditions of an electoral alliance with them which will pay off in specified reforms or in measures of protection or favours of some kind, general or particular, either for the benefit of the working class as a whole or of its members individually.

This is the present situation. At elections the workers are divided between Conservatives and Liberals. From the former they expect a protectionist régime of higher customs duties and consequently a rise in wages. From the latter, more favour for the popular classes or a more effective policy for the general development of the country. We know already that neither of the two Canadian parties can claim to be more advanced than the other. We know also that both are ready, in order to gain votes, to make the concession of the needed programmes; it is not their political principles that will get in their way.

Both parties are naturally eager to "catch the labour vote," all the more so that both stand in dread of the advent of a third party to upset the working of their electoral machinery. Thus the impossibility of achieving results by means of independent members, together with the ease with which they can barter votes for advantages, and in addition that instinctive anxiety of every Canadian to maintain the national prosperity, have resulted in the immense majority of labour votes being cast for representatives of the two great parties in the general elections of 1904. The small parties, if they may be given the name, succeeded only in carrying a very few seats.

We must mention the socialists simply as a matter of record.

They are infinitely less numerous, and are not to be found in the form of a political group anywhere except in British Columbia. At Vancouver they have formed a small but energetic party, with a weekly organ, *The Western Clarion*; they are revolutionary socialists, similar enough to those in France, and find their inspiration in the fundamental doctrine of the class war. That means that in a country like Canada they cannot expect to have much chance of success. As a matter of fact the five candidates they put forward in British Columbia at the elections of 1904 were all defeated, and secured only a very small number of votes. These are not the best representatives of the average tendencies of Canadian workers, especially of those trade unionists who form part of the Trades and Labour Congress. These latter, as we have seen, are not at all uninterested in party politics; they busy themselves a great deal politically, and, no doubt, will do more of this in future; but as a rule they think that the unions or the Congress should not mix officially or directly in the electoral struggle. For example, the Trades and Labour Council of Montreal declares: "We affirm that the integrity of the unions of workers can best be preserved intact by observing strictly a line of conduct of absolute abstention from all political partisanship, and we declare that it is imprudent for the Council to engage in the support of any political organization – federal, provincial, or municipal. We recommend, however, that every wage-earner should exercise his right to vote for the men and measures he believes most favourable to the interests of labour without regard to party politics."[3] So the tactics of this group, as of the Congress, consists in drawing from either party indifferently all the possible advantages.

Many of the unions, nevertheless, would see with joy the establishment of an independent labour party, or more exactly the nomination of independent labour candidates. Such candidates have already appeared on several occasions. The parliament of 1900 contained two – Mr. Ralph Smith, member for Nanaimo, British Columbia, and Mr. Puttee, member for Winnipeg. In 1904, Mr. Ralph Smith, who described himself as a Liberal Labour candidate, was elected with the assistance of the Liberals against a socialist supported by the *Clarion*. Less fortunate, Mr. Puttee, who stood as an Independent Labour candidate, was completely crushed between the Liberals and the Conservatives, polling only 1,200 votes out of 7,000. Yet his programme was a very reasonable one, amounting only to state

[1] Cited by M. Albert Métin in *Le Travail au Canada*, p. 105.

socialism, and making no reference to the social revolution or the war between the classes. It was the Liberal candidate, Mr. Bole, who was elected by a large majority, thus proving that even in a stronghold of labour such as Winnipeg the chances of a third party are limited.

The situation is not very different in the province of Quebec, though here it is complicated by the fact that most of the workers are Catholics and that the labour leaders cannot at present afford to displease the clergy, for if they did so they would break themselves against its irresistible strength. They are careful, therefore, never to talk against the Church, and it seems probable that it will be a long time before the French-Canadian labour movement becomes anti-clerical, as is the case in France. For fear of losing immediate advantages, they will be afraid to pursue the ulterior end of the intellectual emancipation of the workers. In December, 1904, three Labour candidates, MM. Verville, Latreille, and Kelly, came forward in Montreal as candidates for the provincial legislature of Quebec, with a programme of labour and political reforms going far beyond the programme of the Liberals. Curiously enough, they were supported by the great newspapers of Montreal, though these were little inclined towards advanced ideas, owing to their anxiety to find readers among the working classes. On the other hand, they were opposed openly enough by the clergy, who regarded two points in their programme as of a dangerous tendency – the establishment of a Minister of Public Instruction, and of free and compulsory education. As for the Liberal party, it viewed with much disfavour the appearance of these dissentient candidatures, which threatened to produce divisions within its ranks. It carried the day, however, and the three Labour men were beaten.

Since then the cause of labour has made what may prove a decisive step onwards: at a by-election on February 23, 1906, M. Verville was elected a member of the federal parliament by the big majority of 1073 votes over his Liberal opponent. The recent formation of a Labour party in England had probably something to do with this result, and it is to be supposed that in the near future the Canadian labour world will try to follow suit.

But in the meantime there is no third party in the Dominion. As trades unionists the workmen have won important advantages, but they have not yet attained to any combined political action. The electoral machines of the Liberal and Conservative parties are still almost invincible, and the electorate is so used to these traditional divisions that it seems incapable of inventing new ones. It must remain so probably as long as the country continues to be so prosperous, for prosperity does not induce political changes. But if the colony some day runs into a crisis, the two existing parties will have to strengthen their programmes, or other parties will assuredly come to take their place, and no machinery will serve to prevent it.

PART THREE

THE BALANCE OF RACES AND CIVILIZATIONS IN CANADA

28: The French-Canadian Race and Its Programme for the Future

After having studied the psychological formation of the two Canadian races and the conditions of federal political life which result from their union, it now remains for us to investigate how each of them conceives its proper development, and what destiny each can reasonably hope to realize in British North America.[1]

With the French-Canadian state of mind we are already acquainted. We know their feelings of passionate devotion to their language, their religion, and their traditions. In spite of a classification of federal parties which tends rightly to prevent French aspirations from finding expression in the framework of a special parliamentary group, national or religious, it is none the less evident that there does exist in a latent state a real French party which in hours of grave crisis reveals itself and asserts itself spontaneously, in order to give voice to the claims and wishes of the race as a whole. It is permissible, then, to represent our French-Canadian kinsmen as having a line of action of their own, apart from their superficial divisions. What is this line they take? In what sort of programme is it embodied? This will be the subject of this chapter.

Past and present alike give the French-Canadian race precious pledges for the future. After a century and a half of foreign rule, it survives in all its persistent individuality. Nay, more, it is able to boast of an enormous growth. The descendants of the 60,000 who were vanquished in 1763 have come to number 1,640,000, and form a veritable people in the fullest sense of the word. The province of Quebec belongs to it henceforward almost entirely; it is silently invading the Eastern counties of Ontario; if emigration into New England had not taken away some hundreds of thousands of its members, it would

---

[1] M. Albert Métin is preparing a volume which will be specially devoted to *La colonisation et la mise en valeur du Canada contemporain*.

consist to-day of more than two million souls. And in spite of this great leakage, it holds so important a place in the colony that no serious government can be established with hope of lasting without its support.

It is upon these known and indisputable facts that the French Canadians base their hope of a development still greater. The successes they have already achieved have aroused in them a legitimate feeling of pride, combined with an invincible optimism, and they find satisfaction in applying to themselves as a prophecy the words addressed by one of the founders of Montreal to his comrades-in-arms: "You are but as a grain of mustard-seed, but you shall grow until your branches cover the earth. . . . Your children shall fill the world!"[2] Clearly there is nothing in this but the evoking of a glorious dream. The moment an attempt is made to be more precise, different tendencies and different programmes come to the front.

The enthusiasts when they talk of the destinies of their race cannot and will not separate religion from politics. In their eyes the French Canadians are a Catholic people, whose influence should be Catholic as much as French. Thus is sketched out a sort of mystical conception of the role of this Catholic New France in the New World. Poets like M. Fréchette, who is assuredly no clerical, have expressed it in ardent words:

> La plante qui va naître etonnera le monde;
> Car, ne l'oubliez pas, nous sommes en ce lieu
> Les instruments choisis du grand œuvre de Dieu.[3]

What "grand œuvre" is in question? In his book, *La nation canadienne*, M. Gailly de Taurines, a sympathetic student of Canadian Catholicism, indicates it to us thus: "What is this great work of which the Canadian people is to be the instrument? The Canadians will answer us with one voice, and alike from pulpit and from tribune we shall hear these words given forth: 'Our mission is to fulfil in America, we who are a people of French blood, the part that France herself fulfilled in Europe.'" The France, it should be explained in parenthesis, that was the eldest daughter of the Church: not the France of the Revolution. "Over and beyond this earthly aim," continues M. de Taurines, "there is a divine mission which they must fulfil. A Catholic people, one of those that have remained most faithful to the

---

[2] Cited by Elisée Reclus in his *Geographie Universelle*, xv., 495.
[3] Louis Fréchette, *La légende d'un peuple*, p. 59.

Church, they must win over the whole of North America to Catholicism."[4]

The venerable Abbé Casgrain – whom none can forget who ever knew him – wrote to the same effect in brilliant and enthusiastic phrases. "When you have reflected upon the history of the Canadian people," he declared, "it is impossible not to recognise the great designs of Providence that presided over its formation; it is impossible not to foresee that unless it prove false to its calling, great destinies are reserved for it in this portion of the world. The mission of the American France upon this continent is the same as that of the European France in the other hemisphere. A pioneer of the truth like her, she has long been the sole apostle of the true faith in North America. Since her origin she has never ceased to pursue this mission faithfully, and to-day she sends forth her bishops and her missionaries to the extremities of this continent. It is from her womb, let us not doubt, that must issue the peaceful victors who shall lead back under the ægis of Catholicism the errant peoples of the New World."[5]

These extracts, which it would be easy to multiply, disclose the vague kind of enthusiasm to which the French Canadians are so much addicted. In their anxiety to assert their national and religious individuality they dream of the conditions in which they would be free to expand without constraint. Hasty and ill-thought-out ideas are thus conceived. There is talk sometimes of an independent Republic in which the French of America should be self-governing and should develop on their own lines without having to reckon with the English. It is such another dream as the Abbé Casgrain's; idealists alone can believe in its realization.

More practical minds take note of actual facts. Good Catholics, they would doubtless rejoice at the sight of the New World becoming converted, but they know well in their hearts that the event is most improbable. Good Frenchmen, they would delight in independence; but they are obliged to recognize that for a long time to come, perhaps for ever, autonomy is the only possible régime for them. "Some of our compatriots," writes M. Bourassa, "look forward with joy to the day when we shall constitute in America, *de facto* and *de jure*, a new France, a free state in which our race shall rule alone. Assuredly the dream is

[4] Gailly de Taurines, *La nation canadienne*, pp. 282, 283.
[5] Abbé Casgrain, *Histoire de la vénerable Marie de l'Incarnation*, I, 95. Cited by M. de Taurines in *La nation canadienne*, p. 287.

both legitimate and fascinating. And the work of centuries may realize it for us more swiftly than circumstances seem to indicate. But it is a dream, and what we have to do for the moment is the duty of the moment."[6]

Thus the practical people, the responsible leaders, are led to realize that, without renouncing any hope for the future, they must work away in the present with a clear distinction in their minds between what is desirable and what is practicable. They must put aside the vision of to-morrow for the political programme of to-day. In this more restricted field wishes become more precise and methods of action more effective. A policy takes shape and proves to be serviceable based upon two solid factors: the first is the high birth-rate of the French race in the Dominion, the second is the wide extent of liberty – liberty almost complete – that they consider they are entitled to expect from England. With these two elements, they tell themselves, they need have no fear for the future.

The extraordinary fecundity of French-Canadian families is universally known. Times without number allusion has been made in newspapers, speeches, and books to these families of ten, fifteen, and sometimes even twenty children. The official census of the Dominion does not give us precise statistics as to the respective birth-rates of the two races, but it is manifest that the French-Canadian is one of the highest in the world,[7] and that it certainly is much in excess of that of the English Canadians. Thus it comes that the province of Quebec, simply as the result of the French birth-rate, has become almost exclusively French, while from the same cause a part of the province of Ontario is gradually losing its English colouring. As our Canadian kinsmen show no sign of physical decadence, it is easy to understand their boundless confidence in their future: their numbers, they hold, must one day put the power in their hands.

In truth, all, or almost all, French Canadians who live to maturity are destined to become electors, and if the representative system continues to be fairly applied a day must come when the French element, having grown into a majority, at least in certain provinces, must dominate the assemblies, make its way into the ministries, and come to hold a more and more important place – perhaps a preponderant place – in the councils of the country.

[6] H. Bourassa, *Le patriotisme canadien français*, p. 13.
[7] According to the statistics of the Board of Health of the province of Quebec, the rate rose in 1903, to 36.75 per 1000 inhabitants. *Annual Report, 1903-4*, p. 65.

If this reasoning be well founded and if time be working thus for the French Canadians, what would they gain by trying to rush matters, either by demanding an independence which must be contested, if necessary by force, or by offering an uncompromising opposition to the British government? Would it not be better for them to wait, vigilantly but patiently, until times are ripe; to go on permeating the Dominion slowly instead of breaking away from it; and to aim at the real advantages of autonomy rather than the satisfactions, doubtless precarious, of independence?

Here is a programme which ought to appeal to the good sense of practical people. It has been adopted, with more or less enthusiasm, more or less amplitude, by the immense majority – one may say, adopted almost unanimously – of French Canadians. It suits their cautious and patient nature, their innate sense of nuances and combinations, and also their legitimate need of immediate material advantages; for, without involving the least renunciation of principle, it allows them to-day to profit from the present.

This strategy, thoroughly thought out, is pursued with a strong unity of purpose. Yet, according to differences of temperament, it assumes different aspects. Some of the more exalted, the more daring, more whole-hearted spirits are bent chiefly on preserving the French patrimony intact, and, even at the cost of a temporary attitude of intransigence, on ensuring its enhanced integrity in the future. Others, more diplomatic and more conciliatory, also perhaps more eager for immediate results, keep their eyes on the harvests of the moment, and do not hesitate to make certain sacrifices for the immediate acquisition of power.

The former, without properly speaking constituting a party, are represented sufficiently by the group of nationalists of Quebec. Frenchmen and Catholics before everything, they place in the front of their policy the complete and uncompromising development of their race and Church: they recognize in good faith the British supremacy, but they desire to follow their own ways freely, in accord with the English if possible, but in opposition to them if need be. The outspoken kind of language involved in this attitude does not accord well with the exercise of government in an Anglo-French federation like the Dominion. Nationalist politicians are therefore often to be found in a state of half opposition even under a ministry headed by one of their own race like Sir Wilfrid Laurier; compromises thought by the ministry to be called for in the interests of Confederation seem to them regrettable from the purely French standpoint. Thus it was that M. Bourassa wished to dissociate himself from the policy of sending volunteers to the Transvaal, even though it was proposed by his own party. This attitude won him bitter reproaches from those who, more prudent and practical, were chiefly interested in keeping a French prime minister in power, even at the cost of putting principles on one side. The temperament of the true nationalists does not easily adapt itself to such tactics, and in existing circumstances political life is rendered difficult for them.

They feel at ease within the narrow framework of the province of Quebec, which is their home and where they are among their own. In this province, which is almost a little French republic, they can carry on their propaganda without reserve, educate and develop their race, prepare it to play later, if necessary, a more considerable role. Compromise being useless in this special milieu, they can quite comfortably proclaim themselves French and Catholic, and declare openly their desire to see French Canadians multiply, expand, and colonize as much of the land as possible.

Colonize! To the folk of Quebec there seems to be something fateful in the word. To people the vast expanses all around them with their own flesh and blood – there is fascination in the dream! The land is rich and illimitable, their huge families offer a surplus of strong and energetic sons. Why not pour out into the provinces of the west, or to the northwest or north of Quebec, still clamouring for men, this redundance of French vitality, in danger otherwise of losing itself in the human ocean of America?

That is the sermon preached by French-Canadian statesmen and re-echoed by the priests, whose zeal and initiative in this field cannot be too highly praised. Successive ministers of the Department of Colonization have helped the movement in every possible way by the acquisition and occupation of land. The village *curé* follows the settlers to their new abode. There have been priests who have dedicated their lives to this work of leading the workers into trackless regions, there to establish them and help them and watch over them. The celebrated *curé* Labelle earned the honour of giving his name to an extensive district which he was the first thus to open out. This brilliant tradition is still kept on. The priests remain the real leaders, certainly the real centres of the new clusters, and they put forward all their efforts to maintain among the colonists those sentiments of union and patriotism which have enabled their race in Canada to remain so compact and strong.

Thirty years ago it was really believed that the prairies of the far west must be peopled by the habitants of Quebec; and serious efforts were made to direct emigration thither. Nowadays the tendency is rather to concentrate the French-Canadian people in their own province of Quebec – a programme that is more modest but is still gigantic if one considers the vast expanse of land between the St. Lawrence and Hudson Bay.

This policy of colonization, national as it is in some sense, excites all French Canadians. And they are excited because they are at bottom in complete sympathy with the most convinced of their Nationalists. When these latter speak, their fellow-citizens of Quebec cannot help applauding. Nevertheless, when the more moderate statesmen extol the timeliness of some immediate transaction which is necessary for the winning or retaining of power, they cannot resist them either. This is the origin of the success of the Liberal party under Laurier, the party of entente and diplomacy, which avoids imprudent words and too audacious affirmations, but which enables the French race to participate in the government of the country.

Between Laurier the diplomatist and Bourassa the nationalist the French of Canada have never been able to choose. They are grateful to the first for having led them to victory with such incomparable brilliance, and to the second for voicing so well the feelings, even if at times they may be somewhat too lively, that surge in their hearts. Under either formulation, the cause served is the same – the development and expansion of the race.

29: The Future of the French Canadians and British Supremacy

In the preceding chapter we have explained the hopes and the programme of action of the French-Canadian race. It remains for us now to see to what extent these hopes have a chance of realization. Can dependence really be placed on the much anticipated liberalism of the English mother country? Does their marvellous birth-rate suffice by itself to guarantee to the French that one day they will enjoy superiority of numbers in the Dominion? Are numbers the essential and sufficient condition of victory? Such is the complex problem which we must now examine coolly and with full regard to the facts, in order to be able to appreciate judiciously the destiny of our race in Canada.

The arguments drawn from the traditions of British liberalism seem well founded. The period is past and done with during which the British government could think of withstanding colonial claims by force of arms; the province of Quebec is a living proof of this. If other provinces become French in the same way, it is probable that they would be allowed to govern themselves in their own fashion. Even if the entire colony were one day to contain a French majority, it is not easy to see how England, in an attempt to resist, could find a means of openly violating the accepted rules of parliamentary government. There would be, then, for the whole Dominion, as for Quebec, a parliament and ministry for the most part French, and this in accordance with the British North America Act, the constitution granted by the imperial power.

The Anglo-Saxon element in Canada, supported surreptitiously by the English government, would show a strong indisposition to recognize this supremacy; personal influences would be used, and industrial, commercial, and financial concerns would put out all their powers to counteract as far as possible the advantages of numbers. But they would not venture upon a regular *coup d'état*, and constitutional principles would undoubtedly be respected. To this extent reliance may reasonably be placed upon the celebrated liberalism of Great Britain, which consists of a little liberalism and a good deal of wise resignation in the face of irrevocably accomplished facts.

But all this is dependent upon the French acquiring a majority in the Dominion. Will they? If we were to take into account nothing but their birth-rate, it would be mathematically demonstrable that the English would soon be distanced. Wherever the birth-rate is the principal factor the absolute and relative growth of the French race is remarkable.

So the province of Quebec has in the end been conquered by them. The British minority in the province of Quebec, which represented 25.49 per cent in 1851, had fallen to 20.98 per cent in 1881, and to 18 per cent in 1901. Of the 68,840 inhabitants of Quebec City, no less than 57,016 are French.[1] The Eastern Townships, in which the English loyalists fleeing from the American Revolution made their new home, are being rapidly

[1] Census of Canada, 1901.

overwhelmed. Out of sixty-five constituencies in the whole
province, only five – Argenteuil, Brome, Huntingdon, Pontiac,
Stanstead – still retain an English majority.

The part of Ontario which adjoins Quebec Province is in
process of being submerged in the same fashion. In the four
neighbouring counties of Prescott, Glengarry, Cornwall and
Stormont, and in Russell, the French numbered only 32,600 out
of 93,358 inhabitants in 1881. In 1901 they numbered 51,935
out of 111,374. Thus they increased from 34.8 per cent to 46.6
per cent. In the entire province of Ontario they number only
158,671 out of 2,182,947 even now; but between 1881 and 1901
they advanced from 4.8 per cent to 7.2 per cent.

The pacific progress of the race all round the stronghold of
Quebec proceeds silently but steadily. When they are grown up,
the young *Québequois* countrymen cannot all find room in the
village of their birth. Many of them have to pitch their tents
farther afield. Backed by their father, often upheld materially
as well as morally by their *curé*, they buy or rent a farm, marry,
and in their turn become fathers of families. Little by little,
almost imperceptibly, French groups become established thus
in counties which fifty years ago did not contain a single French
family. Suddenly one fine day it is discovered that the French
are in a majority, and the game is won! The British, who are
flooded out in this way, either make off altogether or else become
absorbed, and in some cases, incredible though it may sound,
assimilated. Thus in the province of Quebec one finds families
of Englishmen, Irishmen, and especially Scotsmen, becoming
French Canadians within two generations. They call themselves
Fraser, Barrie, Macleod, but they speak our language with an
unmistakable Norman accent, without any trace in it of British
pronunciation.

If the whole of Canada were developing in the same conditions as reign in the old colonies, the victory of our kinsmen
would not be in doubt. But this, of course, as we have seen, is
not the case. Moreover, the French lose the benefit of their
birth-rate by serious leakages, while the Anglo-Saxon race makes
up for its lower birth-rate by immigration and assimilation.
Thus the relative importance of the French in reality increases
very little or not at all.

The first of the French leakages is through infant mortality.
In Quebec Province the very young children die in great num-

bers,[2] and the large families alluded to above, while remaining imposing, undergo a notable diminution from this cause.

The second leakage, less painful in its nature, is a really much more serious one from the standpoint of the future of the race: it consists in the large and persistent emigration of young French Canadians into the states of New England. Every year thousands of them cross the frontier on their way into Maine, Vermont, New Hampshire, Massachusetts, Rhode Island, and Connecticut. The great manufactories of this part of America are in need of manual labour, and the wages they offer though not high are attractive enough to be very tempting to these young countrymen, dazzled by the dream of a larger and freer existence than that of their native villages.

Nearly a million French Canadians live in this way far from their country, without any real thought of returning.[3] A terrible leakage this and fatal to the future of the race, for it prevents their compatriots in the Dominion from attaining to that predominance in numbers of which we have been speaking. We are told, indeed, that the efforts now being made to stem this current, or at least to turn it to the Canadian west and north, are beginning to be crowned with success, but the results are in reality very modest – a matter of a few thousands, a very small battalion compared with the immense army that is lost. Thus it is that the argument which is based upon French-Canadian birth-rates and which at first sight is so impressive vanishes in part. In the same way certain European races, also astonishingly prolific, the Italians and Germans for instance, see millions of their children disappear and lose their individuality for ever in South America and the United States.

While the French do not reap the full advantage of their fruitfulness, the Anglo-Saxons, as we have seen, increase otherwise than by means of births: immigration works on their side. In 1903, 128,364 immigrants entered Canada; in 1904, 130,331.[4] The government is doing all it can still further to increase the numbers in its anxiety to people that far west which it was vainly hoped by some might have been filled by emigrants from Quebec.

---

[2] Out of 30,914 deaths in 1903, 11,799 were of children under five years of age – more than a third of the total. – *Report of the Council of Public Health*, 1904, p. 54.

[3] Natives of French Canada resident in the United States, 395,427; natives of the U.S.A. with two French-Canadian parents, 266,155; with one French-Canadian parent, 170,077. – *U.S.A. Census, 1900*.

[4] Reports of the Superintendent of Immigration, 1902-3 and 1903-4.

It were vain to hope that this flood of immigrants will serve to make up to the French Canadians for the drain upon their numbers. Among the 130,000 who arrived in 1904, there were only 1,534 from France, 858 Belgians, and 128 Swiss, while there were no less than 45,229 Americans and 50,374 English. The rest – in all about 32,000 – were of various nationalities: German, Austrian, Polish, Russian, Norwegian, etc. Save for some of the French-speaking immigrants, all these are destined to receive the Anglo-Saxon imprint. Germans, Russians, and Norwegians, who would perhaps adapt themselves to a French environment, make haste to assimilate themselves to their Anglo-Saxon environment in the west. They learn the English language only, and their children are taught no other, so that the second generation is barely recognizable, and has forgotten even its origin.

So the Canadian far west has passed insensibly but definitively out of our kinsmen's hands. Towards 1870 it was possible to believe that this immense region, discovered by our explorers, crossed in every direction by our trappers and missionaries, then taken possession of by a vanguard of our Canadian settlers and Indian half-breeds, would perhaps become a new field of action for the French civilization. In 1871 the two races about balanced each other in Manitoba. But since 1881 the French have lost ground: in that year they numbered only 9,949 as against 38,184 English, out of a total population of 65,954 (15.1 per cent). In 1901 the proportion of French was still smaller – 16,021 out of a total population of 255,211 (7.1 per cent). In the other western provinces we are not much better off. In British Columbia there were in 1901 only 4,600 French out of a total of 178,657 inhabitants. In the Northwest Territories we had only 7,040 out of 158,940.

Of course, these figures may not be absolutely accurate. It certainly seems astonishing that the French in Manitoba should number only 16,000. But allowing for error, it must be admitted that the French are in a very small minority. They form compact groups, rallying round their *curés*, and suffering themselves neither to be absorbed nor dominated, and thanks to their high birth-rate they continue to grow, but what can they effect against the great stream of immigrants ever replenishing the Anglo-Saxon flood? The balance could only be redressed by calling into play those hundreds of thousands of French Canadians who prosper in the United States, but who risk being lost in the midst of a people so vast and so implacable towards those who refuse to be assimilated.

Thus the French of Canada have gained ground quickly in Quebec and slowly in Ontario without having made any marked advance in the colony as a whole.

In 1881 they numbered 1,298,929 out of 4,324,810 inhabitants of the entire Dominion – about 30 per cent. In 1901 they numbered 1,649,371 out of 5,371,315 – about 30.7 per cent. From so minute an increase one can hardly derive the hope of final victory!

The French Canadians will have to give up the idea that they will prevail by force of numbers. Their future is assured, but their dream of supremacy is seen to become more and more impossible as the years pass by, shaping the destinies of the Dominion. Canada will not become French again! let us admit it. There are two reasons to prevent it: first, the English are henceforth irrevocably in a majority; secondly – and a more decisive reason still – the weight of history, economic forces, social forces, all combine to favour, no less than mere numbers, the supremacy of Great Britain.

French Canada is still bowed down under the burden of defeat! This observation, which may seem at once paradoxical and hard, comes inevitably to anyone who will study impartially the place accorded to our kinsmen in the Dominion. The Englishman always considers himself a member of the superior race. He carries out loyally and in quite correct manner the obligations entered into with the vanquished of 1763, but he never forgets the rights of victory, and if, for propriety's sake, he does not talk much of them, there is no sign of his having voluntarily renounced them. He does not always succeed in treating his French fellow-citizen as an equal. If in the domain of politics he is forced to make concessions, in other fields where he is not shackled he imposes his ideas and customs masterfully, and often inconsiderately.

A hundred and fifty years of this régime have made the French Canadians too much habituated to giving way in everyday life – even if only in matters which they regard as unimportant – for British supremacy not to have become established as a hard, solid fact. Splendid though they have been in their defence of their political rights, our kinsmen have perhaps been too ready to acquiesce in the predominance which their rivals arrogate to themselves everywhere except in parliament. Too many of them bow down quite sincerely before the superiority of the Anglo-Saxon civilization; they have no love for the English assuredly, but they admire them, sometimes imitate them, and suffer them to assume the general control and management of things in the realms of society and finance.

What Frenchman of France has not been shocked to see in cities so French in their population as Montreal or Quebec a form of civilization other than his own dominating openly, uncontested? Quebec, for instance, does not give the immediate impression of a city of ours; many sensitively observant visitors have felt that. In this city of 68,000, of whom not more than 10,000 are English, there are many parts where French is not understood: perhaps it would be more accurate to say where people *will* not understand it. On the railways it is tolerated at best. At the Château Frontenac Hotel, that marvel of comfort and elegance created by the Canadian Pacific, the principal employees do perhaps understand it, but they refuse to speak it. It is true that in the inquiry office and in the kitchen you can hear it spoken as much as you like, but is it not pitiful that English should be the speech of the managers, and French of the menials? The French Canadians have come to put up with this kind of not very pleasant obstinacy. They learn English, and in that they are wise enough; but they have never been able to get their rivals to learn French. And therein we cannot but recognize a really significant defeat.

It is the same in Montreal. Visitors may pass whole weeks there, frequenting hotels, banks, shops, railway stations, without ever imagining for a moment that the town is French by a great majority of its inhabitants. English society affects unconsciousness of this fact, and bears itself exactly as though it had no French neighbours. They seem to regard Montreal as their property. As they have got to this height, not by force of votes or of numbers, it must be admitted that their attitude is the outcome of the old sense of the rights of the conqueror. Think of the Indian civil service, and you will understand better the rulers of Canada.

It should be added that this strength of the English would amount to nothing if they did not possess the wealth at the same time, and if they had not the control of the economic life of the colony. In this respect, even in the most French districts, the Dominion is thoroughly under Anglo-Saxon domination. We have seen at what a disadvantage the French Canadians are, compared with their rivals, in regard to equipment, for commercial and industrial success; how their traditions, customs, and predilections all tend to make them go in for professions which win them respect, and sometimes even renown, but rarely riches; we have noted how difficult it is for the French-Canadian youth to make a way for himself in this domain of business for which his progenitors have so little fitted him. From this it has resulted inevitably that the wealth of the land belongs for the most part to the Anglo-Saxons, who are thus enabled to rule by as strong a title as the result of the ballot boxes. With some notable exceptions, which are now growing in number, our people have remained outside the great economic current. The principal banks, the leading railway companies, the great industrial, commercial, and shipping concerns belong to their rivals. English is the language of business; Montreal is a satellite of London or New York – a pre-eminently Anglo-Saxon centre, in which the presence of more than a hundred thousand Frenchmen is a factor of secondary importance.

Is it not clear, then, why the French (the question of numbers apart) cannot hope to prevail in Canada? In the long rivalry between Quebec and Ontario, Ontario triumphs. It triumphs, not so much by reason of its numerical advantage as by its resolute affirmation of a civilization which dominates America, and aloof from which – we must regretfully admit – it will be very difficult ever to achieve success.

So the future of the French Canadians is confined within certain limits beyond which there can be no passing for them. However, if complete success eludes them, a more modified success is assured. Let them only give up their hope of making Canada a French country, and endeavour instead, on the one hand to permeate the whole land with their spirit, and on the other to establish themselves strongly and for all time in the province of Quebec, swelling outwards towards the west, the northwest and the north. If in their struggle with British civilization they have not been completely victorious, that is from no lack of intelligence or courage. It is perhaps because – from the beginning and very much through the fault of France – they have been inadequately armed against an enemy strongly armed. Their society, more refined, more distinguished, more perfect, but in some respects grown antiquated and kept too little in touch with the profound changes of modern France, has shown itself, in spite of its superiority in other respects, unable to conquer a society which is more worldly, more vulgar, but incontestibly better adapted to the needs of a new country.

30: The Penetration of Canada by American Civilization

The long rivalry between the French and English in Canada is ending, then, in the victory of the latter. More numerous, more wealthy, finding their strength in a form of civilization more modern than that of their adversaries, the English have distanced the French. But now a new danger threatens the victors, and fresh assaults are made upon their supremacy. By their side – nay, actually within their frontiers, in the very heart of their cities and their farmlands – there is opening out a civilization akin to their own, but more exuberant, more opulent, more modern still. Its powers of absorption are so great that one may well ask the question whether in its character and its customs the Dominion will be able always to remain British.

To begin with, let us state the problem in exact terms. In analysing the feelings of the Canadians with regard to the United States, we saw how they at present dread the idea of annexation. Save in the occurrence of unforeseen events, of some unpardonable blundering on the part of England, it is almost certain that Canada will not willingly and wittingly give herself to her mighty neighbour.

That is not the danger. The danger does not take the form either of an attempt at conquest, a treaty of alliance or a plebiscite. It lies in the imperceptible daily transformation that by a slow steady progress is Americanizing the colony, its men, its investments and its manners. It lies in the slowly changing composition of the immigration which is populating the country – immigration that contains a large British element, it is true, but is in majority American and cosmopolitan. It lies, above all, in the irresistible influence of a prestigious neighbourhood that is already making Montreal a satellite of New York and Winnipeg a little Chicago! It is thus that the individuality of Canada may be threatened. Without any positive act of disloyalty by Canadians toward the metropolitan power, without any formal divorce, Canada is in danger of finding herself one day so completely transformed, so full of Americans and of strangers formed in their image, that the title of British colony, though always true in theory, will cease practically to be applicable to her.

A first reason for anxiety is presented by the present character of the immigration into the Dominion. Formerly the great stream of European emigrants flowed into the United States. Canada, less known, less in favour, wrongly supposed to be colder and less fertile, attracted chiefly a British clientele. Its far west, wild and forlorn, remained the jealously guarded property of a great Company, and was populated chiefly by Indians, with a sprinkling here and there of French and Scots.

Presently, however, the Canadian prairies were opened out. The monopoly of the Hudson's Bay Company came to an end, and the Canadian Pacific traversed the whole Dominion with its ribbon of steel. Manitoba, the Northwest Territories, began to make rapid progress. From 1896 an energetic policy of promoting immigration was pursued by the Liberal administration. A brilliantly able propagandist system was set at work: circulars and pamphlets vaunting the wealth of western Canada were distributed in profusion; agencies were started not merely in England but in the United States and in Europe; a generous administration placed land within the reach of the poorest, every newcomer being able to count upon a grant of 160 acres. As what was wanted was to populate at any price a region needing men, new arrivals were not forced to satisfy many conditions. All that was required of them was good health. No questions were asked as to their origin or resources.

The result of this policy (which is being carried on to-day more zealously than ever) was considerable. Between 1890 and 1896 the total number of immigrants had amounted to 271,216; between 1897 and 1903 it rose to 366,946 – an increase of 95,730. In 1898 the figure was only 31,900; but it went up to 44,543 in 1899, to 49,149 in 1901, to 128,364 in 1903, and to 130,331 in 1904.[1] The progress was remarkable. It was related to the real prosperity of the country, the capable manner in which the propaganda was carried on, and the growing reputation of the northwest provinces.

The government, then, has good reason to rejoice fully over the outcome of its activity. One reservation, however, has to be admitted: from the point of view of the British balance in Canada the composition of the immigration is calculated to cause some anxiety, for the largest element in it is made up of foreigners. It comprises three principal categories – English, American, and cosmopolitan – thus represented in the statistics for the two years 1903 and 1904 published by the Ministry of the Interior:

[1] Reports of the Superintendent of Immigration.

	1903	1904
Total number of emigrants	128,364	130,331
From the United Kingdom	41,792	50,374
From the United States	49,473	45,229
Cosmopolitans	37,099	34,728

Let us study for a moment these three elements.

If we confine ourselves to the figures for 1904, we note that the British contingent takes the lead. It only represents 38 per cent of the whole, however, and one wonders whether it will be strong enough to dominate the two others. This is not a problem which excites the general public of the colony; yet people who look ahead are disquieted by it, and great efforts are made in the mother country to maintain and increase the emigration to Canada. Apart from the agencies of the Canadian government, numerous institutions, conducted by individuals (notably Dr. Barnardo's Homes), occupy themselves with the despatch to the Dominion of "desirable" immigrants, whose fortunes they follow with sympathy and assistance in their new abode. And indeed it is a matter of the first importance that this British influx should be kept up, if only as a counterpoise to the other elements, the assimilation of which would otherwise prove impossible, or else would be the work of the ever-increasing Americanized population.

The invasion from the United States is a new feature. Ten years ago it was the Canadian for the most part who crossed the border. The remarkable prosperity of the Dominion since 1896, the boom in Manitoba and the Northwest Territories, have now induced many farmers of Minnesota, Dakota, and Kansas to sell their lands at a profit in order to buy others at a lower price on Canadian territory. An operation of this kind is quite to the taste of the speculative folk of the West. At first there was an impression that this was merely a craze of the moment, but soon it was revealed by statistics that a veritable migration was in progress. Here are the figures for five years:

AMERICAN IMMIGRATION INTO CANADA

1898	9,119	immigrants
1901	17,987	"
1902	26,388	"
1903	49,473	"
1904	45,229	"

These newcomers, moreover, are not for the most part people without means, or failures anxious for a fresh start; on the contrary, they are generally people who have put by con-

siderable savings and who have already had a long experience
of agriculture. They make excellent colonists, therefore, of a
class that the Dominion is very happy to welcome.

The third element is composed of the most diverse nationalities. Thanks to her system of world-wide advertising, Canada
has now come to know that multiform class of immigrants which
used to flow only into the United States. Their variety comes out
clearly from the statistics giving the number of people passing
through Winnipeg – the gate of the northwest – in 1903:

English	20,224	Jews	605
Eastern Canadians	16,514	Finns	556
Americans[2]	12,698	Belgians	493
Ruthenians	9,514	Danes	481
Germans	7,852	Dutch	381
Scots	7,536	Bohemians	322
Norwegians	4,363	Austrians	297
Swedes	3,877	Welsh	256
Canadians returning		Swiss	156
from the U.S.A.	3,338	Roumanians	129
Italians	2,975	Slovaks	99
Irish	2,521	Greeks	77
French	1,156	Armenians	13
Hungarians	1,047	Australians	8
Russians	932	Bulgarians	5
Poles	725	Arabs	4
Icelanders	692	Brazilians	2

Having now passed in review these three categories of
immigrants, let us look into the triple problem raised by their
presence: How is the British civilization to stand up against this
invasion? What attitude do the Americans take up in their new
country? And what is the line adopted by the cosmopolitans?
On the combination resulting from these heterogeneous elements will depend in great part the political future of the
Canadian West.

The durability of the British civilization is very great, for it
possesses strong trump cards. In the first place, the majority of
the population is still almost everywhere Canadian or British.
The census of 1901 does not, unfortunately, enable us to distinguish the Americans from among the other Anglo-Saxon
actual residents in the colony – these being deliberately classed
together as the same race. The census by nationality is no more

---

[2] The majority of American emigrants enter directly from the Western
States without passing through Winnipeg.

useful, for most of the American immigrants become naturalized. We cannot tell, therefore, how many Americans there are now living in Canada. In spite of this lack of precise figures, however, we can safely affirm that the general character of the people of the Canadian West is still British. The English, Irish, and Scottish form a compact mass, strongly united by political or religious traditions.

It counts for something in the evolution of the customs of this region that the Dominion is an English colony. The political connection, however relaxed it may be, obliges the Canadians to look often towards the mother country, and in this way they keep up such relations with Europe as their American neighbours have long ceased to know. The Americanization of Canada, though it seems inevitable, is thus perceptibly retarded.

What retards it even more is the distinctly British complexion of Canadian Protestantism. The Americans are of course Protestants themselves, but after a fashion much more vague and often erratic as compared with the conservative Protestants of Great Britain. In the domain of religion Great Britain has exerted more influence than America on the population of Canada. Once you cross the frontier from the United States, whether you go to Victoria or Winnipeg or Toronto, you at once feel yourself in a religious environment that is purely British. Without quite knowing in what it consists, you are conscious of a moral atmosphere in the air very different from the joyous anarchy and exuberant gaiety which reigns in the neighbouring country. Winnipeg, for instance, so American in so many ways, is Scottish on Sundays; the Presbyterians exercise a sort of moral dictatorship, just as in Edinburgh, Sydney, or Melbourne, and everyone must submit to it willy nilly. From this standpoint Canada will remain a British colony for a long time to come.

It results from these observations that the Canadian West looks British to those who come to it from the United States. But to those who come to it from Eastern Canada and from Europe it looks American. The habits and customs of the people are entirely those of the States. Regina, Winnipeg, Vancouver are cities built in the American fashion – huge skyscrapers flung up alongside wooden shanties. The railways are modelled exactly on American railways. The way business is conducted, the accent with which English is spoken, the appearance of the people, their hotels and bars and theatres – everything combines to make the visitor feel that he is the guest of Uncle Sam and not of John Bull. You have to look much more closely to see under the surface the strong British current that is still flowing. Thus it is that western Canada may remain politically British, and in some respects even imperialist, while socially it is already practically American.

In this country so like their own, what happens to the immigrants from the United States? Do they become Anglicized, so to speak? No, for they continue to lead exactly the same kind of life they led before. They change neither their habits, their ideas, nor their manners of action. They do not need in truth to undergo any change at all to feel at home in this new region to the north of the purely imaginary frontier which they have crossed. They are perfectly willing to become naturalized Canadian citizens and take the oath of allegiance to King Edward VII, which is one of the conditions of naturalization. It seems clear that these matters of form and convention are to them of minimal importance. Provided they can make money, and are not forced to speak a foreign language, and can secure the kind of education they require for their children, they are satisfied. They go so far, indeed, as to declare that the Dominion is better governed than the Republic. They do not feel at heart that they are in an alien land. Doubtless many of them think that Canada will eventually be American, but this is merely a vague impression in their minds, and they do nothing, so far, to hasten the coming of this union. They must be regarded, then, as excellent Canadians. But they are not becoming British Canadians.

We still have to speak of the cosmopolitans. In America immigrants of all nationalities and races become assimilated within a few years to their new environment. This assimilation takes place in Canada more slowly. The life is not so active, and many of the newcomers remain isolated. For example, entire groups of people of the same origin get hidden away in odd corners of the prairie, where they retain their language and habits. This is the case with regard to many of the semi-Asiatic immigrants sent from Austria and Russia. Sooner or later, however, especially in the cities and along the railway lines, these foreign immigrants of all kinds become Americanized.

To whose advantage will this transformation work? To that of the French-Canadian civilization? We have seen that any such hope must be laid aside. To that of Anglo-Saxon civilization? Obviously, but in its American, not its British, form. The newcomers will learn the English language, but what will their accent be like? They will sign the oath of allegiance to King Edward, but they will become republicans. They will become loyal Canadians at the same time, it may be admitted, but that is not to say that they will ever become Britishers like their English, Scottish, and Irish fellow-citizens.

From a narrowly political point of view, it results from this analysis that the recent flood of immigration constitutes no danger to the Dominion. The new citizens are submissive and well disposed, and harbour as a rule no feeling of regret for their own countries. But as I have been at pains to show, the delicate point of the problem does not lie here. It is as to the future of Canadian civilization that one speculates. It is not a question of men merely. Ideas and customs and capital have to be taken into account.

American capital occupies a considerable place in Canadian affairs. Not that money is lacking in the Dominion, or that the British underestimate the value of their splendid colony, but the natural riches of the land are so colossal that financial aid from the outside is constantly required. The United States are always ready to furnish it. Formerly they themselves had to go to Europe for such assistance, but during the last ten years their affairs have flourished so brilliantly that they hardly know what to do now with their profits. It is only natural, therefore, that they should be willing to turn to the magnificent fields of opportunity offered them by Canada.

They began by mere investments which were warmly welcomed. Then, afterwards, they began to start industries in Canada themselves, bringing with them their plant and staff. Great American industrial houses, which had been hit by Sir John Macdonald's protectionist policy and only in a less degree by Mr. Fielding's, have not hesitated to set up branch establishments on Canadian soil. To-day a large number of industries in the Dominion are thus controlled from without. Economically speaking, the colony is as much dependent upon the United States as upon Great Britain.

It cannot be denied, therefore (though the Canadians themselves do not like to admit it), that there is an American peril for Canada. It does not take the shape of a military conquest – *that* is almost inconceivable; or of a political union – that is not desired by Washington and is sincerely dreaded by Ottawa. It manifests itself in the unceasing and irresistible permeation of one form of civilization by another. It is safe now to predict that Canada will become less and less British and more and more American. The best we can wish for – a wish that may well be realized – is that she may become quite simply Canadian.

PART FOUR

CANADA'S EXTERNAL RELATIONS

31: Canada and Britain

So long as we confined our attention to the domain of domestic affairs we have been able without any great inaccuracy to consider Canada as an independent sovereign nation. But the moment we seek to examine its external relations the point of view changes, and it becomes impossible to forget even for a moment that we are dealing with a British colony.

What is the significance, in practice and in theory, of this term "colony"? What exactly does it cover? We must begin by stating these questions precisely in order to appreciate the nature of the bonds that exist between British America and its European metropolis. It is a question involving fine shades of meaning and implication, for the English have a way all their own, of bending without breaking under the force of circumstances, of smoothly substituting customs for laws, and of voluntarily disregarding written provisions when their application appears difficult or inopportune.

The legal nature of the Anglo-Canadian bonds involves no ambiguity. Canada is neither independent nor sovereign; it constitutes only a portion of the British Empire, and the terms habitually employed to describe it emphasize, rather than attenuate, this state of dependency. For while Australia takes to itself proudly the title of "Commonwealth," the Canadian Confederation contents itself with the more soothing designation of "Dominion," and permits itself to be described in current parlance as a "colony," or actually as a "dependency."[1]

In theory, then, the subordination of Canada is strict and uncontested. In practice, however, it is considerably relaxed, as we shall see, the mother country displaying remarkable tact in the way it gives and keeps – giving with a good grace when this is inevitable, but also keeping when necessary, and to a greater extent than is generally supposed. In the first place, she has kept the real essence of sovereignty. All the actions, legislative, executive or judicial, of the Dominion are done in the name of the

[1] "It [Canada] is properly called a Dependency," (Sir John Bourinot, *How Canada is Governed*), p. 10.

King, who is King of Canada by exactly the same right as he is King of England, Scotland, or Ireland. His accredited representative, the Governor-General, is the sole official intermediary between the metropolis and the colony.

The functions of the Governor-General are of a complex character, and we have to see in him two different personalities. In regard to domestic affairs, he merely plays the role of a president of a parliamentary republic; some writers have refused to consider him in any save this capacity, and have taken pleasure in depicting his post as purely decorative: they have gone so far as to predict the time when the office could be elective and nothing would prevent its holder from being chosen from among the colonists themselves.

Such a supposition misconceives the second aspect of his function, at least as the British understand it. If he may be compared to a constitutional president, and if absolute impartiality in regard to the two parties be thus imposed on him, he is also a British official, subordinated to the Colonial Office and in correspondence with it, receiving secret instructions from London, and sometimes entrusted with special missions. In the field of imperial politics, therefore, he may be compared rather to an ambassador, or more accurately to a high type of resident.

His influence in this diplomatic capacity can be exercised, of course, only with the most scrupulous discretion; for colonial sensitiveness is extreme, especially in regard to a Governor-General who without being a foreigner in the unfriendly sense of the word may yet be described as a stranger. The British representatives have generally understood what fine tact their position required, and for nearly half a century their interventions (if that be the word to use) have nearly always been coloured by an infinite discretion. In the course of recent years, however, this wise tradition has sometimes been abandoned. Lord Minto, for instance, Governor-General from 1898 to 1904, allowed it to be too clearly seen that he was an imperialist at the time when imperialism constituted a burning subject of discussion between the two Canadian parties. Many of the speeches he delivered on the occasion of the South African War overstepped the limits of constitutional impartiality. He thus created the impression — be it right or wrong — that he had been nominated for this very purpose, and behind the correct president of the Canadian Confederation there was visible the imperial proconsul. Nothing is less pleasing to the colonials than that.

The presence of one British dignitary is assuredly no menace to colonial liberties; it is, however, a symbol of a certain subjection, for as long as there is a Governor-General at Ottawa there can be no attaining to complete independence. The species of control exercised in theory and in practice by this imperial functionary will enable us to understand to what extent the Dominion is really a colony.

From the legislative point of view Canada possesses autonomy, not independence. The power to make her own laws has been granted her by England, the sole sovereign authority, and in theory could be withdrawn from her. In the same way, no Canadian Act of Parliament enters into force without the consent of the Crown or its representative, and in theory this consent can be refused upon any pretext or even without pretext of any kind. Such is the letter of the constitution. But in reality the metropolis allows every latitude to the colonial legislator, whose freedom is in no way shackled. Frequently the Governor-General appends his signature to laws which he does not approve, and which in some cases are unfavourable to British interests. The force of tradition, as well as the spirit of the régime he represents, imposes on him this necessity. Resistance on his part would be impossible: in Canada it would cause an uproar; in England it would be disavowed.

There are, however, cases in which the imperial government reserves to itself the right to intervene effectively; it would oppose, for instance, any measures which would be in contradiction with the general legislation of the Empire, or even such measures as would have the effect of preventing the execution of a treaty. In view of this control, all laws voted at Ottawa and signed by the Governor-General are forwarded by the latter to the Colonial Office, which for a period of two years is free to veto them.

The line of conduct of the mother country is thus determined by a very precise rule. If Canada alone be in question, abstention is imposed on the imperial government. If the Empire is involved, then intervention is justified. With this dual attitude correspond the two aspects of the Governor-General's position already described. In one respect he acts as the correct president of a republic and renounces all personal opinion; in the other he conducts himself as a responsible diplomat. And this distinction enables us to appreciate the distance that separates even the fullest autonomy from complete independence.

With regard to the judicial system a similar state of things is to be noted. The Dominion possesses a complete system of tribunals and courts, which deliver their judgments and sentences in entire freedom. The source of judicial power, however, is elsewhere than in Canada. The appeal to the Privy Council in England, which is far from having fallen into disuse, presents itself in this domain as a tangible proof of a suzerainty which is not abdicated.

In the conduct of Canadian foreign affairs similarly the metropolitan authority maintains the right in theory, and sometimes in practice, of asserting its sovereignty. In law, the British Empire has only one foreign policy, one Minister for Foreign Affairs, one diplomatic representative. The treaties which concern more particularly, or even exclusively, this colony or that, are none the less negotiated and signed in the name of the King. Canada does not exist as a power in the eyes of the various powers, and has no ambassadors or consuls to represent her with them: the regular representatives of the United Kingdom are the sole official intermediaries. In Paris, as is well known, the Dominion has an Agent. But the important post now filled by M. Hector Fabre is something apart. He is, indeed, a veritable Consul-General, entrusted at times with strictly political missions. He is, however, not accredited to the French government, which, by reason of the British sovereignty, can only deal with the British Ambassador.

M. Hector Fabre, moreover, is the one and only delegate of this kind that Canada possesses abroad.[2] She has, for instance, never had a permanent embassy at Washington: any such institution would run counter to the constitutional principles of the Empire, and the imperial power would doubtless oppose it with all possible force. In truth, the day that Ottawa has a separate diplomatic body the colonial bond will have been broken.

It is impossible, however, for the British ministers or ambassadors to handle in all their details such complicated foreign affairs as those of great and distant colonies. It was through embarking upon such an experiment that England lost the United States. Therefore she has made it her rule to leave the greatest possible freedom of action to all autonomous portions of the Empire in their negotiations, whilst reserving to herself an attenuated and discreet, but carefully exercised control. To this end she gladly accords to Canadian statesmen all the powers they require to enable them to negotiate with foreign powers.

[2] The Canadian "High Commissioner" in London cannot be regarded as a diplomatic or consular representative, as he resides in the capital of the Empire.

This has come to be a tradition which could not now be departed from. It is also tacitly understood nowadays that the imperial government will not sign any treaty which affects Canada without having obtained her assent. On several occasions Sir John Macdonald, Sir Charles Tupper, and Sir Wilfrid Laurier have entered into a kind of conversation, now with the United States, now with France; England did not fail to stand behind her colony at once to support her and keep her eye on her, but it was Canada that conducted the proceedings.

This *modus vivendi*, which works without too much friction, thanks to a remarkable spirit of conciliation on both sides, is based merely on a tradition, and if the Canadians are thus in enjoyment of independence *de facto*, there is no document to show that they possess it *de jure*.

The imperial government, in other respects so accommodating, has never abandoned its right to append the signature, which after all is the essential part of a treaty. Nor has it given up its right to have a say in the choice of the plenipotentiaries, and it sometimes attaches to the colonial personages who are proposed for the mission some diplomat or some eminent lawyer of its own. We shall see later how in the Alaska affair the presence of a special British representative by the side of the two Canadian negotiators resulted in nullifying in a singular way the efficacy of their action.

Colonial public opinion does not always accept these imperial interventions with a very good grace. Certain Canadians of high rank have even allowed themselves to express openly their regret that Canada lacks the "treaty-making power." These complaints, which have found their way even into the Ottawa House of Commons, have given rise there to a very delicate discussion. What in truth is the right to make treaties directly, if it be not independence? If the colonials name their own diplomatists, if they themselves sign their treaties, the word "colony" becomes absolutely devoid of meaning. Are they ready at Ottawa to cross this Rubicon? I think not. They realize that there are certain necessities in international politics, and no one at heart is desirous of a rupture. What they do ask firmly is that the diplomatic autonomy of the Dominion shall be respected and shall be suffered to come as near as possible to independence without being given the name.

If the imperial government is able and willing to carry out this programme, it will have no difficulty in maintaining a status quo which, despite some friction, seems on the whole to the

Canadians very acceptable. But if it intervenes indiscreetly it may imperil the strength of the most sincere loyalty. We shall see in the following chapters that the line taken by Great Britain has at times seriously disquieted the prudent and thoughtful guardians of the traditional colonial autonomy.

32: Political Imperialism – The Heroic Age

The British Empire was a reality long before the word "imperialism" had found its way into the current vocabulary of English politics, and the great self-governing colonies had indicated the kind of union they favoured with the mother country before Mr. Chamberlain ever came to the Colonial Office. Without dreaming of independence or rebellion, they had declared out loud their profound desire for autonomy, having learnt in the course of the nineteenth century to put before any other consideration that of freedom. The history of the last few years goes to prove, especially in regard to Canada, that this disposition has not changed. So much it is well to bear in mind, whenever one approaches the study of the problem of imperialism.

The outburst of imperialism in the Dominion was sudden. The doctrine had long been familiar there, but it had not aroused enthusiasm. In 1891, in 1893, even in 1896, the burning question of the relations between Canada and the United States was still being discussed in the frankest and freest manner: limited reciprocity, unrestricted reciprocity, a customs union–these were the solutions which were advanced publicly every day under the indulgent eyes of the Liberal leaders who were to form the ministry of the morrow. In 1897 these same leaders introduced the preferential tariff in favour of England, and took part enthusiastically in the celebrations of the Diamond Jubilee. An absolutely irresistible wave of feeling had carried them along. But when the wave had passed by they recovered themselves, and it was possible to note that the country had been but little affected, and remained, as before, essentially autonomist. Such were the two phases of Canadian imperialism: let us now study them in turn.

In conformity with his traditional policy, M. Laurier, when he became prime minister in 1896, turned first towards the White House, in the hope of obtaining that treaty of reciprocity which had been the dream of an entire Liberal generation. But it did not take long for him to realize that the barrier of the American tariff would prove insurmountable to the efforts of his diplomacy. The effect of this repulse was very deep, not only on himself, but on all his fellow-citizens. Hurt alike in their interests and their *amour propre*, Canadians, as one man, turned deliberately towards England, there to look for support and a market. On April 25, 1897, Mr. Fielding presented to parliament a new tariff, which reserved a preferential treatment for Great Britain.

By a happy coincidence, the imperialist movement was then going through a phase of splendid expansion. The campaign which had been skilfully carried on for years by the most powerful men in England was now bearing fruit. The colonies, until then very reserved, were joining in the general enthusiasm. The ruin of the Liberal party and the Little Englanders had resulted in the rejuvenation of the Conservatives, heirs of the great imperialist idea, and Mr. Chamberlain, the new Secretary of State for the Colonies, was flattering the colonials with words such as had never before been addressed to them, and that went straight to their hearts.

The Diamond Jubilee of 1897, with its marvellous stage-setting, which appeared to have been conceived by the semi-oriental imagination of a Disraeli, brought the pride of the Queen's subjects to a climax. Moreover the spectacle presented by the Empire at this moment was calculated to turn the heads of everybody, and the official panegyrists celebrated it grandiloquently. The sun never set on the British possessions. Everywhere had the Anglo-Saxon race become supreme, and established a Pax Britannica as grandiose as that of Rome, under which all the peoples were called upon to come and be enriched. The colonies, like grown-up daughters, pressed round their mother, full of admiration, affection, and deference. It seemed as though we were present at the birth of a new order of things, destined to surpass in splendour the Roman Empire itself.

Very few were able to withstand this species of inebriation, and although there were exceptions among the French of Quebec, the majority of Canadians became infected with the pride of belonging to so great a nation. M. Laurier's journey to London as delegate of the Dominion was a triumph. Among the colonial ministers, come together from all parts of the world, he soon attracted remark by his great gift of speech, his imposing personality, and the eloquent expression he gave to his imperial patriotism, all the more grateful to his hearers by reason of his being French. No one had succeeded better than he in seizing the spirit of the hour; no one voiced in tones more lofty, in words better chosen or more brilliant, the immense hope then permeating the Empire.

In Liverpool, Manchester, Edinburgh, Birmingham, and London, he set forth in a score of speeches the passionate loyalty of Canada, the fidelity of the French Canadians to the Crown, the imperialist sentiments of the colony he represented. Yet he contrived with consummate art to celebrate the coming of the new Empire without ever committing himself in favour of definite measures. Thus at the very moment when he seemed to be the greatest imperialist of all the colonials, he was jealously guarding the liberties and the autonomy which his own people had tacitly placed under his care.

"The time will come," he said in Edinburgh, June 14, 1897, "when the present relations of the colonies to the motherland, satisfactory though they are to-day, will not be satisfactory; and when that time comes, my fellow-countrymen, these relations must become one of two things – either they must break altogether or they must become closer. Shall it be breaking the present relations, or shall it be a closer union than that union which now exists? Gentlemen, the answer has to come from England, Scotland, and Ireland. The answer is not in the mouth of the colonies, because the colonies are ready to stand by the motherland so long as the motherland acts to the colonies as she is doing at the present time."

Indeed, as separatist ideas disappear, sentiments of closer union take their place. "We are free to-day, but we are only colonists. Will I break your heart if I say that we aspire to be a little more than colonists; we aspire to play a greater part than we are now playing in the Empire of Great Britain. If I tell you that our ambition is to remove what disparity there may be between an imperial subject and a colonial subject, I am sure that when the day comes we may count on your support. It is the intention of the colonists at the present time not to go backwards but to go onwards until we have a fully united empire – the British Empire."[1]

Thus the general note of these speeches is that of enthusiasm; but it is an enthusiasm that is kept always under control. Hailing, for instance, in a fine flight of oratory, "the dawn of the day when the imperial parliament shall shelter under its solemn

[1] Speech in Glasgow, June 15, 1897.

arches the elect of the human race," the Canadian prime minister seems on the point of touching upon future plans, but prudently stops in time. "What is to be its [the Empire's] future? It is a subject, I must say, on which I would hardly venture an opinion. Men there are in the colonies, who, recognizing this sentiment in favour of a closer union, have endeavoured to crystallize it into shape, to bring it, to reduce it, or rather to promote it, into actual form. . . . But all their efforts in that direction have so far had a barren result. . . . Gentlemen, what is the cause of this? To me the cause is very obvious. To me the cause is quite recognizable. It is not in the genius of the British race, it is not in the traditions of English history, to write constitutions and to devise theories; but it is in the genius of English history and it is in the genius of the British race to proceed slowly, never to disturb the existing condition of things until the existing condition of things has become heavy, burdensome and inadequate, amounting to grievance; and it is to proceed only so far as may be necessary to meet existing exigencies. To-day there is a colonial aspiration for a closer union, for a broader citizenship; but there is no grievance. We are satisfied with our lot."[2]

These extracts suffice to show how ably, moderately, and sincerely M. Laurier expressed himself. The majority of his English listeners, however, would only see in his words the kind of declarations that suited them – the wise reservations they ignored. Created Sir Wilfrid Laurier on the occasion of the Jubilee, the initiator of the preferential policy soon became in the eyes of Great Britain the most authoritative representative of colonial imperialism. Carried away by their undiscriminating enthusiasm, many jingoes went so far as to assume that he shared their views and in this was followed by all his fellow-Canadians.

In truth, during this heroic age of imperialism public opinion did not trouble much about defining in precise terms the questions at issue. The English Canadians, for instance, were in too great a state of enthusiasm to reason matters out: they were all, or almost all, imperialists – the word meaning little else just then than patriots. The French Canadians, without inquiring much into Laurier's attitude towards England, were content to say to themselves, "He is a Frenchman, let us support him." Thus Sir Wilfrid had worked the miracle of pleasing everybody. The movement, however, could not be left for ever in this stage

2 Speech in Liverpool, June 12, 1897.

of speechifying and demonstrations. The formulating of actual projects was bound to arouse violent opposition and to cause all the divergent views to be defined in black and white.

It was the South African War that produced this second phase of the imperial movement in Canada. As long as it was a question of celebrating the Queen's Jubilee, all were agreed. But when it was a question of taking part in the war, by reason of the principles of imperialism, the Ottawa government found behind it a country violently divided.

Sir Wilfrid Laurier was a Frenchman and a Catholic, but in lofty conception of his duties he thought of himself only as prime minister of the Dominion. If his natural feelings, as we may suppose, inclined him towards a peaceful policy and caused him to look with disfavour upon aggressive jingoism, he realized that as a French prime minister of a British colony he must act with special prudence and diplomacy. The freedom of carriage, in so far as London was concerned, which would have been enjoyed by a member of the other race in his position, was not possible for him. In spite of his distinguished services to the state, suspicious opponents would be able, at the slightest sign of weakness on his part, to cry out, "Treason of the Frenchman Laurier!" and raise up against him a section of public opinion; whereas if he seemed to be giving in to the jingoes, he risked being abandoned by the French of Quebec. He took stock of the situation carefully, like the experienced statesman he is. He understood that the imperialist current was irresistible and that any endeavour to oppose it at that moment would only damage his French compatriots, perhaps depriving them in a day of the fruits of fifty years of loyalty. He decided, therefore, that he must yield to the exigencies of English-Canadian opinion.

Should Canada participate in the war by sending troops? That was the problem. The idea of a banding together of the colonies was in the air, and a clamorous agitation in favour of it was in full blast in the Dominion, especially among the English Conservatives, Laurier's opponents, who thus hoped to put him in an embarrassing position, prove him to be lukewarm in his loyalty, and thus regain by their own jingoism a very dubious form of influence. Of course these people did indubitably represent the general feeling of the British population of Canada, whose patriotic frenzy was but intensified by the marked coldness of the French of Quebec. The latter were almost all pro-Boers, and made no secret of it, despite the efforts of their parliamentary chiefs to restrain them.

Not since 1837 had the opposition between the two races been so bitterly manifested. However, confronted with the unanimous wish of the British element, the prime minister, despite French disapproval, felt forced at least to adopt the principle of giving military support to the mother country. After hesitating for a time to come to any decision while parliament was not sitting[3] (it was in October, during the recess), he thought better of it, as the result of the irresistible pressure brought to bear on him by British public opinion: Canadian volunteers were authorized to go to South Africa, the colonial government paying for their equipment and transport; on arrival, they were to be incorporated in the imperial forces. Fearing, however, that this measure of co-operation might be invoked later as a precedent, the prudent statesman took care to explain, through the medium of a note communicated to the press (October 13, 1899), the reasons and the precise scope of the step he had taken. "The Prime Minister, in view of the well-known desire of a great many Canadians who are ready to take service under such conditions is of opinion that the moderate expenditure which would be thus involved for the equipment and transportation of such volunteers may readily be undertaken by the Government of Canada without summoning Parliament, especially as such an expenditure under such circumstances cannot be regarded as a departure from the well-known principles of constitutional government and colonial practice, nor construed as a precedent for future action."[4]

The English Canadians exulted, and their glee found vent in uproarious demonstrations. At bottom their minds were perhaps not so full of the war itself as of the theatrical affirmation of their patriotism in the face above all of their French fellow-citizens. As for England, she insisted upon seeing nothing in the incident but what was satisfactory. "This is imperial federation!" her people exclaimed with one voice. In his reply to the Canadian offer, Mr. Chamberlain, rendering thanks on behalf of the Empire, was careful to make no allusion to the reservation by which Sir Wilfrid Laurier had guarded himself from creating a precedent. Rendered bolder still by the prevalent enthusiasm, two high English officials resident in Canada, the Governor-General and the Commander-in-Chief of the forces of the colony, by way of welcoming the adhesion of the Dominion to imperialism, indulged in words which certainly went beyond

[3] *The Globe*, Toronto, October 3, 1899.
[4] Communication of the prime minister to the press, Oct. 13, 1899.

anything their positions entitled them to say.[5] This transgression was afterwards made a matter for bitter reproach. At the moment, however, the English Canadians could think of one thing alone – their rally round the flag. And that not merely against the Boers, but also against the dissidents of Quebec, against whom some professional patriots launched anew the charge of treason.

There was, of course, no real question of treason. But the French Canadians did display their feelings with a kind of insolent frankness. Without putting aside their loyalty to England, they rejoiced openly over her first defeats, thus deliberately giving offence to the English. Understanding that Laurier's hands had been forced and that his line of action had been inevitable, they continued to support his ministry. Moreover, their political finesse, sharpened by a hundred years of contests, told them that if they were free thus to voice their sentiments unhindered, they could only lose by a change of administration. So the Liberal party remained grouped around its chief.

There were, however, as I have mentioned already, isolated cases of opposition, the most conspicuous being that of M. Henri Bourassa, M.P. for Labelle, grandson of the famous French-Canadian patriot Papineau. In an open letter (October 18, 1899) to Sir Wilfrid Laurier, he protested strongly against his policy: "Is the British Empire really imperilled and praying for our help to defend it? Or are we face to face with an attempt of military federation of the Empire, a scheme dear to Mr. Chamberlain? These are questions that the Canadian people have a right to put and to have answered clearly before they are driven into war, the causes and legitimacy of which I am not going to discuss now. . . . The principle at stake is the axiom *par excellence* of British Liberalism; it is the very basis of parliamentary institutions – no taxation without representation. . . . The question is to decide whether Canada is ready to give up her prerogatives as a constitutional colony, the freedom of her Parliament, the compact entered into with the Motherland, after seventy-five years of struggles, . . . I shall never consent to uphold such a retrogressive policy."[6] And by way of emphasizing this protest, the courageous member resigned his seat in order to challenge the judgment of his constituents upon his action.

Returned again to parliament by a great majority, M.

---

[5] Speeches of Lord Minto and General Hutton at Quebec on the departure of the Canadian volunteers for South Africa, Oct. 30, 1899.
[6] Montreal *Gazette*, Oct. 21, 1899.

Bourassa raised the whole question in all its aspects: Was the Canadian people to sanction the conduct of its government in involving it in a great war without even consulting the House of Commons? Was it not realized that this participation would be invoked in the future as a precedent? In the name of justice, openly disregarded by a war of conquest, in the name of the autonomy that had been won after a century of struggling, it was necessary that a protest should be raised against a policy that was unjust, and above all prejudicial to the real interests of colonial freedom.[7]

To these strong and eloquent attacks Sir Wilfrid Laurier replied in the Canadian House of Commons in some of his ablest and finest speeches. Never had the tone of this English Assembly been raised to such a height as by these two Frenchmen. The prime minister began by reaffirming his admitted loyalty. He then recalled the unanimity with which the British Canadians had urged the authorization of the departure of the volunteers. Could he resist such an appeal? Yes, perhaps, but only by involving the Dominion in a fiercer racial conflict than it had ever known. Now, the whole of his life had been dedicated to the policy of union — he gloried in it, and would never abandon it. Moreover, he had not been as imprudent as his censor seemed to think. By his communication to the press of October 13, 1899, he had formally safeguarded the future. Canada was therefore bound by no precedent, and later should it be called upon to play its part in other imperial wars, it was the Canadian people, in its all-powerfulness, that should decide upon its answer, and should decide alone.[8]

Sir Wilfrid Laurier achieved in this discussion the most brilliant success of his whole career. He extricated himself from a difficult position with the mastery of a consummate statesman. The French, none the less, despite his eloquence, supported him from other motives than conviction. In this memorable episode of Canadian history it was M. Bourassa who was incontestably the real spokesman of his race. He alone dared to say out openly before the English majority of the House of Commons what so many of his colleagues felt in their hearts; he alone dared to affirm, in the face of official hypocrisy, that the Boers were citizens fighting for their liberty; he alone had the courage, in the course of a sitting that was at once shameful and splendid, to

---

[7] Sittings of February 13, March 13, June 8, 1900, and of March 12 and 28, 1901.
[8] Sitting of March 13, 1900.

humble the pride of his adversaries amid a storm of hoots and threats. The tones of his bitter, passionate oratory acted as a balm to his compatriots' feelings; but, in spite of all, the political needs of the moment prevailed over the promptings of indignation.

Talking one day with Sir Wilfrid Laurier, M. Bourassa said to him, "And yet, Mr. Prime Minister, our French compatriots think with me!" With the smile of the politician, Sir Wilfrid replied, "Yes, my dear friend, they think with you, but they vote for me!" This witty frolic sums up the situation. M. Bourassa's views were shared and his boldness admired, but the French Liberals blamed him a little all the same for putting principles before the interests of the party. "You are, of course, not in the wrong," they said to him, "but what use is there in breaking windows? You are only damaging the ministry." And the party organs took him to task severely. "People are too apt," wrote Le Soleil, the Liberal newspaper of Quebec (Oct. 21, 1899), "to forget the social condition of our country and the need of mutual concessions involved by the fact that our population is composed of heterogeneous elements. . . . Why in these circumstances make public display of a kind of chauvinism which can only result in the intensifying of discord? The lamentable action of M. Bourassa should have for effect the determination of all French-Canadian Liberals to draw closer their ranks round the eminent compatriot whom we have for leader."

Thus the various views of imperialism came to be clearly defined. Nevertheless, the political positions of the two parties remained curiously interwoven. The general election of November 7, 1900, reflected this complex psychology of the Canadian electoral body: it gave Sir Wilfrid Laurier a majority of about 60 in a House of 213 members. The Liberals, therefore, carried off a complete victory, all the greater that certain Conservative leaders, Sir Charles Tupper at their head, were beaten in their own constituencies. The ministry was not, however, victorious everywhere. Ontario put it in a minority of 20, out of 92 seats, whereas in Quebec the Conservatives retained only 7 seats out of 65. It is necessary to analyse closely the results of this important appeal to the country in order to understand exactly the attitude adopted by the two parties towards imperialism.

Ontario has declared against Laurier, though in England he passes for the best of imperialists. Why has the pre-eminently English province abandoned him? The reason is simple. Race jealousy. Jealous of a French prime minister, the jingoes of

Ontario have wished to protest once more against "French domination"; and in the midst of the brutal excitements of war cries of violence and hate have prevailed. To the pure British nationalists Laurier and the French have not appeared pure enough, and they have been repudiated because they are not English.

In Quebec, on the contrary, there has been a mass vote for the prime minister. This is not because the French Canadians have meant in the least to approve of imperialism, but they have said to themselves that it is better to maintain one of their own in power than to play into the hands of the real English imperialists by opposing the Liberal cabinet. So they have found themselves in appearance the most faithful supporters of a policy to which they are opposed.

What conclusions are to be drawn from this confusion? "Victory of the French!" cry out angrily the English of Ontario, disappointed at their defeat. "Victory of Imperialism!" exclaim the London newspapers, in whose eyes Sir Wilfrid is the colonial incarnation of the cause. Which is the truth? The real success lies manifestly with the French, for they have got almost all their candidates elected, and have consolidated in power a minister of their own race. This is the feature of the struggle which in their eyes counts for most, and they have made no secret of their lack of love for Mr. Chamberlain and his ideas. Yet the imperialists of the mother country have some ground for their interpretation of the contest and for entertaining the view thus expressed, for instance, in the *Westminster Gazette*: "The success of Sir Wilfrid Laurier is a matter for congratulation; he is completely devoted to our policy, and he is the only Canadian statesman who is able to make it acceptable to his French fellow-citizens."

A regrettable ambiguity thus results from this election of 1900. It deceives Britain in making it believe that the Dominion and her prime minister are more committed to the path of imperial union than they are in reality. But let us wait until the warlike enthusiasm of a moment has died down and the angry feelings that were evoked have been appeased, and we shall be able for the first time since 1897 to realize how superficial the whole movement has been, not only amongst the French, but also among the English of Canada. In truth, now that the war is a thing of the past, their imperialist ardour is abating very perceptibly. For the cause of imperialism the era of difficulties has begun.

33: Political Imperialism – The Era of Difficulties

The South African War had brought the tone of British patriotism to a pitch of exaltation at which it could not maintain itself for long. Peace re-established, the atmosphere became cleared again. Henceforward, it is to be no longer passion but interest that will determine the attitude of parties towards the already less burning subject of imperialism.

The French Canadians retain the sentiments that they have cherished all along, but that M. Bourassa alone, or almost alone, has ventured to express. Loyal subjects of the Crown, they declare themselves satisfied with the present, but for this very reason opposed to all change. They recognize that they owe certain duties to England, but admit none at all to the Empire. Sentimental arguments such as the English invoke are the very last to appeal to them, for their loyalty is the fruit of careful reasoning, and the glories of the British name have absolutely no interest for them. What they have at heart is the maintenance of their autonomy and the confirmation of the liberties which they have won after a century of struggling. Anyone who will not begin by reassuring them on this point will find them resolute opponents.

From whatever point of view they look at it, imperialism either frightens them or leaves them indifferent. Is it a commercial union that is in question? Devoting themselves chiefly to agriculture and the learned professions, they do not give the first place in their thoughts to economic problems. What they desire most is to have a free hand, and the idea of a *zollverein* does not attract them, for by it they would lose their independence in regard to customs duties. A policy of treaties of commerce does not raise the same objections in their eyes, but they do not seem disposed to negotiate with Great Britain exclusively, and failing that, there is no question, strictly speaking, of imperialism.

Is it a military union that is talked of? Here their alarm takes a definite shape. True descendants of our Western peasant folk, they are not of the militarist temperament. If they are ready to take up arms for the defence of Canada against aggressors of all kinds, they are not anxious to set out for distant battlefields in support of a cause in no clear sense their own. "Everyone for himself" might well be their motto: that, in truth, is their reply to the proposal of imperial solidarity.

Is it a political union that is the goal? Their opposition is more resolute still. Thanks to the indomitable energy of several generations, they have won complete constitutional liberty. Absolute masters of the legislature of Quebec, they hold an important place in the parliament of Ottawa. Nothing durable can be accomplished in the Dominion without their support; and they form the almost necessary core of every ministerial combination. Would an imperial parliament, supposing it possible, assure them of an equivalent influence? They cannot hope so for a single instant, since they know very well that there they would no longer number two out of five members but at most five out of a hundred.

In these conditions it is logical that the French Canadians should be opposed to all forms of imperialism. Their traditions, their past struggles, their actual interests, impel them to the obstinate defence of the status quo which in their view is satisfactory.

The English Canadians, in their turn, are reaching their hour of reflection. The war had thrown all of them, or almost all, on to the same side. In a moment of crisis they all had rallied round the Union Jack, with all the more passion because their fellow-citizens of Quebec affected to stand aloof from the movement. They called themselves, they sincerely believed themselves, imperialists. At bottom they were in reality only patriots – which is not the same thing. Now, after the period of acute crisis, the dithryambs in honour of imperial union continue; they have become the inevitable conclusion of every speech and banquet. But the positive affirmations of this policy remain vague, while the objections are precisely stated. Canadian sentiment, properly so-called, which had remained in the background for several years, now revives. And it is in the name of colonial autonomy that the English Canadians themselves begin to make reservations about the necessity – or rather, since they want to save face – about the timeliness of imperialism. The moment is not far off when it will be English-Canadian opinion that Sir Wilfrid Laurier will invoke against Mr. Chamberlain.

Not that the intransigent imperialists have disappeared. They are always very numerous, but they are specially recruited from certain classes and certain localities. Toronto naturally remains their centre. It is there that they organize jingo manifestoes, invite statesmen from the mother country to come and make speeches, and undertake agitation which, it must be said, is no longer entirely spontaneous. The imperialists, in short, are not everybody; they have become a party.

As a party they have influential backers. Imperialism is the would-be official doctrine of the day; and the high British officials in the Dominion do not hide their sympathies for it. Thus Lord Minto, the Governor-General, seems often to forget that he resides in a colony with responsible government, in which he cannot constitutionally express political opinions. "Imperialism is a national movement," explain the jingoes. "Why, then, cannot the Governor-General make reference to it?" This kind of reasoning shows a misunderstanding of an essential shade of meaning. In speaking of loyalism and patriotism the representative of the Crown remains in his proper role, for he is evoking the unanimous sentiment of Canadians. But, in wishing to draw Canadians into the path of imperialism, he clearly become a partisan, since the problem is a serious subject of controversy. This is what Lord Minto is not always ready to understand, and two or three times Sir Wilfrid Laurier has been obliged to remind him.

The prime minister's cautious attitude has become much easier for him now that he has the English Canadians behind him as well as the French – in a word, the whole of Canada. Canadian public opinion is asking itself now whether it really wants to make any change in the relation between the colony and the mother country. "Canada comes first" is becoming the cry, and no one seems disposed to sacrifice the least fraction of colonial freedom on the altar of Empire. Let us cite, for instance, the words used by Mr. Ross, the Liberal premier of the province of Ontario, at a meeting of the British Empire League at Toronto, May 14, 1901: "In a federated parliament of the British Empire, Canada would be subjected to the decisions of the representatives of all parts of the Empire – of men, that is to say, who have no knowledge of our social conditions or of our national aspirations. . . . What we desire is rather a change of attitude and sentiment than a change in the conditions of the Empire." Some weeks later, Mr. Ross expressed himself more clearly still. "We in Canada," he said, at a subsequent meeting of the Council of the League (July 15), "are satisfied with the government of the Empire as conducted from Westminster. We are satisfied with the representatives of the Crown who have come to us as Viceroys since the Confederation. But as for abandoning any of our privileges of self-government, we are unable to see what advantages we should thus derive."

Thus, among many British Canadians, the imperialist movement is weakening from the mere fact that it lives on without strengthening or producing any results. It tends more and more to become rather a desire for an *entente cordiale*, involving no legislative changes; the colony merely manifesting towards the mother country all the goodwill of which she is full. Since the end of 1901 England has scarcely been in a position to ask for more.

We find proofs of this change of view in the discussions of the Colonial Conference, which met in the month of July 1902, on the occasion of the coronation of King Edward VII. The Laurier ministry is to be seen adopting an attitude of opposition which Canadian public opinion does not disavow. This signifi-cant page from the story of imperialism deserves closer study.

On the 23rd of January, 1902, the Colonial Secretary, Mr. Chamberlain, sent to the Governors-General of the self-governing colonies the following despatch: "It is proposed by His Majesty's Government to take advantage of the presence of the Premiers at the Coronation to discuss with them the ques-tions of political relations between the Mother Country and the Colonies, Imperial defence, commercial relations of the Empire, and other matters of general interest. Should your Ministers desire to submit definite proposals or resolutions on any of the above questions, or should they wish to suggest any further subject for discussion, I should be glad to be informed of the purport by cable, in order that the other Governments can be communicated with."

The invitation was precise: the idea was to engage in a discussion not on generalities but on points clearly specified; the colonies were to indicate how far they were prepared to go in the matter of an imperial union. Canada's reply was disconcert-ing in its guardedness. Out of all different questions mentioned in Mr. Chamberlain's despatch, there was only one which in the opinion of the Canadian government could be profitably dis-cussed, namely, the question of the commercial relations be-tween the various parts of the Empire. The existing relations between the self-governing colonies, Canada especially, and the mother country were, the government considered, quite satisfac-tory, save in some small details of very slight importance. They did not think that in view of the circumstances of the various colonies any system of defence could be established that would be applicable to all. They held, however, that it was desirable to make use of every opportunity that offered for the discussion of problems of imperial interest by English and colonial states-men, met together for the purpose, and the Canadian representatives would be ready to consider any proposals put before them either by His Majesty's Government or the representatives of the other colonies.[1]

These few lines sum up concisely and just a trifle curtly the attitude taken up by the Laurier ministry in regard to imperialism. Language of this kind would have given rise to an outbreak of indignation in 1897. In 1902 it aroused only a mild opposition, a fact that bears out what has been said in preceding pages of the evolution that had been in progress. The leader of the Conservative party, Mr. Borden, brought the matter before the Ottawa House of Commons on the 12th of May, but he scarcely showed himself a greater imperialist than Sir Wilfrid Laurier. After deploring the stiffness of the Canadian despatch, he declared that of the three kinds of future open to the Dominion – independence, annexation, or the continuance of the actual state of affairs – it was the last-named that he preferred. By these words he in some sort buried political imperialism, but he fell back on economic imperialism, and called upon the government to obtain, in return for the Canadian preferential tariff, some measure of favourable treatment on the English market. Sir Charles Tupper had already put forward this thesis in 1897.

In his reply, Sir Wilfrid Laurier was even more downright than in the despatch which he had presented for the signature of Lord Minto. He naturally disclaimed the slightest shadow of discourteous intention towards the British government, but he formally maintained his guarded position on the subject of military and naval imperialism. On the other hand, he declared himself to be resolved to go thoroughly into the economic problem and to endeavour to secure important advantages for Canada on the British market. Thus, of all the great imperial questions, that of a commercial preference alone seemed suited to practical discussion.

While the responsible leaders were thus defining their views, the genuine imperialists did not depart from the normal tone of their propaganda. The British Empire League asked for a complete expression by the representatives of the colonies of their views in regard to the establishment of closer relations. The Canadian Manufacturers' Association, a league which is at once protectionist and imperialist, declared itself in favour of a soothing composite programme, including economic preference, together with the adoption of the metric system. Public opinion

[1] Despatch from the Governor-General of Canada to the Colonial Secretary, February 3, 1902.

generally did not go beyond vague formulas already out of date, or else favoured precise reforms which could not be described as organic. The ministry had, in fact, accurately enough represented the ideas of the electorate in its reply to the Colonial Secretary.

The Conference held ten sittings, beginning on the 30th of June and ending on the 11th of August, 1902.[2] Reserving for subsequent chapters its work in regard to military and economic matters, let us here examine only into its political debates and into the general impression produced in Canada and in England by its transactions.

From a political point of view, it is no exaggeration to say that the prime ministers entertained no illusions when they met. The colonials had too often declared themselves satisfied with the existing régime to display now any great desire to change. Mr. Chamberlain was not unaware of this. In his opening speech, he sought nevertheless to draw the attention of the Conference to the question of political imperialism. He might be thought a dreamer, he said, or an enthusiast, but he did not hesitate to affirm his belief that the federation of the Empire was a possibility. He recalled the striking proof of the Empire's solidarity afforded at the time of the South African War. He recognized, however, that the bonds of union should not be fetters, and therefore he was disposed rather to await definite proposals than submit them. The offer should come from the colonies: the mother country would welcome it cordially. He quoted Sir Wilfrid Laurier's phrase of some years before, "If you want our aid, call us to your Councils." Mr. Chamberlain thus concluded: "Gentlemen, we do want your aid. We require your assistance in the administration of the vast Empire which is yours as well as ours. The weary Titan staggers under the too vast orb of its fate. We have borne the burden for many years. We think it is time that our children should assist us to support it; and, whenever you make the request to us, be very sure that we shall hasten gladly to call you to our Councils."

The Colonial Secretary proceeded to develop the idea of an enlargement of the British Privy Council into a sort of Council of the Empire. Pending the realization, not to be achieved easily or soon, of such a project, he proposed that Colonial Confer-

[2] All the official documents relating to this conference have been published by the British government in a bluebook: *Papers relating to a Conference between the Secretary of State for the Colonies and the Prime Ministers of the Self-Governing Colonies*, June-August, 1902.

ences should be held at stated intervals. This programme was a very modest one, very unambitious. Doubtless Mr. Chamberlain would have wished for more, but in view of the marked reserve of the colonies he could not well be more definite in his suggestions. Sir Wilfrid Laurier, for instance, did not at all want that effective phrase of his, "If you would have our aid, call us to your councils!" to be taken literally; in 1897 he had seemed (quite wrongly, as we have seen) to be the leader of the Canadian imperialists. In 1902 he proved himself the man of sense and reason who held back his colleagues on a perilous path. Without saying much, he did in fact play a very important role on this occasion. When the discussions concluded, Canada had lost no particle of her liberties. The only resolution of a political kind that had been carried was that which provided for future conferences of the same kind every four or five years. But as this same resolution had been already adopted in 1897, the Conference of 1902 resulted in no innovation whatever.

From the standpoint of political imperialism, then, its outcome was purely negative. As usual, there were many banquets by way of celebrating the glory of the Empire and the growing union between all its different parts, but in private conversations Mr. Chamberlain declared himself "profoundly disappointed." In the colonies Sir Wilfrid Laurier's attitude was attacked in imperialist circles, but he found a large number of Canadians – and not only among the French – to congratulate him on having firmly defended the traditions of colonial autonomy. The English newspapers, with some exceptions on the Liberal side, made no mention of this fact; the optimistic pictures they gave of the situation could not, however, deceive the attentive observer. The real position of affairs was this: the colonial governments might perhaps desire an economic or military rapprochement; they manifestly were afraid of any kind of political rapprochement calculated to restrict the least of the liberties.

Thus the year 1902 marked the moment at which the pendulum began its backward movement. This movement soon became accentuated. The farther the Jubilee receded into the past, and the memories of the South African War and all its tragedy and renown, the more Canada began to think of her own special interests. The glory of the Empire, which at the hour of crisis had awakened her enthusiasm, became now quite a secondary consideration. In 1903 a significant event served to show this clearly: the question of the Alaska boundary revealed the existence in the colony of a violently national feeling ready to turn at need against Great Britain itself.

This question had been long a matter of dispute between the governments of Washington and Ottawa. There had always been disagreement as to the interpretation of the Anglo-Russian Treaty of 1825, which had defined the boundary line, and the purchase of Alaska by the United States had not advanced matters. From year to year, from Commission to Commission, it had dragged on, down to the time when the sudden development of the Yukon gave it an interest of the first moment; there was question of important territories and of the approach to the hinterland towards the Pacific. On the 24th of January, 1903, after many difficulties and delays, the United States and England at last signed an agreement by which the dispute was referred to a judicial commission, composed of six impartial and eminent jurists, three for each side. Their decision was to be of a juridical character, and to be confined to the interpretation which should be given to the Treaty of 1825.

The American government selected three personages of note – Mr. Root, formerly Minister for War, and Senators Lodge and Turner. They were not very much like judges, however, for they had not hesitated repeatedly to give expression to the most uncompromising views upon the question at issue. Great Britain nominated two distinguished Canadian jurists – Sir Louis Jetté, Lieutenant-Governor of Quebec, and Mr. A. B. Aylesworth, together with the Lord Chief Justice of England, Lord Alverstone. Everything was to depend upon the latter, for if he voted with the two Canadians, things would come at least to a deadlock and the question would remain undecided; whereas if he were won over to the American views, Canada would definitively lose her case.

The affair, regarded in England as one of minor importance, at once began to inflame Canadian opinion. The Canadians knew well the brutal obstinacy of the Yankees, and they asked themselves whether the British representative would be able and disposed to stand up to them in the same spirit. Their newspapers recalled to mind the way in which, for some years past, the British government had shown itself conciliatory and at times even humble in its attitude towards the United States, from the idea that so powerful a friend must not be offended at any price. "You will see," people began to say in the Dominion, "that England will sacrifice us on the altar of American friendship!" And a general feeling of anxiety came into being, which was to be only too well justified by events.

On the 20th of October, 1903, the decision was made public. Save on certain secondary points, it was in favour of the American contention. Sir Louis Jetté and Mr. Aylesworth re fused, by way of protest, to affix their signatures to it; but the vote of Lord Alverstone being added to the three votes of the Americans gave them the victory. Lord Alverstone had doubtless voted in accordance with his conscience. What was certain was that English diplomacy had served Canadian interests in the matter badly.

The result was an explosion of anger, almost of passion, throughout the colony, not so much against America as against England. "We can quite understand the position of the American government in standing up for what it considers its rights," the Canadians exclaimed, "but the English government should have backed us up, instead of siding with our opponents." Sir Louis Jetté and Mr. Aylesworth had declared the judgment to be manifestly unjust. Public opinion went further and talked of betrayal, asserting that the English representative had acted not as a judge but as a diplomatist, charged with the task of flattering a friendly nation. The newspapers added fuel to the fire. They returned to the tones of violence that had been in disuse since the South African War. "Canada has been sacrificed on the altar of diplomacy in order to cement the Anglo-American alliance," wrote the *World* of Toronto. "The interests of Canada have been sacrificed by Lord Alverstone!" asserted the Toronto *Globe*. "Robbed of our rights!" was the exclamation of the *Times* of Peterborough. The Halifax *Herald* suggested sardonically that perhaps the independence of Canada would be the next thing to be submitted to arbitration. The Vancouver *World* talked of being led like a sheep to the slaughter-house. The French press chimed in, but without coming up to the pitch of English excitement. Everywhere there were indignation meetings, in which men of all sorts and conditions took part – politicians, professors, merchants, shopkeepers. All England's backslidings in regard to Canada were passed in review. A professor of law, Mr. John King, addressing his students in Toronto, October 24, 1903, delivered himself of the following severe remarks: "We cannot forget that this transaction is only the latest of many similar ones. The entire history of British negotiations and treaties with the United States is punctuated with a series of tombstones beneath which our rights have been buried." Certain members of provincial administrations indulged in expressions of unheard-of violence. And when Mr. Aylesworth came to Toronto on the 2nd of November, 1903, to be present at a great banquet in his honour, he had but to give the cue for the whole evening to be transformed into a clamorous anti-British demonstration; he was urged to do so, and it was his own good sense alone that stood in the way.

Carried along by the general indignation, Sir Wilfrid Laurier allowed himself to have recourse to declarations that were perhaps somewhat too strong. Questioned in the House of Commons on the 23rd October, 1903, in regard to the verdict, he committed himself (incidentally, it is true) to the following views: "The difficulty as I conceive it to be," he declared, "is that as long as Canada remains a dependency of the British Crown, the present powers that we have are not sufficient for the maintenance of our rights. It is important that we should ask the British Parliament for more extensive power, so that, if we have to deal with matters of a similar nature again, we shall deal with them in our own way, in our own fashion, according to the best light that we have."

These words coming from so responsible a statesman produced a real effect throughout the Empire. The right to conclude treaties! – that meant independence! There could be no mistake about it. Was the Canadian prime minister really about to adopt this programme deliberately and at once? It was not to be believed, and as a matter of fact a new departure of this kind would have been too serious a matter. But thoughtful people recognized that Sir Wilfrid Laurier's attitude went flat in the face of all the schemes of political imperialism. Lord Rosebery, for instance, in a speech at Leicester (Nov. 8, 1903), spoke out thus: "It is proposed to free us from the responsibility of negotiating treaties on behalf of others. That is an offer that will not tend to draw closer the bonds of imperial union."

Imperialistic dithyrambs were now no longer to be heard in Canada. Vague threats of independence were more to the public taste. "We should not be surprised," declared, for instance, the Mayor of Vancouver, Mr. Neelands (Oct. 22, 1903), "if all this brought about a strong and widespread movement in favour of the establishment of Canadian independence." And the *Eastern Chronicle* of New Glasgow (Nova Scotia) asserted its opinion that Canada should now fly on her own wings. On every side people began to discuss a subject which had for many years been laid aside and even forgotten.

One must know something of the Canadians or something at least in a general way of Americans and colonials at large, to realize the significance and scope of this agitation. Colonials, who have all something of the Gascon in them, do not expect you to take literally everything they say. On this particular occasion the Canadians, for all their cries of "Independence! Independence!" had probably not the slightest intention of separating from Great Britain, and would not even have liked Great Britain to believe it. They were merely having recourse, by way of venting their legitimate indignation, to a method of proceeding which is always easy and sometimes effective, and which amounts in vulgar parlance to the familiar cry, "If that's how I'm to be treated, I'm off!" Consequently, the Alaska affair led to nothing.

It left its mark behind it, however. Since then, Canadian imperialism has ceased to be what it was. If no one, absolutely no one, wishes to break the bonds that attach the colony to the mother country, those who seriously wish to draw them closer are few indeed. Brilliant disquisitions on the theme of imperial union are no longer attuned to the ear of the public. After seven years of vague imperialism, the Canada of 1903 we find returned to very much what we found her in 1896 – a colony essentially loyal, essentially British, but passionately jealous of her liberties, and quite determined not to yield into any other hands whatsoever the least particle of her autonomy.

34: Economic Imperialism

Economic imperialism is the supreme hope of the advocates of imperial union. The realization of political or military federation being delayed, it is towards a tariff federation that they turn their eyes. Hence the impassioned ardour which they bring to the discussion of the commercial relations between the mother country and its colonies. It was commerce, they say, that made the greatness of England. Are we not justified in expecting it to make the greatness of the Empire?

The attitude adopted by Canada in this grave debate is particularly interesting to note. We may comprehend it best if we study it at three successive dates – 1897, 1902, and 1903. In 1897, Canada makes England a present of a preferential tariff. In 1902, on the occasion of the second Colonial Conference in

London, she allows it to be clearly understood that she expects a similar favour from England in return. In 1903, Mr. Chamberlain openly declares for protection, and for the first time in the whole campaign the Canadian government is enabled to enter on a discussion if not of actual proposals at least of certain more or less clear-cut ideas. The position taken up by the colony at these three moments will serve to show us the curve of economic imperialism in the Dominion from 1896 down to to-day.

The project of tariff reform, which was submitted by the Laurier ministry to the Ottawa House of Commons on April 22, 1897, marked a decisive stage in the history of Canada, and in some respects in that of the Empire as a whole. It substituted *ad valorem* duties in a general way for specific duties, and effected reductions in the case of a certain number of articles, while remaining distinctly protectionist. On the other hand, it created, beside the general tariff, a reciprocity tariff which should serve as a bait for treaties of commerce. Finally, and this was the great idea of the new administration, it granted straight away and without preliminary negotiations a 12½ per cent preference to Great Britain.[1] To be precise, the name of Great Britain was nowhere explicitly mentioned; but a clause, as to the meaning of which there could be no doubt,[2] reserved this tariff to those nations according similar privileges to Canada, and only Great Britain and perhaps New South Wales could lay claim to it. The authors of the Bill intended this, and Mr. Fielding was free to conclude his speech on the subject with the following words: "I speak with pride when I say that to-morrow morning (the 23rd of April 1897) at every custom-house office in Canada, from ocean to ocean, the doors will be open on terms of preferential trade with the mother country."

Annoyed at seeing themselves outdistanced by the Liberals in their imperialist zeal, the Conservatives embarked on a species of factious opposition which manifested clearly their ill-humour. Sir Charles Tupper reproached the government for having exacted nothing from England in exchange for the preferential tariff. He would have liked to see England put a duty on wheat or corn, for instance, with a preference for Canadian products. But Sir Wilfrid Laurier and Mr. Fielding had satisfied themselves that such a suggestion would at least have been premature; very prudently, they reserved themselves for later negotiations, satisfied for the moment with having won England's goodwill.

[1] Increased to 25 per cent in 1898 and to 33½ per cent in 1900.
[2] Sixteenth Clause, Schedule D.

A more serious objection was the existence of the Anglo-Belgian and the Anglo-German treaties of commerce (1862 and 1865), which contained the most-favoured-nation clause in favour of Belgium and Germany, and which consequently bound Canada in this case. Was the colony, then, to extend to these two countries the advantages conceded to Great Britain? Questioned on this point, Sir Wilfrid Laurier replied quite openly in the negative, which amounted to saying that he hoped for, nay even counted upon, a withdrawal of the inconvenient treaties in question, which as it happened lapsed that same year.

The condition of English public opinion justified the prime minister in this venturesome hope. It had welcomed the new Canadian tariff with the utmost enthusiasm, and as usual exaggerated its significance. The *Times* declared that there had been few recent events calculated to produce more fruitful results than the measure introduced by Mr. Fielding, and that it was the most decisive step that had yet been taken towards the economic federation of the Empire. And the great organ of the City, anticipating Canadian desires, went on to declare that if the Belgian and German treaties stood in the way of this dream, it would be well to consider the desirability of withdrawing them.

Encouraged by the goodwill, one may almost say the gratitude, exhibited by English public opinion, Sir Wilfrid Laurier, from the moment he arrived in England for the Diamond Jubilee in June 1897, ventured to express himself in terms that were scarcely veiled. "I claim for the present government of Canada," he said at Liverpool (June 12, 1897), "that they have passed a law by which the products of Great Britain are admitted on the rate of their tariff at 12½ per cent reduction, and next year at 25 per cent reduction. There is a class of our fellow-citizens who ask that all such concessions should be made for a *quid pro quo*. The Canadian government has ignored all such sentiments. We have done it because we owe a debt of gratitude to Great Britain. . . . Let me tell you this: the Canadian people are willing to give this preference to Great Britain; they are not willing to extend it to other countries at the present time. We claim that treaties which are opposed to us cannot stand in the way of our policy. . . . If the treaties apply, a new problem will have to be solved; and this problem, what will it be? The problem will be, that either Canada will have to retreat or England will have to advance."

The British government, thus called upon either to accept or refuse the Dominion's gift, decided on the 30th of July 1897

to withdraw the two conflicting treaties of commerce. Henceforth, preference became something exclusively imperial. The
Ottawa parliament emphasized the importance of this modification by replacing the reciprocity tariff of 1897 by an exclusively
British tariff of 25 per cent on the 1st of August 1898. Two years
later, this was to be raised to 33⅓ per cent. The chorus of praise
was universal; Sir Wilfrid Laurier found himself designated as
the leader of colonial imperialism, and Canada came to be
looked upon as the eldest son of the Empire.

This enthusiasm was somewhat hasty, as it proved, but
English public opinion had perhaps some excuse for seeing in
the Fielding proposals the first stone of the imperialist edifice,
and for thinking that others would be forthcoming in due course.
The Canadians as a matter of fact remained protectionists after
1897, just as they had been before. They were ready to accord
a preferential tariff to England, but they wished it to have a
protectionist character. In these conditions intercolonial free
trade is a myth; indeed, in the eyes of the colonies it is a bogey,
for English manufactures are just as much rivals to theirs as are
the American. So that Canada had given the mother country in
the first instance all the advantages she had to give. Since 1900
she has rested on her oars, seeming to say. "I have done all I
could." Presently she will go on to add, "Now it's your turn!"

The years which separate the jubilee of Queen Victoria
from the coronation of Edward VII served but to confirm this
attitude. And the English at last came to perceive that Canada
was defending herself even against them. "This preference,"
said Sir Michael Hicks-Beach, Chancellor of the Exchequer, in
a speech in the House of Commons (June 20, 1901), "still
involves a protectionist duty against the English manufacturer
in favour of the Canadian."

The manufacturers of the Dominion, for their part, reckon
upon the maintenance of this state of things, and say so openly.
We find the annual Convention of the Canadian Manufacturers'
Association, assembled at Halifax in August 1902, voting the
following significant resolutions: "In the opinion of this Association the changed conditions which now obtain in Canada
demand the immediate and thorough revision of the tariff upon
lines which will more effectually transfer to the workshops of
the Dominion the manufacture of many of the goods which we
now import from other countries; . . . that while such tariff
should be primarily framed for Canadian interests, it should
nevertheless give a substantial preference to the Mother Coun-

try, . . . recognizing always that under any conditions the minimum tariff must afford adequate protection to all Canadian producers."

The Association which expresses these ideas is principally composed of English Canadians; it is anglophil, and passes generally for being imperialist in its feeling. Yet the demand for "adequate" protection even against the mother country comes unceasingly, like a refrain, into the speeches of its most authoritative members. There is then no question of new advances towards England. On the contrary, the moment has come for her to make response. The Dominion government is aware that a notable change has been coming over English public opinion, and that from imperial and national considerations the Conservatives and imperialists are moving slowly towards protection. The policy of reciprocity which Sir Charles Tupper advocated in 1897 may thus become possible, and Sir Wilfrid Laurier has declared himself in its favour. He sets out for the Colonial Conference of 1902 declaring that he will do all he can to obtain a preferential treatment of Canadian merchandise on the British market.

It is in these circumstances that the Conference opens, June 30, 1902. Officially, New Zealand alone has recorded a wish in the direction of a preferential system between the different parts of the Empire. Canada suggests, unofficially, a favourable treatment for Canadian wheat by means of a deduction from the import duty established by England on the 14th of April, 1902. The other colonies refrain from committing themselves. As for Mr. Chamberlain, the presiding genius of the meeting, he has taken his bearings, and estimated without illusions the distance separating what is desirable from what is possible. His inaugural address is prudent, moderate, full of suggestion, but remarkable also for what it holds back. The Empire, he began by saying, should become economically autonomous, and the final form of this autonomy should be imperial free trade. How far was this practicable? It was for them to say. He knew that customs receipts were the keystone to their financial systems, and that a complete *zollverein* was therefore not possible at the moment, but let them all seek at least to develop the commerce of the Empire upon the basis of reciprocity.

There is a certain vagueness and absence of assurance about this language. Mr. Chamberlain, in truth, cannot and dare not make two essential observations, though they are undoubtedly in his mind. The first is that the colonies remain more protectionist than ever, and that in consequence payment will have to be made in the shape of serious advantages on the British market for the tariff concession sought from them. The second is that the mother country is really unable to give those advantages without herself going over to protection.

Not being able or not venturing to make any official promises in this sense, the imperial government suffered the Conference to dissolve without results. New Zealand and South Africa did indeed promise, and at once introduced preferential tariffs, but by means of an increase of the duties upon foreign imports, not by a decrease of those on imports from Great Britain: this was little else than an accentuation of colonial protection. Australia refused to take any immediate steps, and Canada only entered upon somewhat vague engagements which did not bind her. Great Britain, for her part, had refused favourable treatment to Canadian wheat, and soon (April 25, 1903) even the duty upon foreign wheat which had given rise to such hope among the imperialists was taken off by Mr. Ritchie, Chancellor of the Exchequer. In such circumstances the word "reciprocity" conveyed no distinct meaning. The check was complete, and thinking people did not deceive themselves on the subject; since the memorable day when Canada had instituted its new tariff, economic imperialism had made scarcely any progress. It was then that Mr. Chamberlain saw clearly the price that would have to be paid for its realization. Audacious and resolute, he burnt his boats, and in May 1903 deliberately declared in favour of protection.

There is no need for us to analyse Mr. Chamberlain's new attitude at length. It will suffice to state it briefly. For the first time, in his speeches during the summer and autumn of 1903, the Colonial Secretary (soon to resign his office) spoke out freely and without restraint. His programme, traced out at once and scarcely to be altered at all afterwards, may be condensed into few words. The economic question is the knot of imperialism, and if it cannot be untied satisfactorily the permanent union of the Empire may be despaired of. With free trade the mother country is defenceless; she cannot retaliate against foreign provocation, and on the other hand she has no concessions to offer the colonies in exchange for the preferential tariffs which she asks from them. Under such a system the word "reciprocity" is meaningless. The establishment of a protectionist system is therefore necessary if England wishes to pursue the policy of imperialism. Only thus will she be able to negotiate with the colonial governments. Never before had the subject been dealt with so freely and boldly. The impression produced was extraordinary alike in England and in the colonies, in Canada especially, where the tariff had been for five years a topic of perpetual discussion. All shades of opinion began to find expression in articles, speeches, interviews, resolutions. Amidst the diversity of judgments two notes were almost always to be heard: first, warm praise of Mr. Chamberlain and imperialism, together with a sincere desire to improve commercial relations with Great Britain; second, a manifest wish to do nothing precipitately, and above all not to lower the existing tariff. It was clear that Canada clung to her protective tariff, and subordinated even economic imperialism to its maintenance.

It was among the manufacturers especially that this guarded attitude was shown. As Englishmen (not many of them are French) they did not fail to sing the praises of imperialism. But having gone through with that rite, they offered a downright opposition to a revision of the tariff involving the lowering of certain duties even to the benefit of England. "And first I will say," declared one of them, "what she will not offer and that is the destruction or curtailment of her manufacturing industries. We must amply protect our own Canadian industries. Free trade within the Empire is an impossibility. . . . But what we can give is a more substantial preference on the goods we do not manufacture."[1] A little later, Mr. W. K. George, President for 1904 of the Canadian Manufacturers' Association, spoke with equal precision. "We are accused of duplicity," he said, "because we wish the preferential tariff to continue to be protective for our Canadian industries! But we adhere to this position, and we assert that there is nothing extraordinary about our proposal. Any other basis would be harmful to Canada, and for this very reason, harmful to the Empire. For the more powerful and prosperous Canada becomes, the more the Empire will profit by it."[2] Finally, on the 6th of February, 1906, before the Committee of Inquiry appointed by the Laurier ministry to study the question of the revision of the tariff, the Canadian Manufacturers' Association defined its economic policy in terms that leave no room for misunderstanding: "We favour the offer of a substantial preference to the other portions of the Empire,

[1] Address delivered by Mr. J. D. Rolland to the Canadian Manufacturers' Association, August 10, 1903.
[2] Speech at a banquet of the Association at Montreal, Sept 22, 1904.

but we are strongly opposed to any policy which will prevent or limit the development of our own resources.

"With regard to the proposed policy of a maximum, minimum and preferential tariff, we have only to say that, so long as it encourages Canadian enterprise to make everything we can at home, and to buy our surplus requirements as far as possible from British sources, we believe it to be in the best interests of the Canadian people."[3]

These various quotations reveal very accurately the attitude of most Canadian manufacturers, and their programme may be thus simply stated: Against the foreigner, prohibition; against England, protection. And they point out, with no thought of irony, that this is undeniably a preference in England's favour.

There are even people who are frank enough and surly enough to declare that all this agitation in regard to differential tariffs is a bit of a nuisance. They declare they are as good imperialists as anybody, only it is better to keep politics apart from business. Let Canada resume her commercial freedom, and if she wants to do something for the Empire, let her offer it three men-of-war instead, and allow her merchants and manufacturers to mind their own affairs. "I have always thought," declared Mr. Cyrus A. Birge, President for 1903 of the Canadian Manufacturers' Association, "that it would be better for Canada to have only the one tariff for everybody. If we wish to take our share of the burdens of the Empire, let us rather make some contribution to the Imperial defences."[4]

It is chiefly among the manufacturers, as I have said, that these views predominate. Generally speaking, Canadian public opinion, without wishing to commit itself to anything in a hurry, is all in favour of negotiations on the subject. The Liberal ministry, the traditional advocate of treaties of commerce, shares this feeling, but as it is in continual intercourse with manufacturers who ask it for increased duties, it realizes that it would be difficult to find any customs concessions that could be offered to the mother country. By its triple tariff proposal it does, however, initiate a policy of reciprocity by which England would be the first to benefit. But it is setting about it with caution and prudence, and it is not to be induced to go farther than it chooses. Sir Wilfrid Laurier in asserting the colony's freedom of action in this respect displays the same faculty of vigorous and downright speech with which he safeguarded Canadian auto-

---

[3] Evidence given before the Committee, Feb. 6, 1906.
[4] Interview in the *Toronto News*, May 18, 1903.

nomy in 1902. At a banquet given by the British Chambers of Commerce in Montreal, August 20, 1903, he thus puts the matter in somewhat hard fashion. "In certain remarks made by the Duke of Devonshire I find a phrase which I am obliged to object to. He has said that whatever may be the immediate advantages that the colonies will gain, it is beyond doubt they will be led to abandon something of that independence and complete liberty of action in their fiscal, commercial, and industrial legislation to which they seem to attach so much importance. I am sorry, but I cannot subscribe to this doctrine. If the advantages that we may expect from the mother country have to be paid for by the abandoning of any of our political rights, I shall say merely: Let us go no farther, we have come to the point where our roads separate."

The attitude of the Canadian ministers is, then, clearly defined. Strongly attached to colonial autonomy, they do not propose to lend themselves to any line of policy calculated to restrict it. In consequence they oppose absolutely any kind of customs union that would tend to establish free trade within the Empire. On the other hand, by virtue of its very cordial relations with England, Canada is perfectly ready to negotiate a treaty of commerce with her, whilst retaining an adequately protectionist tariff. If that is economic imperialism, we may conclude with a section of British public opinion, that Canada is sincerely imperialist. But projects of reciprocity will undoubtedly fail of realization until England has adopted protection.

35: Military Imperialism

The brilliant part played by the colonies, especially by the Dominion, in the South African War, gave rise to dangerous illusions in English minds in 1900. "This is the realization of imperial federation!" they told themselves. And their most eminent public men began to evoke pictures of future wars of the Empire in which the colonials would be fighting side by side with the citizens of the old country. They ignored such significant warnings as that explicit message in which Sir Wilfrid Laurier, while announcing the organization of a corps of volunteers, combatted in advance any attempt that might in the future be made to use it as a precedent.

On this point the responsible prime minister of the colony

was alone qualified to speak in its name. British public opinion preferred to accept the less measured declarations of British officials who had no claim to represent accurately the views of the Dominion. "This contingent," said Lord Minto, in the course of a speech to the senior officers of the force setting out for the Transvaal on October 29, 1899, "is the first present which Canada has given in the great Imperial cause. It is a new departure and the future is filled with possibilities." General Hutton, Commander-in-Chief of the Canadian forces, went farther still, with the naïve simplicity of a gallant soldier. "This is in its way a matter of satisfaction," he said, at a dinner at the Garrison Club in Quebec on October 28, 1899, "but, gentlemen, what after all is the contribution of a thousand men to the requirement of a great Empire? This is numerically nothing; and what Canada has to look to, if she is to fulfill her role . . ., is that the time may come when not 1,000 men, but 50,000 or 100,000 may be required to maintain the unity, the integrity, nay, the very existence of our Empire."

The contrast was striking between the prudence of the colonial prime minister and the boldness of the British officials: the former spoke with responsibility, the others without. When, at the Colonial Conference of 1902, the military constitution of the Empire came under systematic and detailed consideration, it became clear which of the two, Lord Minto or Sir Wilfrid Laurier, had truly expressed the Canadian sentiment. It was for many Englishmen a cruel disillusionment.

Before setting out for the Conference Sir Wilfrid placed before the Ottawa House of Commons the line of policy he intended to maintain (May 12, 1902). It amounted to a frank condemnation of militarism. "There is a school abroad, there is a school in England and in Canada, a school which is perhaps represented on the floor of this parliament which wants to bring Canada into the vortex of militarism, which is now the curse and the blight of Europe. I am not prepared to endorse any such policy." Accordingly he refused, courteously but absolutely, to discuss the question of imperial defence.

Despite this formal abstention on the part of Canada, the question was put upon the minutes. It came under two headings: the imperialization of the navy and the imperialization of the army.

At the first sitting Mr. Chamberlain approached the naval problem in an eloquent address, and declared himself in favour of colonial contributions to the fleet of the Empire. He reminded his listeners of the protection accorded by the mother country to the colonies without return, and insisted especially on the immense increase of this burden of recent years. "No one will believe," he concluded, "that the United Kingdom can, for all time, make this inordinate sacrifice. While the colonies were young and poor, in the first place they did not offer anything like the same temptation to the ambitions of others, and, in the second place, they were clearly incapable of providing large sums for their defence. . . . But now I think it is inconsistent with their dignity as nations that they should leave the mother country to bear the whole, or almost the whole, of the expense."

The appeal was a direct one, and the colonies were either not inclined or not able to ignore it. The Cape, Natal, Newfoundland, Australia, and New Zealand, all promised subsidies – very small subsidies, in truth – thus accepting the principle put forward by Mr. Chamberlain. Canada alone turned a deaf ear. Her representatives explained that the Dominion did not propose to shirk the expenditure rendered necessary for her own defence, but that she preferred to see to this herself, on her own responsibility and without departing from the principles of autonomy which had contributed so much to the building up of imperial unity.

In regard to the army, a suggestion of great importance had been submitted by the prime minister of New Zealand. The English government supported it strongly – perhaps had even inspired it. It was to the effect that in each colony an imperial corps of reserves should be organized ready to serve in case of need outside the colony to which it belonged. The scope of this proposal could not be mistaken: it involved the participation of the colonies in the future wars of Great Britain. To accept it would have meant, to use Sir Wilfrid Laurier words, being drawn into the vortex of militarism.

The representatives of the Cape and of Natal seemed disposed to follow New Zealand in this direction, but Australia and Canada deliberately abstained from assent. The Canadian delegates in particular recapitulated with much firmness and political common sense their reasons for opposing it. In a memorandum admirably drawn up, they defined the conception of colonial autonomy, which dictated their attitude. Their opposition, they explained, was not due to financial considerations, but to their conviction that the scheme would constitute a dangerous departure from the principles of colonial self-government.

Sir Wilfrid Laurier and his colleagues declared themselves ready to give their attention to the grave problem of the military organization of Canada; they solicited the co-operation of the imperial authorities to this end; but they maintained stoutly their position on the ground of self-government, and in this domain would not lend themselves to the least concession.

This action was much discussed, and in England disapproved. In Canada the imperialist leagues and leaders attacked the prime minister hotly, but the French and a large section of the English congratulated him on the prudence and vigour with which he had defended the great principles of colonial liberty. The reform of the Canadian militia served, moreover, to demonstrate that the country did not propose to look abroad – even to England – for its political inspiration.

The Dominion has never contemplated shirking the military duties imposed on it by the necessities of defence against possible invasion. After Confederation a fairly complete militia system came into existence. Under this régime the military forces included –

1. A permanent corps of 1,000 to 1,200 men, soldiers by profession.
2. An army composed of citizens undergoing regular periods of active service.
3. A reserve force, liable to be called up in case of need.

The Commander-in-Chief, it was enacted, should be an officer in the imperial service, nominated by the colonial government.

Immediately after the 1902 Conference, the Canadian ministry declared itself ready to introduce important improvements in the organization of this force. The pay was to be increased, for in a rapidly developing country the military career with low pay does not offer much attraction; and the effective body, by general agreement, needed to be increased. The colony understood, in short, the necessity of facing boldly the undeniable possibility of a war. Nevertheless, wedded indissolubly as it was to a policy of peace, it took no satisfaction in this task. This fact led to grave differences between the minister responsible for the militia and the Commander-in-Chief sent from London. The former represented the supremacy of the civil power, the latter the spirit of militarism. Let us devote a few minutes to this significant crisis.

In the month of June, 1902, the British government proposed Lord Dundonald to the Canadian government for the post of Commander-in-Chief. As the result of various incidents, General Hutton, his predecessor, had been obliged to leave Canada. Lord Dundonald was an officer of great gallantry, who had won fame on many battlefields, notably in South Africa. Accepted by the colonial ministry, he arrived in Montreal in July 1902. He was to be the last English Commander-in-Chief in Canada.

Lord Dundonald's attitude soon affected the susceptibilities of a section of Canadian opinion. Like most of his predecessors, he did not succeed in realizing that he was in a colony that was self-governing and mistress of its own destinies. The English army has never been noted for its respect for civil power; like all armies, it sometimes seeks to place itself, on the pretext of the national defence, above the authority of chosen representatives of the nation. It is, moreover, somewhat aristocratic in its constitution. British officers who come to Canada are, in consequence, not always able to adapt themselves to their surroundings. They find themselves in a country much more democratic than their own, and lacking the conservative influences of royalty and the nobility. They have to deal with ministers who are sons of the people, and who are very jealous of their authority, and not at all disposed to be "bossed" by men from outside. Finally, they are confronted with an army of militiamen very different from the permanent armies of Europe. The colonial soldier is hail-fellow-well-met, capable of obedience up to a point, but manifestly incapable of discipline *à la Prussienne*. If, unfortunately, the Commander-in-Chief happens to be a peer, he can scarcely fail to be shocked by a kind of familiarity to which his feudal habits have never accustomed him. It is annoying for him, too, to be under the orders of a civilian minister, whose social rank is generally inferior to his own.

These were Lord Dundonald's feelings. Assuredly no one could have had better intentions, but his ideas ran counter to those of the colony. Alarmed at the condition – in truth, not first-rate – of its defensive resources, he hoped to give it a really effective army. He wished – a wish praiseworthy but impracticable – to introduce rigorous discipline. He sought in the name of the national defence to overrule the ministers and take out of their hands the duty of nominating officers. He believed himself to be personally responsible to the country, whereas in reality he was a subordinate to the civil authorities.

Very popular in imperialist circles, he spoke well and often.

At numerous banquets, given by his sympathizers in his honour, he put directly before the public the matter which had aroused his enthusiastic zeal. His untiring brain thought out innumerable bold and expensive schemes for military reform. When the responsible minister pointed out to him that he could not constitutionally address the public otherwise than through him, he at once took it into his head that he was being made the victim of a deliberate persecution, whereas he was merely being kept within the limits of his functions.

Things were bound to come to a crisis sooner or later; they did so in the matter of a promotion of militia officers. Lord Dundonald had drawn up a list of names, and Mr. Fisher, acting Minister of Militia, had found among them the name of a political adversary and crossed it out. This proceeding was calculated to annoy, but the minister was within his rights. The Commander-in-Chief, deeply offended, made no effort to disguise his indignation. In a public speech, which was reported in all the papers, he gave full expression to his feelings. He was certain that if it had been Mr. Fisher's lot to occupy himself with military matters he would have been offended, if only on personal grounds, by the extraordinary breach of etiquette involved in deleting the name of an officer from a list drawn up by his official chief. Personally, Lord Dundonald declared, he felt no annoyance. The breach of etiquette affected him very little – he had been two years in Ottawa! But he was profoundly desirous of keeping the Canadian army outside the influence of politics.

The Canadian government took the view that Lord Dundonald was without justification for his complaints, and above all in the publicity he had given them. Without maintaining that Mr. Fisher's action had been well advised, Sir Wilfrid Laurier took up his stand on the principle at stake, and asserted firmly the authority of the Minister of Militia over his subordinate, the Commander-in-Chief. "I give every credit to Lord Dundonald," he declared in the House of Commons (June 10, 1904), "for good motives. But we are not accustomed to be dragooned in this country. Lord Dundonald, with all the respect that I have for him, must learn that this is a responsible government and that, when he sends a recommendation to Council, it is the right of the minister in charge of the department, if he does not approve of the recommendation, to strike out any name." The government was on solid ground constitutionally, and despite the violent opposition of the Conservatives and imperialists, it dismissed Lord Dundonald with an expression of deep regret that an officer of such high rank should have permitted himself conduct to tolerate which would be fatal to that discipline and respect for constituted authority not less essential in the civil department than in the military.[1]

The debate went far beyond the merely personal question. By this stern measure, Sir Wilfrid Laurier and with him his entire party sought to affirm the supremacy of the civil power, and at the same time to maintain Canadian autonomy in the face of Great Britain. By an unlucky but significant slip, the prime minister in one of his speeches had alluded to Lord Dundonald as a "foreigner." He had corrected himself at once, and substituted for this hurtful expression the more harmless designation "stranger." The unpremeditated term that had escaped him, however, pointed clearly enough to a nationalist attitude which very few Canadians fail to share. Canada wishes to be ruled by Canadians, and not by Englishmen.

The new Militia Act voted in 1904, during and after these events, bears traces of the different tendencies of Canadian opinion on the subject of the military question and of the relations with England. In addition to certain technical modifications, such as relate to increase of pay and of the effective force, it introduces two notable innovations into the military system of the Dominion.

The first is the suppression of the post of Commander-in-Chief and the substitution of an Inspector-General of Militia, who may be (and probably will always be) a Canadian. While thus diminishing the authority of the military head of the army, the government adds to that of the Minister of Militia, the representative of the civil power, by attaching to his post a War Council. This important change was not the result of the Dundonald incident, though its opportuneness may have been emphasized thereby. Nor was it due to any desire of accentuating the separation of Canada from the mother country. It was merely an imitation of a system recently introduced in England and in Australia. Nevertheless, whatever its origin, it tends to restrict still further the share taken by Englishmen in the administration of the colony, leaving but one British functionary, the Governor-General. It is another step on the road of colonial autonomy, not of imperialism.

The second innovation is the definite solution of the delicate problem of the participation of the Canadian militia in wars not directly affecting Canada. The imperialists, taking up the

[1] Order in Council of June 14, 1904.

proposal made by New Zealand in 1902, would have wished that the Canadian troops could be despatched into any part of the world in defence of the Empire. A vigorous opposition was maintained against this idea by the staunch advocates of autonomy. The latter insisted upon restricting within clearly defined and narrow limits the conditions in which the militia forces might be called upon for service beyond the frontier. Henceforth the regular troops of the colony can only be employed abroad in wars directly affecting the Dominion. If parliament should be in recess at the time of mobilizing the reserves, it must be convoked within fifteen days after the mobilization. It is true that the government retains the right to authorize volunteers to take part in any wars of the Empire of any kind, so that the co-operation of 1899 may be repeated; it cannot, however, be effected on a larger scale. The Militia Act of 1904 expressly prevents it.[2]

Thus Canadian military policy leans towards nationalism rather than towards imperialism. Growing more and more jealous of any kind of English interference, the Canadians grow more and more determined to keep all the wheels of their administration under their own control. It was in this spirit they dismissed Lord Dundonald and abstained from giving him a successor. It is in this same spirit that they have recently replaced the British garrisons of Halifax and Esquimault by Canadian garrisons. Instead of imperializing the national services, they seek rather to nationalize the imperial services. From the military point of view it is, if not the insolvency, so to speak, of imperialism, at least that of imperial centralization.

36: Canada and France

The present political relations between France and Canada, such as they have been made by the century and a half of history since the conquest, are very clear-cut and free from ambiguity.

On the one hand, the French Canadians have no wish to come back to us. Left to their own resources, they struggled splendidly to carve out a place for themselves in the sun amidst the new surroundings into which their destiny had taken them. They succeeded, and to-day they are sufficiently accustomed to

[2] Militia Act, 1904.

their present condition to be able to declare themselves unreservedly satisfied. And it would be painful and difficult for them to readapt themselves to the ideas and customs of modern France.

On the other hand, our government cherishes no illusions. It is not unaware of this condition of mind that I have depicted, and fully recognizes that it is natural and legitimate. It considers quite sincerely that our political supremacy in North America belongs to a past which it would be idle to wish to see revived. Never at any moment do we dream of reconquering our ancient colony, any more than Canada herself desires to be reconquered by us!

Does this mean that our relations with the French Canadians are destined gradually to become less close? Not at all! If for nearly a hundred years we were so culpable as to forget almost completely these far-off kinsmen of ours, we have fortunately recovered from that state of indifference, and we are beginning now to understand – somewhat late in the day, but not *too* late – that, putting aside all regret for the irrevocable, a fine and pleasant programme is still before us: that of furthering the interests of this civilization, sister to our own; of extending the sphere of our economic activity by our relations with it; and by availing ourselves of it, to a limited but appreciable degree, of defending certain of our political interests.

In the first place, it cannot be a matter of indifference to us that nearly two millions of our countrymen – more than two millions, if we include those resident in New England – are proudly maintaining in this northern section of the American continent their own language and customs and ideas. These French islands still afloat upon the Anglo-Saxon flood demand our liveliest sympathy, and within the measure of our power it is our duty to help to prevent them from being submerged. Though the French Canadians be no longer united to us by any political bonds, they remain none the less a branch of the great French family, constituting a real source of strength for our cause in the world. It is then our duty to remain in close contact with them, and to create this contact wherever it does not already exist.

The rapprochement is of a kind, however, that calls for the most delicate handling. In many respects we are too different to understand each other completely. A large section of French-Canadian public opinion stands in fear of our influence, and that is only natural, it must be admitted. Can we ask practising

Catholics, or moderate men of the English type, to come for their inspiration to the most advanced country, politically, in Europe? It is not only distance that divides us, but also the force of time, and it would be a mistake to imagine that it would be possible to cover up the effects of so long a separation in a few years. That is why the influence of our present form of civilization must make itself felt so gradually among the French Canadians, and with every regard for their susceptibilities. In the fields of philosophy and politics it is natural enough that we should not find it easy to understand each other, but we could and should agreed upon the ground of a broadly conceived patriotism. Nothing will then distinguish the French of France from the French of Canada, and we shall remember merely that we are true compatriots, by origin, by language, and above all, at heart.

Great progress has been made in this direction during the last thirty years. Under the Second Empire, Canada was still unknown to us. The war of 1870 and the outburst of sympathy for our cause which it provoked among the French Canadians revealed to our minds the profound love which they had retained for their old country in spite of its having abandoned them. Then, thanks to increasing facilities of communication and the development of the travelling habit, the two peoples made acquaintance. We learnt – for we hardly knew it before – that the 60,000 colonists of 1763 had become multiplied into immense numbers. We saw with admiration their proud resistance against all efforts to assimilate them. The French Academy emphasized this growing intimacy by crowning the poetic works of a French Canadian, M. Fréchette. The great public began really to understand what our North American brothers had developed into when they were enabled to see for themselves in France, in 1897 and 1902, a Canadian prime minister, French by race and language, in the illustrious person of Sir Wilfrid Laurier.

Meanwhile in Paris some faithful friends of Canada were carrying on an active propaganda in her favour. Numerous books and newspaper articles without number made their appearance, and lectures were organized. M. Hector Fabre, the distinguished Agent of the Dominion, helped by his tact and dignity to give his country a strong diplomatic individuality, while the untiring activity of M. Herbette, familiarly styled "L'oncle des Canadiens," obliged even the most indifferent to become conscious of the existence of this France of the New

World. Nor was the movement confined to the capital. Normandy and Brittany, in particular, showed their anxiety to enter into relations with this colony to whose peopling they had contributed so much. Rouen, Honfleur, Saint-Malo, and many other towns began in this way to receive visits from Canadians of note and distinction whom they had invited, as well as from obscurer people come on a pilgrimage to the homes of their ancestors.

A similar current drew French visitors to Canada. Tourists, merchants, politicians began to make more frequent trips to the Dominion. French lecturers achieved immense successes there; conspicuous among them, M. Brunetière, not only in his capacity as Frenchman but also by reason of his strong Catholic tendencies, was accorded an enthusiastic welcome.

Thus were re-established the bonds of sympathy which had been burst asunder by the Treaty of Paris. Their first result was to develop the economic relations between the two countries. It is only logical, indeed, that they should have close commercial intercourse, though history has kept them politically apart. England, when she lost the United States, still maintained her commerce with them, thus helping them to attain in the nineteenth century a marvellous degree of prosperity. On a smaller stage and smaller scale, why should not France follow this example?

There are in Canada 1,650,000 French who by their origin, speech, and civilization are all favourably disposed towards us. They have, indubitably, a good head for business, and will not be disposed to grant a preference to our products for our *beaux yeux* alone. But without making any appeal to half sentimental considerations, are we not peculiarly well fitted to be their providers in the many fields in which our similarity of tastes renders easy an understanding between us? Everyone thinks so, everyone writes and talks to this effect, and yet we are a long way from having realized such a programme.

From the standpoint of economics, we hold but a very small place in Canada. Out of a total of $472,733,038, French commerce figures only at $7,887,290, while that of the United States amounts to $230,170,729, and that of England to $179,552,285; Germany, who ought certainly not to distance us on this market, attains to $9,847,767. Thus we come fourth, with quite a small total.

It is true that these statistics do not give France credit for her full amount, many of her goods being carried by lines of navigation that are not direct. Thus it is that articles are ascribed to England, though of French origin, when they are despatched from London or Liverpool; and the same thing often happens with regard to Canadian products coming to us via England or the United States. If note be taken of this, simply as concerns such goods as silks, wools, wines, novelties, jams, and wood, it will be found that our figure suddenly rises to one of several millions. Authorities so high as M. Kleczkowski, French Consul-General in Canada, and M. Poindron, President of the French Chamber of Commerce at Montreal, assure us that this is so. Yet even when we have made this rectification, we have to admit that our economic activity in regard to Canada remains far from great.

The $7,887,290 worth of Franco-Canadian commerce is thus made up: $6,289,362 of French exports to Canada, and $1,597,928 of French imports from Canada.

These exports consist largely of expensive products which are light in weight. Among the more important let us note the following: books and stationery, $121,588; manufactured cotton goods, $113,106; dyes and chemical products, $233,132; *articles de Paris*, $344,683; fruits, $173,695; prepared furs, $134,325; glass ware, $71,224; gloves, $280,980; skins, $395,065; metal work, $134,519; silks, $616,523; wines and spirits, $894,036; woollen goods, $1,092,934.[1]

There is question in this list, it will be seen, not of raw material, but of manufactured goods, and especially luxury articles. It is in this field that France has won its greatest reputation and secured its best clients. The American market, whether Yankee, British, or French, is the last on which we should allow ourselves to be distanced in this respect. Our admitted superiority need only fear competition in regard to cheapness, not in regard to quality. Now, Americans pay little attention to price; they do not understand economy, and always want to buy the best, whether from force of habit or from love of display. The Canadians are not very different from their neighbours in this, and they are the more favourably inclined, therefore, towards our products.

Canadian exports to France amount in value to $1,597,-928. They consist for the most part of raw materials, cumbersome goods at somewhat low prices: grain, $191,310; fish and fishery products, $591,556; metals, $365,607; wood, $212,502. These figures give no idea of the natural riches of Canada,

[1] Report of the Department of Trade and Commerce, 1904.

which are beginning not to be known but to be suspected. According as the United States are being filled up, and certain of their riches, their forests for instance, cease to seem inexhaustible, people are turning more and more towards Canada and its resources as yet scarcely touched. We may then look forward to a time, probably not far off, when the economic development of the Dominion shall have come to immense proportions, in some ways comparable perhaps to that of its gigantic neighbour. Let us show ourselves ready for this change, which at the same time that it will be enriching the Canadians will be making them into first-class clients for those who are clever enough to secure them.

Such, then, is the general aspect of our commerce with our ancient colony. To what degree is it affected by the customs systems of the two countries? The Canadian tariff introduced in 1897 is, it will be remembered, a protectionist tariff taken as a whole, and grants a 33⅓ per cent preference to British products. Franco-Canadian commerce is subject to a special system resulting from the Franco-Canadian Convention of February 6, 1893, in operation since October 8, 1895.

Here is the gist of this Convention: According to Article 1, non-sparkling wines, showing at least 15 degrees on the centesimal hydrometer, and all sparkling wines, are exempted from the *ad valorem* surtax of 30 per cent; the existing duty upon common soaps, Marseilles soaps, is reduced by one-half; the duty on nuts, almonds, prunes, and raisins is reduced by one-third. According to Article 2, any advantage granted to any other state by Canada, notably in regard to tariffs, is fully extended to France, Algeria, and the French colonies. According to Article 3, on entry into France, Algeria, or the French colonies, the following goods, coming from Canada, imported direct and accompanied by certificates of origin, are admitted to the benefit of the minimum tariff: preserved meats in boxes, pure preserved milk, freshwater fish, eels, fish preserved *au naturel*, lobsters and crabs preserved *au naturel*, apples and pears, fresh or dried, preserved table and other fruit, wood for building purposes, sawn or rough, wood paving-blocks, stave wood, wood-pulp, extracts from chestnuts and other tannin saps, common machine-made paper, prepared skins, other pelts, boots and shoes, ordinary wooden furniture, furniture other than chairs, rough timber, stair-rods of fir or soft wood, sea-going vessels of wood. And it is understood that the benefit of any reduction in duties accorded to any other state on any of the articles enumerated shall be also fully extended to Canada.[2]

Since this Convention was signed the fiscal system of Canada has undergone important modifications, notably by the introduction of the differential treatment in favour of England. This fact, unfortunately, has not had a good effect upon our interests. The first combination of Mr. Fielding's new system created a reprocity tariff (that of April 23, 1897) which in the intention of the Finance Minister was to apply solely to English products. However, Article 2 of the Convention of 1895 gave us also the benefit of this treatment. As the Dominion government had England exclusively in view, it was not slow to withdraw that tariff, to replace it on August 1, 1898, by a British preferential tariff, confined expressly to the United Kingdom.

The Convention between France and Canada is still in operation, but on the strength of the economic policy inaugurated by Sir Wilfrid Laurier in 1897, and of his frequently expressed desire to conclude treaties of commerce, we have entered into definite negotiations with him with a view to improving still further our commercial relations. Without contesting England's peculiar situation *vis-à-vis* the Dominion, we have considered that France also, as a former American power, might lay claim to special advantages in its former colony, in view more especially of the fact that the French race in the Dominion numbers over a million and a half.

It was in this spirit that the negotiations, both non-official and official, took place in 1901 and 1902. They went some way. France showed herself ready to accord Canada the benefit of her minimum tariff upon all goods. She asked in return a rebate for her products on the general Canadian tariff. The French government at first suggested for this rebate the figure of 33 per cent – that is to say, the figure of the British preference. But the Canadians held back: according to them, a concession of 33 per cent was impossible, first because Canada could not put a foreign nation on the same footing as the mother country, but also because France only offered in return her minimum tariff (still in part protectionist), whereas England gave practically all the advantages of free trade. In the presence of these arguments, the fairness of which it recognized, the French government consented to lower their demands, and began to talk of 30 per cent

[2] Arrangement, destiné à régler au matière de tarifs douaniers les relations commerciales entre la France et le Canada, signé à Paris le 6 février 1893, ratifié le 4 Octobre 1895 (Journal Official du 9 Octobre 1895).

or 25 per cent, and it seems at this point as though an understanding would be come to on the basis of the latter figure. At this time the Canadian government may be supposed to have been the more favourably disposed in that the Newfoundland question, not yet settled, was being simultaneously negotiated, Canada thus playing the role of intermediary between the two great powers engaged in the dispute.

In 1902, Sir Wilfrid Laurier and Mr. Fielding came to Europe on the occasion of King Edward's coronation. On the 29th September and 2nd October, Sir Wilfrid saw our Minister for Foreign Affairs in Paris. All the elements required to bring the matter to a head had been brought together, and it seemed that the treaty might very well be concluded on the spot. Yet, two or three days later, the prime minister of the Dominion left Paris with nothing signed!

What was the reason of this check? Was Sir Wilfrid Laurier frightened by a protectionist campaign which was being started just then, and without his approval, by M. Tarte, his Minister of Public Works? Or did he think that France was displaying too great eagerness over a scheme that had not become mature as the result of years of study? Or was there not perhaps some discreet exercise of pressure on the part of England, then still our rival, and jealous at the idea of her colony coming to too good an understanding with us? In any case, the psychological moment was lost, and the negotiations have never since been resumed.

And yet the Canadian government is very favourably disposed towards France. If it is afraid of displeasing certain protectionist interests, we must not forget on the other hand that its economic quarrel with two great nations imposes on it the need of new openings. The United States, since McKinley's time, have shut themselves up as though behind the Great Wall of China. As for Germany, jealous at not benefiting by the preferential tariff of 1897, she subjects Canadian imports to the least favourable treatment. The Dominion retaliated in 1903 by putting on German products a surtax equal to a third of the duties imposed by the general tariff. The result is a tariff war. It is for us to turn it to account. Sir Wilfrid Laurier has clearly evinced his goodwill towards us by favouring to the utmost possible extent the creation of a direct line of navigation between France and Canada. At his proposal, the Ottawa Parliament has promised to grant an annual subsidy of $103,600 for ten years to any Franco-Canadian or Anglo-French line plying direct between the two countries, on condition that it guarantees eighteen crossings each year with an average speed of twelve knots. Thus encouraged, a French line was organized in 1903 and 1904 between Le Havre, La Pallice, and Canada, with vessels of small tonnage. Unfortunately, it did not succeed, owing to the peculiar difficulties of the situation. The amount of commerce involved proved, indeed, insufficient to ensure regular traffic, especially as many articles gained by being sent through England, there to be denationalized, so as to have the benefit of the preferential tariff of 33 per cent. More recently, the great Allan Steamship Company has created a service from London to Le Havre and Montreal. By a special arrangement with the Canadian government, it receives a subsidy of $130,000, although it is a purely English line, and not Franco-Canadian or Anglo-French. It has prospered in every way. The Company not being obliged to ask for more than a share in French exports, is placed on a much more satisfactory basis than if it were limited to Franco-Canadian traffic. It is regrettable, however, that such an enterprise should have nothing French about it. Perhaps it might be possible for us to participate in it, even on a small scale, in some way or another.

This question of a line of navigation between France and Canada, her former colony, is, in truth, of the first importance, for it goes hand in hand with the extension of our business. It is not natural for our products to pass so frequently via England or the United States. We lose our commercial individuality and damage our credit by resigning ourselves to this state of things and showing ourselves incapable of modifying it.

The economic policy for our country in regard to the Dominion is then clearly indicated. It should form a natural sequel to that rapprochement which I have described in the first pages of this chapter. Let the French of France and of Canada get to know more and more of each other, and let our business men seek resolutely to achieve that place on the Canadian market which logically they should be enjoying; then let the two governments come upon the scene and further the movement by means of mutual tariff concessions: that will be the best method of developing the economic relations which it is sad at present to see so restricted.

Beyond this economic and moral rapprochement our political relations with Canada necessarily remain restricted. We must remember that all negotiation between Ottawa and Paris has to be carried on through the British government as intermediary. The latter, it is true, has made it a rule to hamper as little as possible the freedom of the colonial governments, but Canada remains a portion of the British Empire, and can only act in accord with the imperial power. As we have loyally accepted the *fait accompli* in North America, we cannot deliberately ignore England when discussing matters with its colony. Thanks to the *entente cordiale*, the British government will not seek to discover any disquieting reserve in our desire, so often manifested, for such a policy as this.

In these circumstances it is natural that we should seek to benefit by the real and special sympathies which we possess on the banks of the St. Lawrence. In the foreign policy of our time intermediaries do not play a less important role than of yore. We may be able to find able and friendly intermediaries sometimes among the French of Canada. In 1901, before the question of Newfoundland was settled, the Laurier ministry would willingly have given us its good offices. Similar conditions may arise in which it may not be an unimportant matter that a Canadian statesman of this type speaks our language and is of our race. In discussing these political relations we must confine ourselves, of course, to generalities. But it is desirable to point out that wherever the flag of France has flown, wherever our race survives and our tongue resounds, our attitude can never be one of forgetfulness or of abstention.

37: The Future of Canada in North America

We have seen the objections, probably insuperable, which Canada raises against the more pronounced forms of imperialism. On the other hand, we have seen also that her relations with France, although very cordial, can never again become what they were in the distant past. What, then, is to be the future of the Dominion in the continent of North America, in face of the overwhelming immensity of the United States? To an examination into this grave question I shall devote the concluding chapter of my book.

There are three possible solutions. Either the present state of things will continue indefinitely, Canada remaining a British colony; or this link will be broken and she will become independent; or, finally, she will be annexed by the United States. It should be added, however, that beneath the surface of this cut-and-dried statement of the problem, the situation in reality (as generally is the case) is so involved in its character that the final issue may very well be some kind of blend of all these three eventualities.

The status quo stands a good chance of lasting. The colony is satisfied with its relations with the mother country, provided that the latter does not return, under the pretext of an imperial union, to that policy of intervention which succeeded so ill in the past. This fear laid aside, Canadian loyalty, after a moment of disquietude, resumes its complete sincerity. The thing is easy to understand. To form part of a mighty empire without having to share, save in a minute degree, in its military and naval expenditure, to have all the benefits of its protection, its influence and its prestige, to be able to lean on it in difficult situations when at issue with sometimes formidable adversaries – these advantages are real enough and cheap enough for the Canadians to appreciate them thoroughly. They render the management of the affairs of the Dominion a much easier task for the Canadian ministers, who personally are by no means indifferent to the wider fame they derive from their connection with an empire numbering four hundred million men. The French Canadians, for their part, ask for nothing better than the continuance of a rule which has enabled them to expand so wonderfully.

In these circumstances, it would take some tremendous blunder on the part of England to precipitate a rupture – a thing talked of sometimes after the fashion of an empty threat, but a thing that no one at heart really desires. For a long time to come, then, no solution will accord so well with the real needs and the real wishes of the Canadians as the maintenance of the colonial connection, so long as it does not retard the evolution of the Dominion towards that fuller autonomy aspired to, which shall border upon independence without being given the name.

This leads to the second possibility, which it will be found difficult in practice to keep distinct from the first. Without breaking away from the Empire, without ceasing to be an integral portion of it, Canada is developing a swift tendency towards actual independence. For a long time past she has regarded herself as a nation with a distinct personality, a policy and a destiny of her own: we may add, indeed, a sovereignty of her own, for despite the not insignificant restrictions we have noted, she is possessed to-day of almost all its advantages. Is it not the "sovereign will" of the Canadian people that determines the attitude of its government, not only in domestic affairs but also in military, diplomatic, and economic matters? Have we not seen Lord Dundonald recalled, and Sir Wilfrid Laurier standing up to Mr. Chamberlain? If it is true that the signing has to be done by England, the deciding rests with ministers responsible to a parliament with the election of which the people of Great Britain have nothing to do. Should the Ottawa parliament choose, to-morrow, to accord to imports from France a differential treatment yet more favourable than that now enjoyed by the mother country, nothing could prevent it from so doing. Should it choose, with the approval of its electors, to vote for an economic, or even a political, union with the United States, in what way would England be able to offer any effective opposition? She would protest, of course, but it is well known that she would not attempt to maintain her suzerainty by force of arms, and that she must needs acquiesce in the decision taken by her colony.

It is easy to understand that in these circumstances, recognized on both sides, the autonomy of Canada must evolve naturally towards sovereignty. In accordance with her prudent practice, which consists in silently accepting the inevitable, the British government pretends to see nothing to complain of, and consistently gives in all along the line, bent principally on preserving the letter of the union. Under cover of this, Canada does more or less as she likes, and as the Canadians are very sensible folk they are careful not to provoke a rupture which would leave them diminished and weakened, and much at the mercy of their too powerful neighbour. It is almost certain, therefore, that if the rupture does come it will not be due to their initiative.

Is it to be deduced from all this that the third contingency will not come about? That would be too much to say. All that can safely be affirmed is that it is scarcely probable in the near future.

For we know that the Canadians, English and French alike, will not hear of annexation at any price just at present. We know, too, that the Americans entertain no notion of conquering Canada, either now or at any time. They believe, undoubtedly, that by the force of a manifest destiny the Dominion will cease to be British and pass under the Star-Spangled Banner; but, like the vulture sure of its prey, they show no disposition to precipitate the event, or even to discount it in advance. The annexation of Canada may very well be a topic of public discussion in the United States, but it is not, and doubtless will not be for a long time to come, a matter for the government. It is the less likely to become so for the reason that the excellent Anglo-American relations, which date from some years back, will thus be the more easily maintained. Whether we inquire into the declared and immediate desires of the two governments of Washington and Ottawa, or into their private and ultimate aspirations, we find no trace of any tendencies towards annexation: they are not being drawn in this direction, either by a friendship so intimate as to lead to union or by a state of tension so acute as to lead to war.

Is it a question of friendship? The *entente cordiale* between the two neighbours hardly exists. Their recent history is marked by an endless succession of abortive efforts at a satisfactory understanding, of negotiations that come to nothing, of arbitrations that leave behind them only grudges and ill-will. Is there, on the other hand, such a feeling of coldness between the two capitals as could imperil their peaceful relations? Surely not. One must, indeed, be familiar with the diplomatic ways of the United States and of the British colonies in general to realize how utterly they differ from ours: they can go to great lengths in what they say, they can have recourse to methods of procrastination that amount almost to incivility, they can almost refuse to talk, without there being the slightest danger to peace. As a matter of fact, a war between the two countries seems hardly conceivable, and the Canadians resolutely condemn any policy that could tend to provoke it. If, then, the Americans do not take the first step – and they do not seem disposed to do so – there is nothing to suggest that Canada and the United States will not long continue to live side by side, as they have done for a century or so, without any shock to the unstable equilibrium that exists to-day.

I do not wish to imply that the danger of annexation has disappeared. It still exists, but, as we have shown already, in a different form from that of a military or political conquest. It is not the American nation that threatens the Canadian nation; rather is it the American form of civilization that threatens to supplant the British.

We are thus led back to the first solution, but under different conditions; and it is doubtless in this direction that the future lies. The Canadian nation, even though it shall have become

American in its ways, may yet remain indefinitely a British colony. This means a victory for America, it will be said. Assuredly. But it means a victory also for English statesmanship, which will thus have achieved its masterpiece. And in this destiny, at once so diverse and so tragic, let us take care not to forget the old French civilization which faces the future with a joyous cry of hope.

INDEX

SUGGESTIONS FOR
FURTHER READING

The most recent, and one of the best, of the many one-volume histories of Canada is W. L. MORTON, *The Kingdom of Canada* (Toronto, 1963). A good shorter history is J. M. S. CARELESS, *Canada, a Story of Challenge*; this is now published in a paperback edition (Toronto, 1963). PROFESSOR MORTON has also written a short book of interpretation, *The Canadian Identity* (Toronto, 1961). The Canadian Historical Association (Ottawa, Public Archives of Canada) publishes a series of booklets on various topics in Canadian history. The classic historical account of the triangular relationship of Canada, Britain and the United States is J. B. BREBNER, *North Atlantic Triangle* (Carleton Library, 1966).

Useful books on French Canada are: MASON WADE, *The French-Canadian Outlook* (Carleton Library, 1964) and *The French Canadians* (Toronto, 1955); and MICHEL BRUNET, *La présence Anglaise et les Canadiens* (Montreal, 1958).

Lives of Laurier are: O. D. SKELTON, *Life and Letters of Sir Wilfrid Laurier* (Carleton Library, 2 vols., 1965) of which a critical review is contained in J. W. DAFOE, *Laurier: A Study in Canadian Politics* (Carleton Library, 1963); and J. S. WILLISON, *Sir Wilfrid Laurier and the Liberal Party* (Toronto, 2 vols., 1903. The latter work was heavily drawn upon by Siegfried in *The Race Question in Canada*.

F. H. UNDERHILL in the Massey Lectures over CBC radio in 1963, *The Image of Confederation* (Toronto, Canadian Broadcasting Corporation, 1964), gives an account of the chief discussions about the significance and destiny of Canada that have taken place since 1867. Some of the most readable of these discussions during the generation in which Siegfried's *Race Question* was written are: GOLDWIN SMITH, *Canada and the Canadian Question* (Toronto, 1891); SIR CHARLES DILKE, *Problems of Greater Britain* (London, 1890); J. A. HOBSON, *Canada Today* (London, 1905); RUPERT BROOKE, *Letters from America* (London, 1916); J. S. EWART, *The Kingdom of Canada* (Toronto, 1908); JAMES BRYCE, *Modern Democracies* (London, 1922). *The Image of Confederation* contains a bibliography of the more important books in this field that have been published in the last hundred years.

NOTE ON THE AUTHOR

André Siegfried (1875-1959) was one of the most distinguished modern French students of politics. His interests covered a wide field, including not only politics in the narrow sense but also economics, geography, sociology, social psychology and religion. He became known especially as an expert on the English-speaking communities.

His first book, published in French in 1904 and not translated into English until 1914, was *Democracy in New Zealand*. He was the author of two works on Canada – the present volume, *The Race Question in Canada*, published in 1907; and a later volume, entitled *Canada*, published in 1937. This volume was revised and brought up to date in 1947 in a second edition entitled *Canada: an International Power*. He also wrote two books on Britain: *Post-War Britain* (1924), and *England's Crisis* (1931); and two books on the United States: *America Comes of Age* (1927), and *America at Mid-Century* (1955). In addition he was the author of many other books on a wide variety of subjects, including his own country, France; Switzerland; the Mediterranean; Latin America; South Africa. He was a frequent contributor to the Paris newspaper *Le Figaro* and to many periodicals in France and abroad. In 1944 he was elected to the Académie Française.

THE CARLETON LIBRARY